GENTLEMAN IN THE
SHADOWS

GENTLEMAN IN THE
SHADOWS

BENJAMIN C. EVANS JR. AND THE CENTRAL INTELLIGENCE AGENCY

DOUGLAS A. WISSING

Indiana Historical Society Press
Indianapolis 2019

©2019 Indiana Historical Society Press. All rights reserved.

Printed in the United States of America

This book is a publication of the
Indiana Historical Society Press
Eugene and Marilyn Glick Indiana History Center
450 West Ohio Street
Indianapolis, Indiana 46202-3269 USA
www.indianahistory.org
Telephone orders 1-800-447-1830
Fax orders 1-317-234-0562
Online orders @ http://shop.indianahistory.org

The paper in this publication meets the minimum requirements of American National Standard for Information Sciences—Permanence of Paper for Printed Library Materials, ANSI Z39. 48–1984 ∞

Library of Congress Cataloging-in-Publication Data

Names: Wissing, Douglas A., author.
Title: Gentleman in the shadows : Benjamin C. Evans Jr and the Central
    Intelligence Agency / Douglas A. Wissing.
Other titles: Benjamin C. Evans Jr and the Central Intelligence Agency
Description: Indianapolis, Indiana : Indiana Historical Society, [2019] |
    Includes bibliographical references and index.
Identifiers: LCCN 2019033874 (print) | LCCN 2019033875 (ebook) | ISBN
    9780871954367 (cloth) | ISBN 9780871954374 (epub)
Subjects: LCSH: Evans, Benjamin C., Jr., 1924-1987. | United States.
    Central Intelligence Agency—Officials and employees--Biography. |
    Intelligence officers—United States—Biography. | World
    politics—1945-1989. | Cold War—Biography. | Houser, Jan A. K. Evans. |
    United States. Army—Officers—Biography.
Classification: LCC JK468.I6 W585 2019 (print) | LCC JK468.I6 (ebook) |
    DDC 327.12730092 [B]—dc23
LC record available at https://lccn.loc.gov/2019033874
LC ebook record available at https://lccn.loc.gov/2019033875

No part of this publication may be reproduced, stored in or introduced into a retrieval system, or transmitted, in any form or by any means (electronic, mechanical, photocopying, recording, or otherwise) without the prior written permission of the copyright owner.

"I wish to be useful, and every kind of service necessary to the public good becomes honorable by being necessary. If the exigencies of my country demand a peculiar service, its claim to perform that service are imperious."

CAPTAIN NATHAN HALE

This book was made possible
by the family of Benjamin C. Evans Jr.

Contents

Author's Note		ix
Acknowledgments		xi
Chapter 1	Havana, 1959	1
Chapter 2	Indiana Beginnings	3
Chapter 3	The Dividends of Culver	13
Chapter 4	West Point	19
Chapter 5	The Earthquake	27
Chapter 6	Aide-de-Camp	33
Chapter 7	Washington	41
Chapter 8	The Payback	51
Chapter 9	The Agency	59
Chapter 10	Tradecraft	65
Chapter 11	Cuba and the Revolution	71
Chapter 12	Crisis	83
Chapter 13	The Bomb	91
Chapter 14	World of Spies	97
Chapter 15	Limited Hangout	109
Chapter 16	The Seventh Floor	117
Chapter 17	Family Jewels	129
Chapter 18	Denouement	149
Chapter 19	Retirement	159
Image Gallery		165
Notes		185
Index		247

Author's Note

Gentleman in the Shadows is a biography of Benjamin C. Evans Jr., a Central Intelligence Agency executive who operated at the top levels of the U.S. intelligence community during the darkest days of the Cold War. After serving as a covert case officer in revolutionary Havana, Cuba, and then managing The Asia Foundation, a sprawling CIA front organization, Evans was promoted to the CIA headquarters' seventh floor, where the executive directorate team managed world-changing intelligence missions. A socially adept administrator, Evans was the CIA Executive Secretary for seven Directors of Central Intelligence under four presidential administrations. Spooks said Evans was the traffic cop of the CIA.

As a military intelligence and CIA officer, Evans was part of the tumultuous period that included America's crusade to democratize occupied Japan, the Korean War, nuclear standoffs with the Soviet Union, the anti-Castro counter-revolutionary movement that climaxed in the Bay of Pigs invasion, the Vietnam War, Watergate, and the Family Jewels furor after the CIA's dirty secrets were revealed. Although he had global CIA responsibilities, Evans was among the coterie of top federal executives who operated out of the limelight—extraordinarily significant officials whose names were virtually unknown to the American public.

Through his marriage, Evans was a member of America's elite that figured so prominently in the U.S. intelligence services. Born and raised in a prosperous family in Crawfordsville, Indiana, Evans was imbued with conservative Hoosier values that celebrated servant-leadership. Following his graduation from the U.S. Military Academy at West Point, Evans's social savvy and encultured mores stood him in good stead in occupied Japan, where he served as aide-de-camp to General Eugene Harrison, a decorated World War II intelligence officer and occupation administrator. It was in occupied Japan that Evans and the general's stepdaughter, Jan King, fell in love, and later married.

Jan King Evans came from old Washington aristocracy—self-described "cave-dwellers"—who allied with the powerful thronging the nation's capital. The family connections shaped Evans's career. When President Harry Truman recognized he needed a foreign intelligence service, General Harrison was on the commission that established what came to be the CIA. Not too many years later, Harrison and his cohorts insured that his son-in-law Evans, by then a respected military intelligence officer, was offered a position in the agency.

So this book is also about CIA families, who not uncommonly led double lives of sequestered thoughts, unasked questions and intimate deceptions. An empathetic family man, Evans paid a psychological price for his emotionally isolate life in the clandestine service.

The primary source material for this book is based on family archives, on-the-record interviews, and available declassified CIA documents. Given Evans's covert career and long executive service near the apex of U.S. intelligence, it is not surprising that the CIA has declassified only a small portion of the enormous volume of documents connected to his CIA career. As such, this book is incomplete; a contribution to the larger story of a remarkable gentleman spy, who remains partially in the shadows.

Acknowledgments

I am indebted to the experts who shared their deep understanding of the Central Intelligence Agency and Benjamin C. Evans Jr.'s role in this peculiar service. Many others have helped me understand Evans as a man. I am particularly indebted to his widow, Jan King Evans, whose amazing memory, storytelling prowess, and remarkable family archive informed my understanding of Washingtonian "cave-dweller" high society's connection to the institutions of U.S. national security, as well as her eventful life as a CIA wife that ranged from a covert posting in revolutionary Havana to momentous Washington years among the powerful and connected.

Many thanks to Karla Evans, Louise Evans Turner, David S. Evans, Daniel F. Evans, Charles "Chip" King Jr. and Nan King for their recollections of family life with a CIA official. My research into Evans's early life received able assistance from Crawfordsville District Public Library local history specialist Dellie Craig, Culver Academies Museum curator/historian Jeff Kenney, and Culver Academies director of alumni relations Alan Loehr and research manager Deb Fox. Carol Somerville provided insights into the Lake Maxinkuckee holiday-home culture that leavened the Culver military academy experience. My thanks also to Wabash College archivist Beth Swift, West Point Association of Graduates director of communications Kim McDermott, and the U.S. Military Academy's Stephanie Greene. Fellow United States Military Academy graduate Corbin Davis shared memories of Evans at West Point and beyond, as did Margaret Gresham Livingstone.

Veteran foreign correspondent and Indiana University professor Joe Coleman provided insights into occupied Japan. Heurich House executive director Kimberley Bender explained the Heurich family's rise and enduring prominence in Washington. Columbia University archivist Jocelyn Wilk and Bill Santin in the registrar's office assisted with documentation of Evans's graduate study in psychological warfare.

Oscar Echevarria, Evans's covert Havana agent and lifelong friend, provided crucial information about their clandestine counterrevolutionary work in the years after Fidel Castro took power, as well as insights into his friend's personality. Fellow counterrevolutionary agent Elena Echevarria recounted tales of derring-do she experienced with her CIA handler, Evans. Professor and author Maria de los Angeles discussed the CIA psywar campaign that precipitated the Pedro Pan movement. Knox County Public Library director Emily

Bunyan assisted with historic documents that illuminated the lives of Cuban Pedro Pan children displaced to an orphanage in Vincennes, Indiana.

I wish to thank Doctor Mary Curry of the National Security Archive at George Washington University for her crucial archival assistance with declassified CIA documents. National security author Doctor John Prados of the National Security Archive also provided important advice. Thanks to IU Social Sciences Librarian Mary Alford for her assistance with the documents, as well as research assistant Boryana Borisova, who ably aided document processing. My appreciation to investigative journalist Emma Best of muckrock.com for her groundbreaking work on the CIA connection to The Asia Foundation, as well as her guidance with my further archival research into the CIA-TAF linkage. My thanks to TAF vice president Nancy Yuan, who discussed Haydn Williams, longtime TAF president and Evans family friend.

West Point graduate Tom Cormack recalled his long CIA career, during which he served with Evans. My thanks to Ambassador Donald Gregg for his views on his early CIA days, and his memories of Ben and Jan Evans. Meg Gregg, also a former CIA officer, provided invaluable insights into the dynamics of CIA families. Retired CIA officer Sally Lilley drew on her family's long service in the clandestine services to offer nuanced perspectives on agency family culture. Shirley Cornett, who served with Evans on the CIA's seventh floor, discussed the everyday working environment. CIA psychiatrist Doctor Barney Malloy discussed the stresses that impact CIA officers and families. Retired CIA spy and IU emeritus professor Gene Coyle regaled me with Hoosier spook lore. Director of IU Archives Dina Kellams and archivist Mary Mellon helped unveil aspects of the university's long relationship with the CIA.

Sandra McElwaine depicted the tenor of Washington during Cold War-era nuclear threats. Norma Richards explained Washington's hierarchical social milieu and the cult of professional confidentiality. Maria Cantacuzene and Penny Denegre informed me about fox hunts, an important social institution of the Virginia horse country where the Evanses' farm was located.

I deeply appreciate the contributions of these experts. None of my informants, of course, bear any responsibility for my errors of fact or interpretation.

1

HAVANA, 1959

The ferry sailed into the Havana harbor with a blare of basso horn; engines reversing as the ship eased toward the shore. On board was a young American family eager for their first sight of Cuba's legendary capital. Tall, blue-eyed Benjamin C. Evans Jr. was a freshly minted State Department officer, the second secretary in the political section of Havana's U.S. embassy. Evans was also a covert Central Intelligence Agency case officer, assigned to counter Fidel Castro's radical anti-American government.

Blond, self-confident Jan King Evans held the couple's eight-month-old daughter as she assessed Havana: El Morro castle looming over the harbor, the old candy-colored buildings curling along the waterfront Malacón, the thickets of church spires, the bayside refinery belching fire and smoke, the thin Cuban boys treading in the tobacco-colored water calling for coins, and the bearded militiamen waiting beside the gangplank. She could smell the sweet stench of a tropical harbor, as well as a certain romance and a certain menace. Soon it was time to go. Gathering their belongings, the Evanses disembarked into a city seething with revolution.[1]

Ben came from a well-to-do business family in Crawfordsville, Indiana. Growing up during the Great Depression, Evans had excelled at Culver Military Academy, which informed his decision to go to the U.S. Military Academy at West Point. During his service in post–World War II Japan and Korea, Evans was assigned to U.S. Army psychological warfare units focused on countering the growing international communist movement. Psychological warfare graduate studies at Columbia University enhanced his skills. Intelligence became his métier; psywar his weapon.

Jan had even deeper roots in intelligence. Her father was a high-ranking intelligence officer, who died in the 1944 Normandy invasion. Her stepfather was a general in army intelligence during World War II and provided critical analysis during the penultimate battles in Italy and Germany. After the war, he advised President Dwight D. Eisenhower's intelligence committee that led to the CIA's formation. She was also a scion of Washington aristocracy, who had long intersected with America's military and government elites, including the leaders of the nation's intelligence services. From the time she was a young girl, Jan intimately knew the culture of intelligence.

The couple had fallen in love when Ben was serving as Jan's stepfather's aide-de-camp during the post-World War II occupation of Japan. Their marriage commingled American upper-class life and the culture of covert intelligence. During the Cold War, the Evanses lived a privileged life of mansions, foxhunts, and exclusive clubs, bifurcated with the shadow world of tradecraft, intrigue, and strict need-to-know dictums. Moral quandaries and untold secrets were part of their shared existence. As Ben rose to the highest levels of the CIA, the peculiar service shaped him, and his family.

2

INDIANA BEGINNINGS

"I am just plain American and proud of it," Benjamin C. Evans Jr. wrote in 1941 during his seventeenth year, telling of his "heterogeneous mixture" of Dutch, German, English, and Scottish forebears, who had included President Abraham Lincoln's secretary of war, a member of Captain William Kidd's pirate crew, and a Hoosier township trustee who butchered ten hogs a year, in part to feed the citizens who came to his monthly institutes.[1] Evans concluded his family was like most others, "partly good and partly bad."

Born on March 14, 1924, Evans grew up in prim, orderly Crawfordville, Indiana, an agricultural entrepôt for the bountiful farmland that surrounded it, with a population of about 10,000.[2] Under a high prairie sky, tidy commercial buildings surrounded the courthouse square and stately Victorian homes and imposing churches lined its prosperous neighborhoods' leafy streets.

The town prided itself as the "Athens of the Prairie." Wabash College, a Presbyterian school, was an important institution. Founded in 1832 by Presbyterian home missionaries, the college was a bastion of conservative mid-nineteenth-century societal norms. A Wabash College history noted, "And through the pulpit and the church press they reiterated the argument for a college where soul and intellect could be trained. They were convinced that only such a measure would save the great Western Country from free-thinkers, atheists, Catholics, and Unitarians."[3]

Crawfordsville's hometown hero was General Lew Wallace, decorated Civil War general, foreign diplomat, and author of the nineteenth-century's best-selling novel, *Ben-Hur: A Tale of the Christ*. During the panic of 1876–77, Wallace organized a local militia to help quell Indianapolis's "Bread or Blood" labor uprising.[4] Wallace's walled study and home anchored the prosperous Elston Grove neighborhood, which was an enclave of Evans's extended family.

Near to the Wallace estate, Evans's family home was a large, comfortable American foursquare with a broad shady limestone porch. Embellished with quarter-sawn oak and beveled glass, the finely appointed interior signified an established family with resources.[5] Most of his family was active in the neighborhood's First United Methodist Church, which emphasized personal ethics, responsibility, and temperance. One relative's obituary read, "Home, business and church was the trinity of his life," a phrase that characterized the family.[6]

Crawfordsville refracted a Hoosier identity that stressed self-reliance, an enculturated normality, and emotional compression—"an Oriental indifference" one nineteenth-century observer, Mary Dean, termed it. "A Hoosier," she reported to her *Lippincott's Magazine* readers, "is unimpressible, incurious, and incapable of awe. He lives at an inaccessible height of self-respect."[7]

Flu and More Flu

Evans wrote, "I regret that the outstanding memory of my young childhood was sickness." His earliest days were fraught with serious illnesses, including pneumonia, mastoiditis, a concussion, and spinal meningitis. Family lore tells of one crisis during Prohibition, when his teetotaler Methodist father drove to Illinois for some illegal, albeit medicinal, whiskey.[8]

An Evans family retainer, Bina T. Sarver, recorded one crisis in late December 1928 when Ben was four years old. Reporting "flu and more flu," she wrote in her diary of "Benjie" having whooping cough and pneumonia.[9] On Christmas day, with Benjie's temperature at alarming levels, the doctor had to puncture his eardrum. It did not work. She wrote a few days later, "Benjie stays as bad as can be. They are using oxygen to keep him alive." It was ten days before Sarver could note, "Benjie is decidedly improved," and another two weeks before he could even sit up in bed.[10]

The young Ben's early afflictions were so severe that his mother, Ruth Fraley Evans, took him and his older brother, Dan, to Florida and Arizona for a few winters to protect his weakened system. Despite his childhood maladies, Ben was among the largest students in his grade school class. He credited his stature for being frequently given "positions of high responsibility."

Spring Ledge and the Natural Life

Ben's Indiana childhood introduced him to the natural world: "During these early years I developed an ardent love for nature, the out of doors and animals." He credited his paternal grandfather, Frank C. Evans, with teaching him the name of every bird, fish, and animal on the Evans family country estate, Spring Ledge. The family patriarch, Frank Evans, had purchased the sixty-acre plot alongside scenic Sugar Creek in 1917.[11]

Ben found a soul mate in his grandfather Frank—a "distillation of congeniality" as a close family friend later described their relationship.[12] Born in 1875 into a Russellville, Indiana, pioneer farm family, Frank had become a wealthy farm financier. Founded in 1907, his farm loan company became Evans, DeVore and Company. Operating from a suite of offices in the Ben Hur Building, the management, which included Frank Evans's nephew, Lawrence E. DeVore, and his son, Benjamin C. Evans Sr., lent out eastern capital from the Mutual Benefit Life Insurance Company to book millions of dollars of farm mortgages across the fruitful prairie lands of Indiana and Ohio, including hundreds of loans secured by the deep loam soils around Crawfordsville.[13]

Frank was a civic-minded man. He was president of the Methodist Church board of trustees, a member of the Methodist Official Board Sessions, the DePauw University Board of Trustees, president of the Indiana Audubon Society, and an early and important supporter of the area Boy Scouts.[14] Frank was also a flamboyant bon vivant with a wide-ranging mind. Young Ben's aunt later wrote him, "Your Grandfather found rare pleasure in so many things: a joke, a fine movie, a preacher, a poem, a scout, the blue gentian, a field of cattle, a lady's slipper, a horse—a horse! Don't you doubt that your love for a horse, perhaps even your easy seat in the saddle is a legacy?"[15] Tall, impeccably dressed, with an impressive mustache and an authoritative mien, Frank was a striking sight as he inspected his Spring Ledge estate, pausing at the trout pools to feed the fish, watching the nesting birds through binoculars, observing flamingos strut by on their erector-set legs, and feeding the elegant spotted Sika deer that clustered about him in the deer park.

As the Evans family's fortunes rose with the World War I price booms for agricultural products and farmland, the exacting Frank, using the plans of noted Chicago landscape architect Jens Jensen, had transformed Spring Ledge, a former pig farm, into a showplace. Spring Ledge eventually had seventeen landscaped springs, waterfalls, fish pools, a menagerie of birds and mammals, carefully preserved natural habitat for dozens of native bird species, and flower gardens so lavish and expansive that garden clubs came for tours.[16] Soon after Jensen submitted his plans to Evans in 1919, Spring Ledge was getting statewide attention, including being the subject of a long 1920 *Indianapolis News* photo feature, "Spring Ledge, A Bird Paradise Near Crawfordsville, Where Man's Kindness Has Been Fully Appreciated."[17] The Evanses' rambling white clapboard house with knotty pine paneling and a fieldstone fireplace became the family country home, the gathering place for the good life, replete with Dresden china and thick monogrammed napkins. Spring Ledge was to provide a natural idyll and cultural training ground for Ben.

Sarver was the Spring Ledge chronicler. She and her husband Clifford began working as the estate caretakers in February 1919. A former schoolteacher, Sarver kept a remarkable diary, which depicted the natural and political world with a sharp observational eye. Written with a literary tone, it was a verse-and-news-punctuated journal of birds, plants, weather, and Evans family life.

Ben's sojourn in the country became a ritual. Sarver noted, "Benjie came today to spend a month with his Grandparents while his mother and father go on their vacation." When Ben left, she wrote, "the place seems lost without him. He has been so dear and sweet the whole time." The memories were imprinted on Ben. Writing his high school essay more than a decade later, he said, "This increasing love of the out of doors is responsible for a great part of the happiness in my life," and he went on to predict, "I am sure it will bring me greater joy as I grow older."

Boom and Bust

In 1928 Sarver recorded the news of the day: Amelia Earhart (later affiliated with Purdue University) becoming the first woman to fly solo nonstop cross the Atlantic Ocean. Celebrating Republican Herbert Hoover's great electoral victory in November 1928, she echoed the temperance-minded Evans family: "This nation did not want whisky given to her boys and girls. It was more a victory for Prohibition and Protestantism than it was for the Republican party." Through 1929 Sarver made no note about the booming stock market, as she focused more on declining rainfall. Nor did she record her thoughts about the great Wall Street crash of October 1929, or the attendant farm finance crisis. She ended her 1929 diary with a determinedly upbeat entry, calling the year "outstanding," with medical and aviation breakthroughs, hope for arms control and world peace, and, closer to home, improved highways. She did have one portentous observation: "the government has extended relief to agriculture and has placed cooperative agencies at the disposal of farmers."

Sarver wrote of 1930 as a catastrophic year, with the Midwest suffering bad weather of biblical proportions.[18] By 1931 Sarver's lyric diary entries gave way to terse notations. January was "gloomy" and "damp and disagreeable," giving way to "very disagreeable" by spring. Precipitation was a tenth of the year prior, auguring poor crops and strained farm finances. "Hundreds of farmers are being forced to haul water to their stock for the first time in history," she reported. The heat killed so much livestock that the local rendering plant had to hire extra help. The local grain elevator was paying farmers thirteen cents a bushel for oats; $7.50 for a load. "A bushel of wheat or three bushels of oats is worth a gallon of blackberries," Sarver reported. The township was so strapped for cash that neighbors had to donate labor to make the backroads safe enough for the school hack to travel. In the fall of 1931, with oats down to eleven cents a bushel and hogs plummeting to their lowest prices since 1908, Sarver wrote, "Farmers in middle west are calling for a 'Farmers Holiday' & refusing to sell anything until it brings enough to pay cost of production and a small profit."

The Farmers' Holiday Association was officially founded in Des Moines, Iowa, in May 1932. By August strikers were blockading Iowa roads and produce terminals. The movement was primarily centered in the Corn Belt states of Iowa, Nebraska, Minnesota, the Dakotas, Wisconsin, Ohio, Illinois, and Indiana, where massive numbers of farms were bankrupt or being foreclosed.[19]

By the time the 1929 stock market crash hit, agriculture had been in a deep recession for a decade and farmers were just holding on. Then commodity prices virtually collapsed after the crash, falling in unprecedented amounts. Only the farm debt remained unchanged. With farmers unable to make their mortgage payments, farm finance companies, Evans, DeVore and Company among them, were busy with foreclosures. Up and down the country roads, clots of people gathered for closing-out auctions as farmers gave up, their implements and household goods going under the hammer. More than 21,000 rural Hoosier families were on relief in 1932, and the relief requests doubled every year.[20]

One Evans, DeVore foreclosure lived on in family memory: at some point during the farm crisis, the firm foreclosed on a four-hundred-acre farm that was owned by Arthur and Daisy Fraley—Ben and Dan's grandparents. Daniel Evans later recalled, "it prompted me to think for the first time about the legitimacy of certain government supports and the possible need for a moratorium on foreclosures."[21]

The Farmers' Holiday Association called for farmers to voluntarily withhold their produce from market to pressure the government to raise farm prices to a level where costs could be met and a small profit earned. One scholar calculated to reach this level in 1932 farmers would need to receive ninety-two cents per bushel for corn, eleven cents a pound for hogs, and sixty-two cents per pound for butterfat. The prevailing prices in June 1932 were ten cents a bushel for corn, three cents a pound for hogs, and eighteen cents a pound for buttermilk. By August 1932 the Farmers' Holiday Association reported more than half a million midwestern farmers had become members.[22]

Indiana farmers were active in the movement. In August 1932 an Indiana state association was founded in Shelbyville.[23] In Vincennes dairy farmers blocked the bridge over the Wabash River to prevent Illinois farmers from transporting milk to the local creamery. When one farmer ran the blockade, the strikers pursued him through downtown, captured and beat him, and then forced him to dump his milk in the river.[24] As hundreds of picketing farmers across the Corn Belt blocked transport of grain and livestock, the *Crawfordsville Journal Record* ran a photo of the Farmers' Holiday Association president, Milo Reno, publicizing the upcoming thirty-day strike.[25] A week later the paper ran an editorial criticizing the movement, calling it "surely one of the oddest strikes ever proposed," given the perishability of farm products. "The striking farmer is up against a profoundly different proposition than the one that faces his brother in the city," the paper stated.[26]

The editorial ran only two days after front-page stories trumpeted that the assessed valuation of Montgomery County property around Crawfordsville had dropped a huge amount, reflecting the disastrous drop in land values. The state tax board had rejected the county assessment and demanded a 15-percent increase, forcing the county Farm Bureau officials to file an injunction.[27] There were a lot of angry Montgomery County farmers. Evans family lore tells of demonstrations in Crawfordsville. Ben's older brother Daniel F. Evans later wrote, "I can recall when many farmers, pitchfork in hand, staged a protest at the county courthouse against foreclosures; I was permitted neither to watch nor to go downtown. Rather, I was assured the protest was not against Evans, DeVore and Company specifically but rather against the presumed injustice of the system."[28]

While the Farmers' Holiday Association strike channeled the farmers' deep frustration, it failed to improve their economic situation. The widespread movement did, however, sensitize political leaders to the farm crisis. Agricultural legislation became an urgent political matter, one that was soon to affect the Evans family.

New Deal; Bad Times

On November 8, 1932, Sarver dryly noted, "Biggest landslide in years gave the Democratic party a clean sweep, national, state and county." Taking office on March 4, 1933, Franklin D. Roosevelt quickly declared a three-day bank holiday. Sarver declared it was "Cold raw gloomy." In October she decreed, "Everyone is talking 'New Deal,' especially in the barber trade where prices have been boosted from 25 to 40 cents for a hair cut. Everyone is buying razors, brushes and shaving soap."[29]

Agricultural reform became one of the Roosevelt administration's top goals, which quickly translated into new laws during its first hundred days. At the behest of major farm organizations, Congress passed the Agricultural Adjustment Act in May 1933, creating the Agricultural Adjustment Administration. Democratic policy makers envisioned the new law would raise agricultural prices and farmers' incomes by reducing total farm production. Then in June of 1934, Congress amended the Bankruptcy Act of 1898. The newly passed Frazier–Lemke Farm Bankruptcy Act restricted banks' ability to repossess a farm from an insolvent farmer by delaying foreclosure for five years. During that period, the farmer could either agree to buy back the property at the currently appraised value over six years at 1 percent interest or could retain possession as a paying tenant if the mortgagor refused to sell. The law was a blow to farm finance businesses, including Evans, DeVore and Company.[30]

Anarchy was in the air. The Bonus Army of disgruntled World War I veterans had disrupted Washington with near-riotous protests in 1932, until federal troops drove them out with tanks, bullets, and tear gas. The next summer a second Bonus Army unsettled the nation. Bank robberies were endemic. On July 22, 1934, Sarver recorded, "[John] Dillinger No. 1 Public Enemy was killed by Federal officers at Chicago tonight." A few weeks later she noted violent strikes and martial law.[31] Disorder was rife; discontent with the established order widespread. Populist movements were growing, with demagogues such as the radio priest Father Charles Coughlin and Louisiana governor Huey Long reaching disaffected millions through the airwaves. The Communist Party of America, drawing on its strength in the labor force, quintupled its membership through the 1930s.[32] Then there was a great rift in the government itself: the Supreme Court ruled Roosevelt's National Recovery Act unconstitutional, triggering a battle between the judiciary and the executive branch. "Everyone is wondering what will happen now," Sarver wrote with alarm.

One can imagine the discussions around the Spring Ledge dining table. The Evans family had conservative Hoosier values, which typically included both a wariness of large government and a deep respect for the rule of law.[33]

Order was part of their worldview. Amid the seeming anarchy, young Ben must have felt compelled to do something. He was on the fourth-grade school patrol, when he saw a driver speed through a stop sign. "Having recently seen a gangster movie, and being quite impressed with my new responsibility, I wrote down his license number," he remembered. After school, the patrol boy stopped by the police station to file a report and "demanded immediate action." The next Saturday he was in court testifying "in a firm voice" in front of most of his classmates. "The poor man in the case got eighteen days or a ten dollar fine with his license revoked," Ben wrote.

Life Goes On

Through the economic upheaval, the bucolic life of Spring Ledge carried on, with Sarver recording peafowl hatchings, first sightings of orioles, visitors coming to see the blooming gladiolas, hundreds of Nature Study and Audubon Society guests to gander at the bird life, and a garden party for 112 and another for 120. The peacocks still strutted the landscaped grounds; the Sika deer still browsed the deer park. Frank Evans still had his chauffer (the only in town); his wife Ruth still had her maid. Fifty golfers gathered at the adjacent country club for the 1931 state championship. In October 1932 Sarver noted that Frank's exotic birds were still making their annual migration from his aviary to protected quarters: "Caught t[w]o flamingoes and karasoo [sic] and sent them to Lincoln Park Zoo, Chicago, tonight." Some years when Frank and his wife went south for the winter, the fowl went to Florida, too.

Despite the New Deal laws, Evans, DeVore and Company remained solvent. In 1936 the firm was managing farm loans valued between seven and nine million dollars. While a big decline from the 1920s peak, the loan amount was more than the combined assets of the two Crawfordsville banks. With all of the Depression foreclosures, the company was also managing about two hundred farms.[34] While no banker wants to manage property, the farms were appreciating with improving commodity prices. From its nadir in the early 1930s, Indiana farmland had risen steadily in value.[35]

But the farm reform laws and lowered interest rates had narrowed operating margins to the point that Mutual Benefit had to eliminate the farm mortgage middlemen. On May 1, 1936, Evans, DeVore and Company dissolved, reopening as Crawfordsville Farm Loan Branch Office of Mutual Benefit. The principals took a hit: salaries for Frank Evans and Lawrence DeVore were one-quarter of their old ones. As assistant manager, Ben's father, got cut 50 percent.[36] Living big got smaller.

The cadences of Ben's life continued: grade school in Crawfordsville, then time at Spring Ledge. Fishing in the summertime; collecting nuts with his brother Dan as autumn set in. Musing on their different personalities, Sarver wrote, "Danny picked up his hulls and all for they filled up [the basket] faster that way. Benjie hulled his as he went."

Ben's traits of meticulousness and responsibility continued to develop through his boyhood. He had role models. His father was a tightly wound perfectionist who demanded a house so clean that he did not even want trash in the trash baskets.[37] Beyond his Evans, DeVore work, Benjamin Sr. obsessively crafted elaborate furniture in his basement workshop, which was so well equipped it became the subject of a 1929 *Popular Science* article: "One Man Who Has Every Tool a Woodworker Needs."

Ben's mother, Ruth, offered another model. Self-effacing with a sweetness of temperament, she was devoted to her sons. Each school day the boys came home for lunch. After the meal, Ruth and her sons would sing together for fifteen minutes or so before the boys returned to school.[38] With her Methodist principles and strong moral character, she quietly adhered to her beliefs. But she was a redhead with occasional flashes of rebellion, such as the time Ruth emptied a basket of trash down the basement steps into her husband's inviolate woodworking lair.[39]

Be Prepared

Ben began to excel in junior high school, realizing "the importance of working, making good grades and entering into as many activities as possible." With his grandfather's staunch support of the Boy Scouts, it was natural that Ben would follow his lead.[40] Scouting, with its emphasis on honor, service, teamwork, and duty, used a ladder of progressive achievements to focus boys on core principles: rule of law, the Scout Promise, hands-on learning, teamwork, Scout symbolism, personal development, nature appreciation, adult support, and community service. Self-reliance and self-confidence were key goals. "Be prepared," British founder Robert Baden-Powell indelibly counseled.

While Baden-Powell's original program retained a few military elements, scouting emphasized individual decision making and creative learning. The divergence from the military's drill-based hierarchical command structure left future scout-soldiers with an implicit tension between following orders and making individual moral decisions.[41] Ben eventually rose to Eagle Scout, scouting's highest rank. Joining this elite group of "servant-leaders" attested to his focused goal orientation, as well as his determination to serve.[42]

Ben found high school equally rewarding. "High school thus far has been very pleasant for me; I have had very few disappointments," he wrote. His teachers stimulated his thirst for knowledge, which he began to see as essential to an interesting life. Ben concluded that history was about human progress; English language skills could help him convey his thoughts, accurately and effectively. His senior year at Crawfordsville High School brought more honors: he was named editor of the school's *Blue and Gold* newspaper and achieved wider recognition when he won a prestigious state oratorical contest.[43]

Standing on the cusp of adulthood in 1941, Ben was in good shape. He was imbued with a moral compass, a strong work ethic, a preternatural self-knowledge, and a heroic normalness that he was willing to subsume to forces bigger than himself. "I am hoping and planning for a good education; I have a helpful and understanding family; I am among friends, and I live in America," he wrote. "What a land of opportunity and how thankful I should be."

3

THE DIVIDENDS OF CULVER

As the storms of war gathered in the summer of 1941, Benjamin C. Evans Jr. received his first command, a captaincy at Indiana's storied Culver Military Academy. On review day, military cadences echoed across Lake Maxikuckee—the heart thump of the bass drum, the rattle of the snare, the rousing timbre of the brass horns, sharp commands from the cadet officers—as Culver Military Academy's uniformed formations wheeled in front of the garrison parade reviewing stand filled with faculty officers, dignitaries and cottagers from their large lakeside summer homes. All eyes were on Culver's magnificent Black Horse Troop—shining mounts in precise parade gait, troopers at attention in polished saddles, and at the head of the troop rode Captain Evans, tall in the saddle in his dress uniform of gray wool shirt, yellow-striped jodhpurs, and buffed riding boots.

The Culver campus, more than a thousand acres of greensward dotted with medieval-inspired structures, was established on the shores of scenic Lake Maxinkuckee, Indiana's second-largest lake. Maxinkuckee was long a summer destination for prominent Hoosiers. While in residence there, Lew Wallace wrote the first two chapters of *Ben-Hur: A Tale of the Christ*, including the climactic chariot race. After visiting Maxinkuckee, Hoosier poet James Whitcomb Riley penned a verse extoling lake life: "would that the world was always so / Always summer and warmth and light / With mirth and melody day and night." Wealthy Indianapolis families traveled north on the Vandalia Railroad (later the Pennsylvania and Nickel Plate) to their sprawling shore-side cottages. The cottagers, and especially their eligible daughters, became part of the academy's social scene.

Culver Military Academy was founded in 1894 by Saint Louis businessman Henry Harrison Culver, who utilized the military system "for the purpose of thoroughly preparing young men for the best colleges, scientific schools and businesses of America." Great emphasis was put on cadet officers being given substantial authority and responsibility. An early Culver catalog stated, "Through them [the cadets] the greater part of the discipline and instruction of the Corps has to be effected."[1]

With its combination of military-inflected rigor and social cachet, Culver was appealing to conservative parents of means. In its catalogue, Culver preened, "The boys of the Cavalry Camp come from excellent homes and from all sections of America," going on to assure parents that "All the boys must meet certain standards regarding character, moral influence, citizenship, and physical fitness before admission to the camp. Only clean-cut, wholesome young fellows, eager to make the most of their opportunity are admitted." Citing the "broadening influence" of meeting well-connected peers as a "distinct advantage," Culver promised camp friendships to be "particularly close and enduring."[2]

Will, Equitation, and Social Diversion

Evans began attending the academy's Woodcraft Summer Camp while still in grade school.[3] Oriented around scouting, the camp counselors trained boys in Indian and woodlore, nature study, handicrafts, sports, and "just enough military to teach boys habits of neatness, promptness, and courtesy," as the camp brochure promised.[4] Through challenging activities, such as learning to swim and start fires without matches, the Woodcrafters embraced the Culver motto, "I can if I will."[5]

The Woodcraft Camp director was Spanish-American and World War I veteran Colonel Robert Rossow, who had recently stepped down from being Commandant of Cadets.[6] Rossow had many tales of Culver derring-do to tell the impressionable young Woodcrafters. There was the remarkable story from 1913, when Culver cadets loaded their naval cutters on railroad cars to rescue 1,400 citizens from flooded Logansport, Indiana, a small city about forty miles away. The grateful townspeople memorialized the rescue by erecting Culver's Logansport Gate. Rossow recounted the tale of Culver officers and alumni battling Chicago gangsters who robbed the nearby State Exchange Bank on May 29, 1933.[7] Armed with Springfield rifles and an automatic weapon, ten battle-seasoned Culver officers and five hundred local vigilantes (who included several Culver graduates) eventually captured the bandits in a swamp about ten miles from the academy.

In 1939 when he was fifteen, Evans enrolled in Culver's summer Cavalry School. Culver's enrollment had dropped to about half during the depths of the Great Depression, but more boys were signing up as the economy improved through the 1930s.[8] Culver was an expensive school. The 1941 Summer Cavalry Camp brochure indicated the eight-week program cost $445 for tuition and uniforms—a substantial amount when the Department of Labor reported American workers were making less than seventy cents an hour.⁹

Culver's summer cavalry course was organized with instruction in "equitation and horsemanship" that advanced over three summers. The first summer, the Culver cavalry officers, most trained at the U.S. Army Cavalry School, focused on teaching fundamentals, including "a good seat," which Evans may have already acquired with his grandfather's assistance. The second and third summers the instructors emphasized jumping, cross-country riding, and trick riding, such as Roman riding astride two horses. The climax of the summer course was the ten-day "Hundred Mile Ride" across northern Indiana.¹⁰

Culver's famous Black Horse Troop dated back to 1897, when Commandant of Cadets Leigh R. Gignilliat, a young Virginia Military Institute graduate, organized the cavalry unit of matched black horses.¹¹ In 1910 Gignilliat took over the academy's command. A former Indiana governor, Vice President Thomas Marshall invited the Black Horse Troop to serve as his guard of honor for President Woodrow Wilson's first and second inauguration parade. The Black Horse Troop appearances gave Culver extraordinary exposure. Over time, the troop became the military academy's most important symbol.

As World War I enveloped Europe, Gignilliat became a leader in the Preparedness Movement, which agitated for civilian military training and expanded armed forces. His influential 1916 book, *Arms and the Boy: Military Training in Schools and Colleges*, argued that military academies prepared boys for martial and civilian life with discipline, physical challenges, and organization.¹² When the United States entered the war, Gignilliat and other Culver teachers volunteered for duty, as did nearly 3,500 Culver alumni, of whom eighty-six gave their lives.¹³

Beyond horsemanship, the Culver teachers instructed the cadets in martial skills, including boxing, fencing, and marksmanship. There was an emphasis on physical development, particularly posture. With constant correction, the cadets learned the "proper set-up" to broaden their chests and straighten their shoulders into a military bearing. The Culver catalogue stated, "The military system also tends to develop in the boy a pride in his carriage and his physical fitness."

Social development was one of Culver's key selling points. The program highlighted music, including a glee club that Evans joined. The singers regularly performed for the cottagers at their summer homes. And then there were "social diversions"—movies and dances. To prepare, the cadets took dancing lessons three times a week; partnering with one another to practice waltzes and fox trots. The protocols of a formal receiving line, dance cards, and decorous behavior were mandatory. The weekly dances provided opportunities for the cadets to mingle with the ladies from the "delightful summer colony of Lake Maxinkuckee," as the catalogue termed it. "The high character of the nearby lake community, populated by summer residents of cultivated tastes, affords an unusual opportunity for pleasant social contacts."[14]

Culver also recruited internationally. The school's first international cadet, Xenophon Kalamatiano, graduated in 1899. Kalamatiano achieved some infamy in 1918, when the Soviet Cheka counterrevolutionary police arrested him for being an American spy.[15] The Soviets initially sentenced Kalamatiano to be executed but released him in 1921 after failing to negotiate a prisoner exchange for Hoosier labor leader Eugene V. Debs, whom the U.S. government had imprisoned for opposing the war.

With Culver's determined recruitment campaign, a steady stream of wealthy international cadets, especially from cavalry-smitten Latin America, began to make their way to northern Indiana. The academy boasted of cadets from Panama, Peru, El Salvador, the Philippines, Singapore, and Cuba, whose first cadet attended in 1919.[16] The Crown Prince of Siam attended in the 1920s.[17] In 1941, when Evans commanded Troop B, two Cubans, a Costa Rican, a Brazilian, and an Argentinian attended Culver. Culver's international cadets, typically from their societies' upper strata, gave their American classmates an opportunity to mingle with powerful families from around the globe.

Summers of Growth

Evans considered his first summer of the cavalry course to be inauspicious. He wrote, "My first [year] I spent as an unimportant, insignificant, third classman, learning to take criticism and never to give it."[18] But he persisted, earning a Bronze Tuxis Medal, the lowest proficiency emblem. During his second summer of cavalry school he served as a sergeant. While he learned the finer points of horsemanship, Evans still termed it "a summer of mediocracy [sic]. His third summer he came into his own, serving as Troop B captain of the Black Horse Troop, commanding troopers from twenty-four states and Argentina.[19] His command was a coveted position, part of what he called "a summer of leadership."

The academy shaped Evans, introducing him to the warrior ethos: integrity, honor, selflessness, and courage. He learned military discipline, the value of competence, and a respect for unflappability. He developed physically. Intellectually, he gained an international perspective. Over the three summers, he polished his social skills, which were enhanced by his equestrian accomplishments. Culver gave him an entré into the world of the powerful and privileged. "I feel that I have spent three very profitable summers at Culver," Evans wrote in 1941. "I am hoping that these three summers will be paying dividends for the rest of my life."

Evans experienced a structured adolescence. Growing up in the cloistral enclaves of Elston Grove, Spring Ledge, and Culver, he learned leadership skills, respect for authority, and an imperative to defend civil society against threats to the established order.

In his senior yearbook photographs, the six-foot, two-inch Evans towered above his classmates, and with his military bearing, blue eyes, and classical profile, it was easy to understand the lead phrase of his yearbook entry: "Makes the girls' hearts beat faster."[20] His school activities reflected his intelligence, talents, and work ethic: honor roll, glee club, editorship of the school newspaper, presidencies of the Audubon and speech arts clubs. He won the Central Indiana Oratorical contest.[21] And with a maturity that belied his age, Evans wrote, "As for myself, no matter how great the depression is, or how prosperous the country is; no matter how may wars are about us, or how peaceful the world is, we get out of life in exact proportion to what we put into it."[22]

4

WEST POINT

West Point during World War II was intense. With battles raging in the Pacific, North Africa, and Europe in 1942, the army crammed the academy's already daunting four-year course into three grueling years—"the war time course" the officers called it.[1] With the war's outcome uncertain, the military needed young officers in the fight.[2]

Cadet Benjamin C. Evans Jr. enrolled in the academy on July 1, 1943, and his class was the first to experience the compressed wartime program. The cadets were joining a storied American institution. President Thomas Jefferson signed legislation in 1802 establishing the military academy at West Point, a battlement that guarded a strategic pinch point on the Hudson River. In the process of teaching the art and science of war, the academy officers inculcated the cadets with an unbreakable code of honor, self-discipline, and respect for tradition. With the West Point motto, "Duty, Honor, Country," as the guiding light, the U.S. Military Academy graduates and cadets formed the Long Gray Line.[3]

Evans's path to West Point was circuitous. After graduating from Crawfordsville High School in 1942, he enrolled in Wabash College, the conservative Presbyterian school that educated many members of his extended family.[4] His older brother, Daniel Fraley Evans, was already at Wabash, building a record as an exemplary student leader, particularly as a champion orator. Graduating with a straight-A average in October 1943, Dan quickly volunteered for the navy.[5]

As he had done in high school, Ben excelled at English and speech, and did middling in science and math. He was in his brother's fraternity, Phi Gamma Delta, ran cross-country, and sang in the glee club.[6] But with America at war, Evans made plans to join his brother in military service.

Senator Raymond E. Willis of Indiana appointed Evans to West Point in 1943. Willis had graduated from Wabash College in 1896. After a career as a northern Indiana newspaperman, postmaster, and state representative, Willis unsuccessfully ran for the U.S. Senate in 1938 as an outspoken candidate of the resurgent Indiana Republican Party, which was battling the New Deal.[7]

Two years later, Willis ran again as a supporter of the Midwest-centered isolationist movement led by "Mr. Republican," Senator Robert Taft of Ohio.[8] This time Willis won his Senate seat, and with it the power to appoint young men to the military academies.

Evans was connected. His uncle, Noble R. Shaw, was active in the state Republican Party and was also a Wabash graduate. According to family lore, Shaw engaged his powerful Washington friends to lobby Willis about a West Point appointment for his accomplished nephew.[9] And it was soon a done deal—Evans was headed to the academy.[10]

Hell on the Hudson

The cadets called West Point "Hell on the Hudson," especially the plebe year when the full weight of the rigorous military system bore down on the heads of eighteen-year-olds. The academy might be a free government-paid education, but it nonetheless exacted a price. With his Culver introduction to military discipline, Evans was undoubtedly better prepared than some of his classmates who came from farms and small towns with little inkling of what awaited them.

Unlike most incoming cadets, the war-years plebes were given basic army training, so were at least spared Beast Barracks, the nickname for the traditional seven-week cadet basic training.[11] The transition from civilian to cadet was still an arduous, character-challenging process. From the moment the day began with shrill bugle calls and the clatter of drums, the plebes endured regimented rounds of five-mile runs, calisthenics, and precision marching in sweltering summer heat. Throughout the day, the plebes marched in mandatory formations and raced double time when not. There were endless bracings by upperclassmen and officers.

With the war-shortened curriculum, the cadet course of instruction was a relentless grind. There were demanding classes in civil engineering and military science (especially hygiene, as disease always took more soldiers than combat), chemistry, physics, law, English, foreign languages, and international relations. "You were so pressed academically and physically," Evans's roommate Corbin Davis said, "you just had to work your heart out to stay."[12]

While the West Point program focused on training cadets to be professional military officers, it included formal academic classes that encouraged discussion and independent thinking. Evans and his classmates were beneficiaries of the West Point curriculum that had evolved to resolve what one commentator termed "the contradictions between Athenian and Spartan goals."[13]

At West Point, Evans continued to excel in language and social science courses. He did marginally well with military subjects and hard science. His classmates termed him a "goat" in mathematics.[14]

To prepare themselves for the rigors of war, cadets were also expected to participate in sports. "Every man an athlete," was part of the West Point ethos. During the war years, West Point was a football powerhouse, going undefeated from 1944 through 1947. (Their opponents groused that their best players were off fighting the war, while the military academy could stockpile its talent.)[15] When General Douglas MacArthur addressed the 1946 academy graduation, he reminded the cadets of the importance of sports: "On the fields of friendly strife are sown the seeds that on other days and other fields will bear the fruits of victory."[16]

Evans was an enthusiastic athlete, running cross-country, the half-mile, and hurdles in track. He was on the lacrosse team and the ski club. Drawing on his equestrian training, Evans was a leading member of the intramural riding team, and an outstanding jumper.[17] His classmates viewed Evans as a composed, low-key leader. "He had a good disposition, a good sense of humor. He was from a family of means and wealth, but he didn't flaunt it," Davis said. "He just knew how to fit into a situation. He didn't look down on anybody." Speaking of Evans's leadership style, Davis noted, "He kept his mouth shut. He could observe people. He kept his cool. He could see a fool when he saw one. He was a learner; he worked."[18]

Affable and easy-going, Evans was sometimes a target of pranks. One day just before room inspection, his two roommates barricaded the door shut, thinking he would panic when he could not enter. Unflustered, Evans enlisted the services of a friend across the hall: All-American football end Hank Foldberg. The roommates inside heard "Mr. Evans, please stand out of the way!" just before the door splintered. Evans calmly entered the room, knowing his roommate, the room orderly, would have to explain the smashed door.[19]

West Point discipline was based on a system of demerits. Behavior was so codified that one 1914 study determined cadets could receive demerits for 18,000 different infractions. Robert E. Lee reportedly graduated without receiving one demerit, but he was the exception. Ulysses S. Grant graduated with 290 demerits; World War I commanding general John Pershing received 200.[20]

A solid, hardworking cadet, Evans had relatively few infractions. The demerits he received were for minor offenses: dusty shelves, a spot on his overcoat, or lint on his cap. But in the spring of 1944, West Point cadet Evans was marching to and fro in the courtyard below the crenelated gray-stone cadet barracks. Marching in his dress gray uniform with white cross belts, his drill rifle at right-shoulder arms, Evans was "walking the area," a punishment tour for failing to salute a senior officer of the guard one night while on sentinel duty. What caused his insubordination while on sentinel duty? According to family lore, while on guard duty, animal-loving Evans had picked up a shivering cat and tucked it under his coat. When the senior officer arrived for inspection, Evans could not salute properly because he was holding up the cat.[21]

The War and West Point

The war's momentum shifted in 1944, as the Allies invaded Italy and commenced a massive bombing of Germany. On D-Day, June 6, 1944, the Allied army invaded Normandy with hundreds of thousands of soldiers soon pouring into France, liberating Paris in late August. On the eastern front, the Soviet forces were advancing toward Germany. In the Pacific, the hard-fought victories in Guadalcanal and Tarawa led to the amphibious landings on Saipan and Guam.

Dan Evans was in the thick of the fighting in the Pacific, where he was a crewmember of the USS *Levy,* one of the navy's first destroyer escorts. During the summer of 1944, the *Levy* supported the invasion of the Mariana Islands, and the carrier-based air battles during the Battle of the Philippine Sea. Later in 1944, the *Levy* took part in the conquests of the western Carolinas and Leyte.[22]

At West Point, the army added military training to the accelerated program that was already challenging Ben Evans and his classmates. For the first time, the military academy offered pilot training, and the War Department authorized West Point to commission 60 percent of its officers into the Air Corps. With the air war strategically crucial, most cadets, including Evans, wanted to be in the air corps. It was the hot ticket. Pilots were considered to be a higher echelon than foot-slogging infantrymen—and the paychecks were fatter. But after starting pilot training, Ben's body sabotaged him. For a month in the summer of 1945, he was on sick leave, recovering from surgery to repair a double hernia. With full-time flight training taking over a year to complete, including four months at the military's primary flight schools, he missed his opportunity to become certified for the air corps.[23]

Despite the war, social activities remained an important part of the academy regimen. Evans served on the *Howitzer* yearbook staff. He joined the glee club and Cadet Chapel Choir, where his clear tenor won him a slot on the "A Squad." His classmates decreed him to be "the most important member" of both ensembles, and enjoyed his trio, which performed serenades by the clock tower on warm spring nights.[24]

Saturday night hops were an academy highlight. From New York City and nearby colleges, gowned lovelies arrived to dance with the uniformed cadets. Circling the ballroom of venerable Cullen Hall, the couples danced the approved waltzes and foxtrots, occasionally spiced with elaborated grapevine and twinkle steps. Like Culver, the cadets knew they were being judged on their social skills. A clumsy "elephant" could get demerits for bad footwork. Evans was not among them "He was a good dancer," Davis recalled. "With ladies, he didn't have any problems."[25]

Tall, socially adept Evans soon had an OAO—a "One And Only" in the West Point argot—a winsome Vassar science and math student named Margaret Gresham from Birmingham, Alabama. The two met at a West Point dance. "They were very regimented," Margaret Gresham Livingston said about these weekends. "They had definite rules about what you could and could not do." The young women were sequestered in a separate dormitory at West Point. "There were row after row after row of beds," she remembered. "They were very careful about what you wore—'Dress properly,' we were told." Livingston noted, "You met your date at the dance. He couldn't take you back."[26] His final year at West Point, Evans was a "king of the walk," who could stroll with his now-pinned OAO along "flirtie," Flirtation Walk, the rustic riverside trail that was the only place on the academy grounds where cadets were allowed sanctioned displays of affection, such as hand-holding.[27]

But in Evans's last years at West Point, the reality of war was never far away. The military history class had a strategic map of the World War II battlefields, and each day cadets tracked the campaign strategies and outcomes on the European and Pacific fronts, before pivoting to the principals of warfare as illuminated in previous conflicts. Antoine Henri Jomini's *Life of Napoleon* illuminated the Russian eastern front. The Civil War offered perspectives on tactics in France, Belgium, and Germany. The Military Art and Engineering classes focused on battlefield construction—and destruction. Instructions on ridges, roads, and field fortifications were commingled with lessons on ordnance and sapper tactics.[28]

In February 1945, 1,200 American and British heavy bombers dropped 4,000 tons of bombs on Dresden.[29] The bombing and subsequent firestorm killed as many as 135,000 people. Kurt Vonnegut Jr., who had also summered on the shores of Lake Maxinkuckee, was a survivor of the bombing and immortalized it in his celebrated book, *Slaughterhouse-Five; or, The Children's Crusade*.[30]

With the Allied forces closing in from two sides, the German Reich was collapsing. On April 30, 1945, Adolf Hitler killed himself in his Berlin bunker. On May 8, 1945, the West Point cadets celebrated V-E Day along with millions of Americans. Germany had surrendered. President Harry Truman announced the victory with a warning to the Japanese: "We are going to be in a position where we can turn the greatest war machine in the history of the world loose on the Japanese; and I am informed by the Chiefs of Staff, by the Secretary of State, and the Secretary of the Navy, that Japan is going to have a terrible time from now on."[31]

The Japanese were already having a terrible time. In March 1945 American bombers began firebombing Tokyo, where 85,000 eventually died. That same month as Iwo Jima fell, Dan Evan's ship, the *Levy*, began bombarding the remaining Japanese-held atolls in the Marshall Islands.[32] In mid-July the United States successfully tested the world's first atomic bomb in New Mexico.

In July 1945 the victorious U.S., British, and Soviet political leaders met in Potsdam to decide the future of postwar Europe. It was not a harmonious conference. The victors' disagreements over Soviet control of Eastern Europe and the disposition of vanquished Germany prefigured a new kind of war—a Cold War, which was to shape global politics for the next decades.

The war against Japan ended with a bang. On August 6, 1945, the *Enola Gay* dropped Little Boy on Hiroshima. The atomic blast eventually killed 140,000 people. On August 9 the second atomic bomb landed on Nagasaki. An estimated 70,000 Japanese eventually died. On August 15, 1945, the Japanese announced their surrender, with the formal ceremony on the battleship USS *Missouri* in Tokyo Bay on September 2, 1945.[33] World War II was over, but a new war was already beginning.

Ben Evans graduated from the U.S. Military Academy on June 4, 1946, ranking 694th out of his graduating class of 875 cadets.[34] The same day the War Department issued him his appointment as second lieutenant in the infantry.

The army assigned Lieutenant Evans to Fort Benning, Georgia's Infantry School for the Basic Officer Course.[35] Evans was to find the curriculum somewhat familiar. During the war the Officer Candidate School there became a veritable officer-making machine under the guidance of West Point officers, whose instructions were suffused with military academy protocols.[36] From July 1941 to May 1947, more than 100,000 candidates enrolled, with more than 67,000 "90-day wonders" graduating as commissioned lieutenants. The Pentagon claimed it was the biggest and fastest commissioning job ever attempted by an army.

Before reporting to Fort Benning, Evans took his well-earned graduation furlough. He and Margaret, first traveled with the Evans family to Indiana. After the pressure-filled academy years, he was once again able to take solace in nature, with days of family, flowers, and hunting.[37] En route to Fort Benning, Evans made a stop in Birmingham, Alabama, to meet Margaret's family. However, by the time he left for his next assignment some months later, the two had decided to part ways.[38] Soon after, Lieutenant Evans was embarking for occupied Japan.

5

THE EARTHQUAKE

On June 28, 1948, an earthquake devasted Fukui, Japan. Lieutenant Benjamin C. Evans Jr. had just showered after an afternoon tennis match when a violent shake overturned his bed and spewed the contents of his locker across the room. Wrenching the jammed door open, he ricocheted down the stairs, "feeling like a billiard ball which had been thrown in a bath tub," he wrote his family. Clutching a swaying tree in the yard, Evans watched a five-story concrete building collapse as people staggered toward open areas. "Then there was an awful snap of the earth, after which every standing thing in sight seemed to fall," Evans wrote. "The dead & bloody were scattered along the streets, and we could hear the moans of those people caught in adjacent movie house."[1] The fires soon began.

A year earlier, Evans had arrived in Japan as part of the U.S. occupation force.[2] When the quake struck, there was a small American contingent of ten officers, seventeen enlisted men, and seven dependent families in Fukui. Evans was the chief of the military government's Civil Information and Education team, which was focused on ingraining Japanese students with democratic and antimilitaristic ideals.

An industrial city of about 85,000, Fukui was situated about 120 miles northeast of Kyoto on the west side of Honshu, Japan's largest island. The 7.0 magnitude earthquake ravaged Fukui and the surrounding prefecture.[3] When the massive tremor struck at 5:14 p.m., the cooking fires were lit, which ignited two dozen conflagrations across the city. Within a few hours the flames could be seen thirty miles away.[4]

The American officers quickly realized that their first impulse to help individuals "would be a drop in the bucket," Evans wrote. Still only clad in boxer shorts, Evans received an order from Lieutenant Colonel James Hyland to alert the higher echelons, including the Eighth Army and the Supreme Commander for the Allied Powers, Douglas MacArthur. Evans was then to act as liaison. But when Evans raced to the railway station to call headquarters in Kyoto, he discovered the lines were down. Dodging fallen wires and huge crevasses in the streets, pushing away dying and injured people, Evans next ran to the radio station, which was also destroyed. "I picked up a bloody baby from middle of the street," he wrote, "and tried to put her where someone would notice her."

Commandeering a jeep and an interpreter, Evans tried to drive out of the city to a working phone, but the roads were blocked. "The fire was spreading from the south part of town; the bridges were out to the north, to the east, and west; the mountains had fallen over the roads," he recalled. The fires eventually subsided enough to the south for him to escape Fukui. "The roads full of debris, house tops & people looking under roofs for their families. The next 4 hrs. drive was Hell," he wrote. Evans finally reached a detachment with a working phone in Tsurga, where he was able to call I Corps in Kyoto and the Eighth Army in Yokohama. For the next days, Evans was Fukui's only link to the outside world.

In Indiana the Evans family learned of the disaster the next day, when they read the *Indianapolis Star* story from the Associated Press, which quoted Lieutenant Evans of Crawfordsville, Indiana, who indicated, "the loss of life might be extremely large." A telegram went out to Japan the same day: "Are you all right. What things do you need most urgently? May God bless you and keep you safe."[5] Evans wrote back that they might replace his tailored gabardine shirt from Rogers Peet, the upscale Manhattan clothing store that had all of his measurements. And he wrote, "There is nothing in this world that means more to me than my home & family."[6]

The earthquake destroyed more than 63,000 buildings in the prefecture, and severely damaged thousands of other structures.[7] The city's two railway stations and the seven-story Daiwa department store had collapsed into contorted jumbles of columns and beams. Hundreds of moviegoers died when the theater floor fell into the basement, and then the crumpling building buried them. Thousands more were feared dead. Adding to the trauma, the people of Fukui were just recovering from an American bombing raid in 1945 that had destroyed 97 percent of the city's buildings. "There's no time for self pity," Evans wrote his family, "for all of those around us have lost everything for the second time—1st Time, B-29s."[8]

The American Experiment

Evans was one of the 250,000 U.S. occupation troops assigned to Japan as part of a unique experiment to transform feudal, militaristic Japan into a pacifist, democratic country. By late 1945 Japan was supine, the Japanese armed forces were devastated, and the Americans had firebombed all the major cities—sixty-six, including Hiroshima and Nagasaki. Around three million Japanese had died in the war, with millions more wounded, ill, homeless, and malnourished. In addition, as many as six million Japanese expatriates in overseas colonies were streaming back to the home islands. Perhaps a third of Japan's total wealth had been destroyed, including four-fifths of all shipping, a third of the industrial tooling machinery, and a quarter of all rolling stock and vehicles. Urban living standards had plummeted to one-third of prewar levels.[9]

When Ben Evans arrived in Japan in 1947, the cities still had nightmare vistas of bombed-out devastation. The streets were filled with traumatized survivors, including the shunned Hiroshima and Nagasaki victims, "polluted" by atomic radiation.[10] Gangs of orphaned street urchins clustered in the rubble. With social and economic networks destroyed, prostitution was rampant. Impoverishment was the norm.

MacArthur, and the 3,200 non-Japanese bureaucrats who served under him, intended to revolutionize Japan—to eliminate the social, religious, and economic conditions that had engendered Japanese militarism.[11] Arguing that Japan's unconditional surrender had given MacArthur autocratic powers, the Americans ran the country.[12] During the six years and eight months of the occupation, Japan had no sovereignty and no diplomatic relations. Japanese were not permitted to make any major political, economic, or administrative decisions without MacArthur's express permission—for most of that period, they were not even allowed to travel overseas.[13]

The Allies had a radical agenda, as they believed implanting antimilitarism and democracy involved changing all areas of Japanese life. Outlined by the Potsdam Agreement, and elaborated through Joint Chiefs of Staff directives, both public and secret, the United States and its allies instituted major Westernizing reforms intended to insure Japan would never again wage an imperial war.[14] Administered by "Proconsul" MacArthur with his absolute powers, the occupation ironically had a New Deal agenda, with an emphasis on equality of opportunity through labor unions, industrial demonopolization, women's empowerment, land redistribution, and education reform.[15] It was intended to create a tectonic cultural shift.

As chief of a prefecture-level Civil Information and Education team, Lieutenant Evans was in the phalanx of MacAuthur's New Education campaign that recast Japanese schools and cultural institutions.[16] The CI&E teams endeavored to reshape the Asian society with myriad programs, from running reading rooms to offering square dancing classes to supplant samurai bushido norms.[17] The CI&E priority was the educational system. CI&E officers oversaw the screenings of teachers, administrators, and education committee members, with the intent of purging former members of imperialist groups, such as the militarized political party, the Imperial Rule Assistance Association, and left-wing radicals.

With help of Japanese interpreters and facilitators, the teams imparted "democratizing" doctrines to Japanese teachers for the reeducation of their students.[18]

As part of the wholesale reorganization of Japanese education, new textbooks extolling democratic and antimilitarist values needed to be published. Until new textbooks arrived, CI&E teams supervised the censoring of the existing Japanese textbooks.[19] The students censored the schoolbooks during class time by inking out militaristic and feudal narratives—a process known as *Suminuri-Kyōkasho*—"blacking-out primers."[20] It was a wrenching experience for young students, who had been meticulously instructed to care for their books. For the students, the blacking-out of previously sacrosanct ideals underscored the finality of defeat, and the unfettered power of the tall, well-fed American soldiers.

Although the Japanese people embraced the democratization agenda with a remarkable zeal, the Allied authorities were increasingly concerned about the growing communist and radical socialist militancy in Japanese unions, including the teachers' union. When broad popular momentum built in January 1946 for a massive general strike, MacArthur canceled the protest, stating he would not permit "the use of so deadly a social weapon."[21] That same month Evans's Eighth Army CI&E officers were directed to teach "democratic" collective bargaining techniques, such as arbitration, mediation, and conciliation.[22] On May Day 1946, 2.7 million Japanese joined 7,000 unions.[23]

Rising social unrest led to increased membership in the Japanese Communist Party. With the rapidly escalating Cold War shaping U.S. foreign policy, the occupation's New Deal-style programs were supplanted with policies designed to contain communism, particularly by rebuilding Japanese industry. The policy shift, which came to be known as Reverse Course, began in 1947, and continued through the occupation. Reverse Course banned strikes by public workers, sharply reduced private-sector union bargaining power, eliminated the previous policies to break up the industrial conglomerates known as zaibatsu, and returned conservative Japanese politicians to power. The Japanese communists were targeted, including being blacklisted during the "red purges," which began in 1949.[24]

In his letters home, Evans wrote of his propaganda work: "Spent the day in Fukui City working with Col. on press release exposing Communist activity and planning a Communist control program. I think we have the Commies right where we want them. Our jails are full of them and outsiders are afraid to step into the prefecture. We all realize that putting them in jail is not going to solve the problem—so we are out to expose their illegal political agitation."[25] A few weeks later Evans wrote his family, "I am now writing a feature news article on how we have been able to control and suppress Communist activity during the disaster period by enforcing existing Jap laws and encouraging the enactment of new laws—as their need appears. I am hoping it will get a lot of publicity for we feel that our handling of the Commies in Fukui can serve as an example to others."[26]

The Relief Train

Fukui earthquake relief became the priority. Evans's phone call to alert I Corps in Kyoto about the damage got a rapid response. Military operators routed the information to the Tudor-style Daimaru Villa across from the old Imperial Palace that had been commandeered for the I Corp's chief of staff General Eugene Harrison and his family.[27] Under General Joseph M. Swing, the decorated airborne commander who had helped to liberate the Philippines, I Corps was responsible for the military government of the southern half of Japan. Swing and other I Corps officers were scheduled to attend a dinner party that night at the Harrison home.

Harrison's fifteen-year-old stepdaughter, Jan King, picked up the phone. When the seismic waves had hit Kyoto a few hours earlier, she had rushed from the bathroom to stand under a doorway, as her maternal step-grandfather, the peripatetic British journalist and informal diplomat Sir Willmott Lewis, had instructed her to do in the event of an earthquake. A tall, self-possessed young woman, she proceeded to act as the phone liaison between the I Corps commanders and their headquarters in Tokyo. She later wrote that she "very much felt part of what transpired in setting up a train taking help and supplies that very night to Fukui. I had the audacity to ask my step-father's boss—the BIG general—if I could accompany him on the train."[28] Most likely bemused, Swing agreed—perhaps so his twenty-two-year-old daughter accompanying him to Fukui would have a traveling companion.

When he had called Kyoto, Evans had dictated a five-page list of needed equipment and supplies—"from bulldozers to splints"—to the I Corps officers, who had prioritized the requisitions. Evans wrote his family, "General Swing called me and said he was taking a special train to Fukui—I told him he could go no further by rail than Tsurga."[29]

Early that next morning, Evans met Swing at the Tsurga railway station. Climbing into Swing's private railway car, Evans proceeded to make his dire report. Unbeknownst to the officers, King overheard Evans's damage assessment through the thin wall of the adjoining bedroom. She later remembered that when Evans reported the death toll might reach 3,000, Swing snapped, "Calm down, Lieutenant It can't be that bad." When the Kyoto contingent clambered into jeeps to view the damage, they found devastation. "It was a real shock," King said. "The town was destroyed—the smoke! There were dead bodies everywhere."[30] She thought Swing, like many generals, had trouble accepting that the situation under his command was in such chaos. The Fukui Prefecture death toll eventually reached more than five thousand.[31]

6

AIDE-DE-CAMP

General Eugene Harrison needed an aide-de-camp.[1] As I Corps chief of staff, Harrison was a key administrator in the military government of the southern half of Japan. It was a big job, with a lot of high-level diplomatic obligations. He needed a savvy aide with competency and social polish.

Beyond needing a new aide-de-camp to assist with military duties, Harrison needed help with his new family. After forty-seven years as a bachelor, Harrison had married a war widow with three young children in 1946. The former Karla Heurich King; her fifteen-year-old daughter, Jan; and two sons, thirteen-year-old Charles (Chippie) and ten-year-old Donald, were living with him at the Daimaru Villa in Kyoto.

Eugene Lynch Harrison was among the last of the old-time horse cavalrymen. Born in 1898 in San Augustine, a small sawmill town in the rough-and-tumble piney woods of deep East Texas, Harrison garnered an appointment to West Point, graduating in 1923.[2] Commissioned into the cavalry, he was posted to the Mexican border at Camp Marfa, where he reveled in the competitive equestrian sports, especially polo, which animated the moribund military years after World War I.[3] It was the heyday of military polo, when the army polo team dominated the wildly competitive sport. George S. Patton Jr., later famous as a hard-charging World War II general, headed the 1922 army team that won the junior championship. Patton wrote: "The virtue of polo as a military accomplishment rests on the following; It makes a man think fast while he is excited; it reduces his natural respect for his own safety, that is, makes him bold; it should teach restraint under exciting circumstances."[4] Harrison excelled at polo, both at West Point and on active duty, and was a member of the 1931–32 U.S. Olympic Equestrian Squad.

Posted to the Third Cavalry Regiment at Fort Myer, Virginia, Harrison also served as a popular aide to Franklin D. Roosevelt's White House, where he often escorted First Lady Eleanor Roosevelt on her cherished horseback rides along the Potomac River. Harrison was an immaculately groomed, socially adept aide with notable composure. After a stint at West Point as an athletics manager, Harrison returned to the Washington crucible during the fraught years between 1940 and 1942, serving as aide to General Jacob Devers and Secretary of War Henry Stimson.[5]

With his military skills, exceptional judgment, and social connections, Harrison was tapped in 1942 to take command of the Forty-Second Armored Regiment, Fourteenth Armored Division. Soon posted to the European theater, Harrison joined General Devers's personal staff in London and Algiers. As the allied armies battled their way up the boot of Italy in 1944, Harrison served as assistant chief of staff in operations for IV Corps, and later in Corsica.

In France and Germany during the closing days of the European campaign, Harrison found his métier: intelligence. While serving as the Sixth Army Group's assistant chief of staff G2 (intelligence), Harrison's analysts had predicted in April 1944 that the German army was no longer capable of forming a last-ditch National Redoubt in the Alps.[6] Later that year, Harrison's officers, working with Office of Strategic Services spies, had forecast Operation Nordwind, the massive attack launched by German army Group G on December 31, 1944. Among other discoveries, Harrison's analysts deduced aerial photos of prepositioned forward artillery emplacements presaged an attack. When OSS behind-the-lines raids to capture prisoners encountered fierce resistance, Harrison had urged OSS officers to persevere. "Thousands of men a day are being killed along the front," he said, urging them to not "hesitate to take any risks with their agents."[7] Based on the vetted intelligence, G2 deduced the Germans would attack on New Year's Eve, when the Americans would be celebrating. Leaves were canceled and defenses stiffened. The intelligence coup saved many American lives during what proved to be the last major Nazi offensive.

Harrison was also instrumental in the success of the Alsos Mission, a secret Manhattan Project mission that captured four crucial German atomic laboratories and the lead German scientist. With Hitler trumpeting a Nazi "super-weapon" that would snatch victory from the jaws of defeat, the Manhattan Project scientists were terrified the scientifically sophisticated Germans were about to unleash an atom bomb. The subsequent investigations allayed the Allied fears that the Nazis were close to having such weapons.[8]

Returning to the United States after the war, Harrison became the Army Ground Forces G2. In late 1945 he served on the Lovett Committee, which was organizing a new intelligence department to replace the OSS and its transitory successors.[9] The new organization was named the Central Intelligence Agency.

The Finest Lieutenant

Harrison's new aide-de-camp, Lieutenant Benjamin C. Evans Jr., arrived at the Tudor-styled Daimaru Villa in January 1949, driving through the gothic stone gate in the snazzy blue jeep he owned.[10] As the new aide-de-camp, he was responsible for all of the help and furnishings. Evans first needed to inventory the house furnishings, so he got after it, surveying the public rooms, taking charge. He had gotten a fair amount of experience taking charge in Fukui, where he was responsible for half of the prefecture in the tumultuous period after the earthquake.

Generals carefully selected their aide-de-camps, considering both their achievements as young officers and their future potential in the military.[11] Evans stood out. The citizens of Fukui had praised his work, calling him "a personification of leading spirit of a true democratic America."[12] Like Harrison, he was a West Point graduate, and the Thin Gray Line stood together. Evans's equestrian skills must have caught the old cavalryman's eye. Tall, handsome, well dressed, and socially refined, Evans was universally praised as bright, even-tempered, and amiable—important traits for an aide-de-camp ensconced in family life. And as a masterly G2 officer, Harrison must have noted that Evans also had experience with intelligence matters. During the course of his work in Fukui, Evans interfaced with military intelligence, and the anticommunist propaganda campaign that he directed was psychological warfare, a crucial tool of intelligence work.[13]

Unbeknownst to Evans, he had a shadow as he surveyed the household: Jan King, now sixteen, had seen him arrive. Hurrying after him as he entered the house, she had a chance to interrogate the new aide-de-camp while her parents prepared for an evening engagement. When she learned his previous posting was Fukui, she instantly realized he was the Lieutenant Evans she had overheard six months before when he reported to General Joseph M. Swing on the relief train.[14]

Being an aide-de-camp was a demanding position with extraordinary round-the-clock responsibilities—and access. An aide-de-camp had a privileged view into decision making at the highest levels of military leadership, and was privy to secrets, military and personal, requiring exquisite discretion and an inscrutable poker face. As an overseas aide-de-camp, Evans facilitated the general's day-to-day military duties and had a plethora of responsibilities relating to the personal needs of the family, from overseeing the sprawling three-story mansion and its twenty servants, to playing cards with the young Kings and teaching teenaged Jan how to horse jump.[15] On Harrison's inspection trips around Japan, the aide-de-camp needed to insure that the general and his family were comfortable in their private railcar, The Clifford. He did well. Jan later recalled that Harrison pronounced Evans to be "the finest lieutenant he'd ever known."[16]

The Catch

The handsome, kind, and accomplished aide-de-camp did not go unnoticed by the general's wife. Karla Heurich Harrison was from an old Washington, DC, family, an heiress of the Christian Heurich brewing fortune. Growing up in the Teutonic-inflected Heurich House mansion on New Hampshire Avenue near Dupont Circle, she had absorbed an appreciation for culture and education. After graduating from Connecticut College in 1928, Karla earned a master's degree in zoology in 1930 from George Washington University. The next year, she married Charles B. King, another Cave Dweller, the DC argot for multigenerational Washingtonians of an elevated social class.[17] The two had been high school sweethearts.

King graduated from West Point in 1928, so the deeply rooted Washingtonian couple joined the itinerant military society.[18] Their first children, Jan and Charles, were born in Hawaii, where Lieutenant King was stationed at Schofield Barracks. He earned a reputation as an empathetic officer who cared about the enlisted men under his command. Son Donald was born at the next posting, Plattsburgh Barracks in upstate New York, where King served from 1935 to 1937. West Point was the next stop, where he served as a tactical officer, and daughter Jan attended kindergarten and her first three grades of elementary school. In 1941 now Major King was assigned to help organize the new Fort Benning Officer Candidate School, where tens of thousands of ninety-day wonders were imprinted with West Point norms.[19]

The three King children grew up as army brats, but somewhat bipolar ones, as they transited between the Spartan life of military bases and the family mansions and upper-crust life of Washington. "I loved being driven around in a chauffeured limousine. It was the cat's pajamas," Jan said of her childhood visits to Washington. "I loved the shopping trips with my grandmother."[20]

Commanding troops in combat was the sine qua non for military advancement. Lieutenant Colonel King accordingly chafed for a command with frontline troops. But first the King family returned to Washington in 1942 for a year-and-a-half posting to the American Ground Forces headquarters. Living in a Heurich family mansion on Woodland Drive near the National Cathedral in northwest Washington, King commuted to his duty station in the G-2 section, organizing the military intelligence for the planned invasion of France. Karla began reintegrating back into Washington society, as the King children attended exclusive schools that catered to the surrounding districts' elite denizens. An avid sportsman, King availed himself of the grand hunting at Sycamore Landing, his family's 2,300-acre "shooting box" on the Potomac River, where top military and civilian leaders, including generals George C. Marshall and Omar Bradley, joined him in the duck blinds.[21] It was one of those places where old established Washington intersected with the powerful military and political elite pulsing through the capital.

King proved to be a whiz at intelligence—so much so that instead of being given command of a regiment, the army assigned him to the crucial G-2 position of VII Corps, which had a critical offensive mission in the Normandy operation. Landing at Utah Beach, the VII Corps soldiers battled their way across the Cherbourg Peninsula in the weeks following D-Day, June 6, 1944. King was there beside them on the front lines, gathering intelligence wherever it was freshest. On the evening of June 22, 1944, King approached the banks of the Ollonde River near the village of La Riviere. His mission was to interrogate a group of German prisoners. However, the Germans were waiting in ambush and King was killed.

King was buried in the Normandy American Cemetery, his grave marked by a simple white cross like the thousands of his compatriots who lay in serried rows in the fields of honor and sorrow. Later that year, his family gathered at the Pentagon so his son, Charles Jr., could receive the Legion of Merit that the army posthumously awarded to King for his "exceptionally meritorious conduct," which "contributed materially to the success of the campaign on the Cherbourg Peninsula."[22]

Karla was desolate after her husband's death. It was only after a long bleak period punctuated by therapeutic massages and a redemptive job at a society florist that she began to return to the world. A year or so later, her mother-in-law Lady Willmott Lewis took her to a party at the French Embassy. Karla saw a familiar face across the ballroom. "Who's that?" she asked. "I know him from somewhere." It was Eugene Harrison, a confirmed and highly eligible forty-seven-year old bachelor whom she remembered from West Point. Her daughter Jan remembered, "She talked to Gene, and started dating—and they were married before you knew it."[23] Harrison had an instant family. "I thought he was so lucky," Jan remembered, "getting these three wonderful children." While epitomizing grace under fire, the phlegmatic Harrison may nonetheless have had other thoughts.

The Harrison-Kings were still blending as a family when they arrived in the ancient capital of Kyoto, which had been spared the American firebombing during the war. It was the heart of traditional Japanese culture, replete with revered artisans, serene temples, and a landscape sculpted to an envisioned essence of nature. The general's new wife, Karla, was an independent woman with wide-ranging interests, from the natural environment to the esoteric culture of traditional Japan. Enlisting some of the cultural masters of Kyoto, she proceeded to learn the Japanese language, collect Japanese antiques, and immerse herself in Japanese arts, including the refined intricacies of classical ikebana, Zen-influenced flower arranging.[24]

Flowers were certainly something that Evans knew. His beloved grandfather (who had unexpectedly died while Evans was at West Point) had been an extravagant horticulturist.[25] He had written his mother from Fukui that he had been pressing Japanese wildflowers for her as a gift. "There are so many interesting wild flowers over here & they have an ancient method of preserving their color & pressing them," he wrote.[26]

Karla decided someone needed to quickly snag this remarkable young lieutenant, so she sent out the call to her favorite niece to hie herself to Japan to meet "the catch," as the family called Evans. But the niece had other romantic entanglements, so instead the Harrison family and their attentive aide-de-camp spent the summer in enchanting Kyoto. Nearby Lake Biwa, long celebrated by poets for its beauty and calm, was close enough for day trips, sometimes by Evans in his blue jeep. On inspection tours, the Harrison retinue traveled on their private rail car, complete with servants and provender. There were excursions around the other main Japanese islands, visiting the general's equally high-ranking friends. They stayed in acclaimed hotels, such as the Imperial Hotel in Tokyo and the Fujiya Hotel, a famous hot-springs *ryokan* near Mount Fuji that dated back to 1878. At the Fujiya, Jan and her visiting American friend played a prank on Evans and his roommate. Amused that the two men had been assigned to the Passion Flower Room, the girls had the front desk dispatch two female masseuses. Hiding farther down the hall, they watched as Evans turned the women away.[27]

It was a good year for Jan. She excelled at Kyoto American High School, at last able to concentrate on her studies without the distractions of American life. She had learned to drive in Japan, the general giving her driving lessons in the new green Cadillac that the family had shipped over with them. In the penury of postwar Japan, there were few vehicles beyond the occasional charcoal-burners that fumed along with cumuli of gray smoke. The roads were empty, even the slender road to Osaka that arrowed past the greening rice fields rank with the smell of night soil. Standing five feet, eight inches tall, Jan towered above the Japanese, who clustered around her when she explored the Ginko-shaded shopping districts. Doe-eyed and discerning with a nimbus of blond curls, she had become a young woman with a strong sense of self. And a young woman in love with the aide-de-camp with the Eagle-Scout rectitude. She confessed her feelings to a visiting friend, and wrote about her crush to friends back in Washington, but it was time to go home. Boarding the SS *President Wilson*, her friend chastely gave Evans a kiss—"for both of us," Jan remembered. "I was in love, but had no idea my feelings were reciprocated."[28]

7

WASHINGTON

Impressed with Lieutenant Benjamin C. Evans Jr.'s performance in Japan, General Eugene Harrison arranged for him to be assigned as the aide-de-camp to General Thomas W. Herren, the commanding general of the Military District of Washington, DC.[1] From his own Washington experience as aide to Secretary of War Henry Stimson, Harrison knew that it was important for Evans to be posted to the epicenter of American power.

Evans's posting also placed him amid the capital's pomp, circumstance, and social whirl. The army was the lead participant in the multitude of public ceremonies and events that crowded the Washington calendar, so there was a need for polished young officers to squire dignitaries and enhance the decorum. During the Cherry Blossom Festival, the debonair Evans served as an escort to a festival princess.[2]

Like his patron Harrison, Evans was stationed at Fort Myer, located on the Arlington Heights just across the Potomac River from Washington. It was historic ground, part of the 1,100-acre estate that the Union confiscated from Robert E. Lee's family after he joined the Confederacy. The heights were also hallowed: Arlington National Cemetery with its hundreds of thousands of military graves stood as silent sentinel on the Virginia hillside overlooking the nation's capital.[3] As the fallen began arriving from the Korean War, Evans served as leader of the Arlington ceremonial company.[4]

The Cave Dwellers and the Government

Not long after Evans arrived at Fort Myer, a car with two young women slowly cruised the lanes of the venerable old military base—looking, looking, looking for a convertible with Indiana license plates. Evans had written a Christmas card to Jan King, now a high school senior at Washington's prestigious National Cathedral School, telling her that he was driving from Indiana to his new posting at Fort Myer in a convertible. But the girls had no luck and crossed the Potomac back to their homes in affluent northwest Washington.

Both sides of Jan's family were Washington, DC, Cave Dwellers. Her paternal grandmother, Lady Norma Lewis, renowned for her beauty, brains, and vivacity, was a social force in Washington. Like other Washington grande dames, such as her friends Marjorie Merriweather Post and Perle Mesta, she had come from elsewhere.[5] Lady Lewis was born in Terrell, Texas, as Norma Bowler. Prior to World War I, she had abandoned her first husband, Ludlow King, in Okemah, Oklahoma, and relocated to Washington with her two sons, Ludlow Jr. and Charles. When living in Okemah, a bleak railroad town on Route 66, she had told a sympathetic pediatrician about her marital unhappiness. Recognizing her attributes, he arranged for Bowler and her sons to live with his father, powerful Iowa congressman John A. T. Hull, longtime chair of the House Committee on Military Affairs, and his wife. While living with the Hulls, she and their army colonel son, John A. Hull, fell in love. When he was posted to Paris during the war, Bowler followed him. "She took her riding boots and volunteered for the Red Cross in France," Jan said. "Or the Red Cross was her cover, anyway."[6] Bowler and Hull married in 1919 at Fort Myer.[7] Hull became a major general and judge advocate of the U.S. Army. Norma was now part of a rich, politically connected family. The Hulls were prominent Washingtonians, living in a finely appointed Massachusetts Avenue house replete with servants, entertaining and mingling with the city's upper crust.

In 1934 Norma divorced Hull in Reno, but she was not done with marriage. In the summer of 1939, *Time* magazine noted a number of society marriages in its "Milestones" section. In Newport, former number one Manhattan debutante Eleanor ("Cooky") Young, twenty-one, married socialite Robert Ogden ("Bunny") Bacon Jr., twenty-seven; "her first, his second." A daughter of a New York financier married a University of Virginia law graduate in Centreville, Maryland. And in Lorton, Virginia, socialite Mrs. Norma Bowler Hull, fifty-one, married Sir Willmott Lewis, sixty-two, the famous *Times of London* correspondent—"both for the third time." Norma Bowler was now Lady Norma Lewis, though still Connie to her many friends.[8]

Adding to her Sycamore Landing estate that she received in the Hull divorce settlement, Lady Lewis soon acquired a mansion in Georgetown, then a rundown African American neighborhood. Built in 1797, the imposing federal-style mansion at 3425 Prospect was known as Quality Hill, which had been abandoned for thirty-five years. When Lady Lewis bought it in 1942, the eight-bedroom mahogany-trimmed house was definitely a fixer-upper. Skirting wartime construction restrictions by declaring her building project "a rehabilitation," she scoured demolition sites to salvage grand architectural elements. "She followed Ace Wrecking around town," Jan laughed. Once revivified, Quality Hill proved to be the perfect setting for Lewis soirees that drew Washington insiders.[9] And the fine hunting in the Sycamore Landing wetlands attracted the top military brass eager to take a break from wartime Washington with the indomitable outdoorsy Lady Lewis. "Grandmother Lewis knew *everyone*," Jan said. "Grandmother was kind of wild—everyone loved her."[10] Evans remembered the first time he met Jan's grandmother—Lady Lewis had her foot on a giant turtle, preparing to slaughter it for dinner.[11]

Jan's maternal side had even deeper roots in Washington. Her maternal grandfather, Christian Heurich, was a German brewer who had arrived in Washington in 1871. It was the dawn of the capital's Gilded Age, when office seekers, lobbyists, parvenus, and aspiring entrepreneurs began to throng the young city. Mark Twain, who wrote the satirical novel that gave the period its name, wrote of men such as Heurich, "Washington gathered its people from the four winds of heaven, and so the manners, the faces and the fashions there, presented a variety that was infinite."[12] The constantly replenished mix provided the newcomers rich opportunities.

The city's southern-dominated society had already been upended after the Civil War, when victorious Union veterans and Republican stalwarts began muscling their way into the social elite. Washington boosters claimed the access reflected the nation's egalitarian ideals. Critics saw the capital's churning social scene somewhat differently. A *New York Times* correspondent wrote, "The truth is that more uneducated, rude, and vulgar men and women find their way into the social gatherings of the capital than those of any other city in the Union."[13]

When Heurich arrived, Washington was still a generally rough-hewn town, though one with pretensions. The half-finished stub of the Washington Monument stood abandoned beside the river, looking, as Twain wrote, like "a factory chimney with the top broken off."[14] The 1871 Organic Act that established the self-ruling District of Columbia accelerated the growth of Washington, already booming from post-Civil War federalization. Laborers were wresting a world-class capital out of the Potomac muck. The pestilential Washington City Canal that ran through the middle of town was covered over, a modern sewer system was built, and roads were graded. Pennsylvania Avenue, long a jarring, flood-prone route of broken cobblestones, was resurfaced—its completion celebrated with a city festival. While not as cultured as Boston, or as prosperous as New York, or as innovative as Chicago, Washington nonetheless pulsed with the raw energy of a yet-untapped continent. It was a time of great promise.

Heurich wrote that Washington "seemed to be on the way up. True enough, I stood on the step of the Capitol one autumn afternoon and saw ahead of me nothing but Virgin forest, but I came back in a very few weeks and the change was, to say the least, startling; streets were being laid out, trees were being planted by the hundreds, sewers were being put in and buildings were going up so fast I could see them actually growing."[15] Among the armies of construction workers and federal factotums, there was a market for beer—especially for German-style brews that had swept through America.

Heurich was born in 1842 in Haina, a hamlet in the Duchy of Saxe-Meiningen, located in what is now southwest Germany. As a young boy he was touched by the progressive fervor of the reformist Revolutions of 1848, whose leaders he continued to respect.[16] Trained by his father as a journeyman brewer, Heurich took to the roads of Europe for his required *wanderjahre* of working under multiple master tradesmen, who trained him in the most current styles of central European brewing. His trip also introduced the young man to the great cities of Basel, Munich, and Vienna, then the grand, glittering capital of the Austro-Hungarian Empire that he came to love. Tramping the roads and floating the rivers from 1859 to 1863, Heurich traveled through what became Germany, Austria, Switzerland, Slovenia, Italy, France, and Hungary.

In September 1872 Heurich and a partner opened their first brewery on Twentieth Street NW between M and N Streets in a sparsely populated part of Washington. They began by renting an existing brewery, one of five in the city—and "the worst," according to Heurich.[17] With his European training and boundless energy, brewmaster Heurich rapidly rejuvenated the brewery. Rigorously brewed under the strict German beer purity regulations known as the *Reinheitsgebot*, Heurich's beers quickly found a clientele among the city's working and middle classes. "It was mighty good beer," Heurich wrote, and contended Washington's workmen "needed good German lager." Within a year he bought out his partner and commenced his rise to success.[18]

It was a very good time to be a German brewer in America. The arrival of lager yeast had revolutionized the country's drinking habits. Up till then, whiskey was king. In the early nineteenth century there were 14,000 American distilleries producing twenty-five million gallons of whiskey annually—six to seven gallons per adult. In contrast, there were only two hundred American breweries, making English-style ales for the most part. Lager beers arrived in America from 1838 to 1840, not long after the brewing breakthroughs in Munich and Vienna.

Lagers quickly dominated American beer production and tastes. By the 1840s the consumption of spirits dropped to two and a half gallons per adult. By the 1850s, when a flood of German immigrants boosted demand, beer was outselling spirits. The Civil War further increased production, as the Union army contracted for rivers of beer, the brews considered to be far healthier than the disease-tainted water that devastated the ranks. With their palates now attuned to light lagers, Union veterans returned home with an appetite for more.[19]

Heurich got rich over the next twenty years. Forever modernizing and expanding his brewery, he built the capacity to craft fifty thousand barrels a year—and was able to sell almost that amount. He was a very big regional brewer, selling about half the beer in Washington, with a standing beer order for the White House that ran through sequential administrations.[20] Beyond his beer empire, Heurich was one of Washington's biggest property owners, second only to the federal government.[21] Brewers typically owned a lot of real estate, most often to lease to saloonkeepers, who contracted to sell the house beer. Like most brewers, Heurich bought corner lots, ideal for saloons. Beyond a large Maryland farm that became his country retreat, he also invested in tracts around the district, including several parcels on Wisconsin Avenue at the far edge of town. And he acquired a large piece of land in a swampy low-lying industrial area near the Potomac known as Foggy Bottom.

By the early 1890s, Heurich's flourishing four-story brewery on Twentieth Street was an industrial relic in an increasingly posh neighborhood, now known as Dupont Circle. Over the previous twenty years, the area had become the elite neighborhood for Washington's powerful. Mansions and multistory stone-clad row houses lined the streets radiating from the circle. It was time to move the brewery.

The new Water Street brewery that Heurich began building in 1894 in Foggy Bottom was the city's largest. With five cavernous lagering cellars and an ice plant that could produce one hundred and fifty tons daily, the brewery could produce up to a half a million barrels of beer a year. And ever the scientific progressive, Heurich made sure his new brewery was state of the art. While Heurich valued modernity and had a soupçon of youthful progressivism that informed his employment of union labor, he was not so liberal as to tolerate ultimatums from his unionized workers, particularly if they challenged his fiscal conservatism and property rights.[22] "He appreciated work being done for him," said his granddaughter, Jan King. "But he wasn't going to be told what to do."[23]

The Heurichs did not leave Dupont Circle. The four-story, thirty-one-room Heurich Mansion at 1307 New Hampshire Avenue NW was already complete.[24] Built of poured concrete and iron for fireproofing, the turreted and elaborately fenestrated mansion was clad in a rustic rough-hewn stone. Two gargoyles peered from the roofline. The palatial interior, which included a drawing room, reception room, library, music room, and formal dining room, was a magnificent expression of high-Victorian esthetics and masterful German woodworking. The late-nineteenth-century house had indoor plumbing and a central vacuum cleaner and communications system. The basement included the sprawling kitchen, where servants prepared the family's meals, and a cozy *bierstube*, a rathskeller-inspired beer room where Heurich and his confidants could relax over beer and skat, his favorite card game.[25] The Dupont Circle mansion was a clear expression that the Heurich family had indisputably made it in America.

The Washington social scene at the turn of the century was still fluid. With America rapidly industrializing, great fortunes were being made. The Spanish-American War won the United States an empire, and swaggering Washington was its imperial capital. Successful businessmen began moving to Washington as newly elected members of Congress or appointed officials. Titillated by proximity to power, nouveau riche from across the country established winter homes in Washington, better to influence the government to serve their interests—and to attain elite social status that might not be possible back home. As a gentleman brewer and successful businessman, Heurich maintained some remove from high society.[26] Nonetheless, he sharply observed the shifting social scene: "The city was practically invaded by well-to-do midwesterners and westerners of the millionaire type [who had] just about nothing to do but spend [money] . . . in some fashion it became known that 'society' could be reached and climbed aboard easier in Washington than anywhere else in these United States."[27] As the gatekeepers to Washington high society, the Cave Dwellers wielded an outsized influence in the workings of the government—albeit often informal and veiled. Jan King said, "Before World War II, I can't tell you how small a town Washington was. You knew everyone. And it was very social."[28] A discrete word meant the right kind of people moved up. It was a pattern that sustained itself throughout the twentieth century.

Smiles Across the Board

As it turned out, Evans had not driven a convertible from Indiana to his post at Fort Myer. In the interests of practicality, he had come out in a station wagon. Nevertheless, within a short time of arriving, Evans reconnected with King after dinner at Lady Lewis's Quality Hill mansion in Georgetown. "He gave me a big hug," King remembered, and they made a date to meet again at Lady Lewis's. "He came the next Saturday night—and said he wanted to spend the rest of his life with me," King recalled[29] She was seventeen years old. "It was kind of a shock for someone who was a senior in high school," she said. "He wasn't proposing. He was telling me his intentions. I appreciated that."[30] Despite the age difference, the relationship persisted. The young couple dated through her senior year of high school, often going on double dates to dinner or the movies. In the early summer she sat down after dinner with her mother and stepfather, and said, "Mother, Ben wants to marry me." The Texan general exclaimed, "Jose Cuervo!"[31]

Though eight years older than their daughter, the Harrisons still perceived Evans to be "the catch." He had a solid pedigree with a West Point degree, no small consideration for the general and his wife, who both had strong connections to the academy. Evans's military record was exemplary, he was handsome and considerate, and, important to Cave Dwellers, he had finely honed social graces. "He had the best of everything. He was used to the best," King said. "At Fort Myer the dry cleaners told him he [had] the biggest cleaning bill on the post."[32] The Harrisons had already shown an extraordinary interest in the young lieutenant, stopping to visit Evans's parents in Crawfordsville, Indiana, on their way back from Japan to Washington.[33] And it was not unusual for an aide-de-camp and the general's daughter to fall in love, especially with duty in occupied Japan, where servicemen were strongly discouraged from dating Japanese women and aides had daily interactions with the generals' families.[34]

Evans and his intended later met with the general and his wife to discuss their intent to eventually marry. There was an agreement that she first needed to go to college. And there was another matter. After reaching some consensus about the potential match, Harrison took Evans upstairs, and showed him his stepdaughter's chaotic clothes closet. He asked the prospective groom, "Can you handle this?"[35]

In the fall of 1950 the couple went different directions. Evans traveled to Fort Riley, Kansas, for the Officer Intel Course, while King went to Connecticut College in New London.[36] "I would have bought the degree if I could," she said about their reluctant parting.[37] But college was a good experience. Her fellow classmate, Norma Richards, remembered, "Jan King was the most sophisticated member of the class. As a freshman, she was a very poised, confident woman."[38] After her scholastic achievements and adventures in Japan, King's

National Cathedral School classmates had elected her senior class president. She arrived at Connecticut College as a worldly, accomplished young woman, who had already learned to deal with life's challenges and changes. And she had the cachet of having an older military officer as her boyfriend.

Their long-distance romance continued apace, with King at college and Evans serving as aide-de-camp to Herren. In the spring of 1951 Evans sent a letter to "Dearest Jan," telling her of his military mission to northern Canada, where he saw "lots of Indians, Eskimoes, bear, and SNOW." He gave her information about George Washington University summer school and urged her to carefully choose her courses to maximize credits toward early graduation. He emphatically wrote, "NATURALLY THE IDEA OF SUMMER SCHOOL APPEALS TO ME. THE SOONER YOU FINISH YOUR COLLEGE WORK THE BETTER. 'guess I don't have to give any reasons for this statement!!!'"[39]

In the fall of 1951 the army selected Evans to attend Columbia University graduate school to study international affairs and psychological warfare.[40] Arriving in Manhattan, Evans rented a room near the university from feminist and suffragist leader Alice Paul.[41] On the weekends, he often traveled to New London to visit with his fiancée.[42] Their engagement became public knowledge in late December 1951. A *Washington Times-Herald* story blared the society debutante's betrothal to the West Point captain, breathlessly calling the engagement and planned September wedding, "exciting third-finger-left-hand news."[43]

By the spring, the couple was making furniture choices. In early April 1952 Evans wrote King an ardent love letter, telling her "you appear as the only thing in my life. Everything in life has taken on a new and wonderful meaning, for it is impossible to have a hope, wish, or dream without your being in it." He delicately alluded to their proprieties in the chaste 1950s, writing, "I am felt the tenderness of your love and though we have the full and real expression of being one together to look forward to, I know that in all of these things we have just scratched the surface of what the years together will prove to be a marriage made not only on Earth but in Heaven." Hailing her "very dynamic spirit," Evans pledged, "You dear, are the most wonderful thing in my life, and I'll love, and cherish you every minute of it!"[44]

The Washington papers covered the impending nuptials of the "beauteous, blond Miss King" and Evans, along with the fêtes thrown in the couple's honor. King's maternal grandmother, Amelia Heurich, hosted a dinner at the Columbia Country Club.[45] Lady Lewis gave a rehearsal dinner for sixty at her

Georgetown mansion. A fellow West Point graduate, Wilson Patrick Hurley, and his wife had a Chevy Chase cocktail party festooned with gladiolas and pompoms. But the lead story was the black-tie dinner party that Chairman of the Joint Chiefs of Staff Omar Bradley and his wife gave the couple and her family at Fort Myer.[46]

The couple had a properly reported society wedding with four hundred attendees, held in chrysanthemum-decorated Saint Albans, the Episcopal church on the northwest Washington heights that overlooked the national monuments far below. The *New York Times* wrote that General Harrison gave away his stepdaughter, who wore a lace-embellished wedding gown of oyster-white taffeta. The groom wore a white tie, Marcella waistcoat and formal black tailcoat decorated with his military medals. There was a (publicized) honeymoon at the Greenbrier resort. A Washington society page ran a photo of the two playing table football with the big headline, "Smiles Across the Board." After the honeymoon, the newlyweds returned to New York, where Evans continued his international relations studies, and his bride enrolled in Barnard College.[47]

8

THE PAYBACK

There was the utilization period, the payback that Captain Benjamin C. Evans Jr. owed the U.S. Army for its investment in his Columbia master's degree. "You don't get something for nothing," his new bride, Jan King Evans, said.[1] He had graduated in the winter of 1953 with a master of arts in public law and government from the Faculties of Political Science, Philosophy, and Pure Science.[2] His focus was on in international affairs and psychological warfare.

Captain Evans was embarking on a promising career. In the early days of the Cold War, psychological warfare (psywar) was a hot ticket. When the Korean War erupted in 1950, the U.S. Army had established the Psychological Warfare Division at Fort Riley, Kansas, where General Eugene Harrison was posted after his stint in occupied Japan.[3] Psywar had gotten a big boost in 1951, when Congress appropriated $121 million for President Harry Truman to launch a "Campaign of Truth" against communism.[4] By 1953 when Evans graduated, there were at least five separate psywar organizations in the U.S. government, operating in different places and at five different levels, even describing their mission with an array of different names, including "ideological warfare," "foreign information," "war of wits" and "the battle for men's minds."[5] Propaganda and attendant "actions," such as State Department activities, U.S. information services, and front organizations were the primary tools of psywar.

Evans's first posting after Columbia was at Fort Benning, Georgia, where he was sent out to give speeches, while Jan went to Red Cross Nursing School. The couple initially resided at 22-A Battle Park, one of the tens of thousands of Wherry Housing units built after World War II. To help house a large-standing Cold War army, Congress had appropriated funds for low-interest loans to private developers to build family housing "on or around military installations." The units were infamous for their grim esthetics, shoddy construction, and cramped quarters. Within months, the Evanses had relocated to the base town of Columbus, Georgia, where they rented 646 Gibson Drive, a low-slung brick-veneered tract house.[6]

In 1954 the Evanses transferred to Fort Bragg, North Carolina, where the Pentagon had relocated the U.S. Army Psychological Warfare School. The center was responsible for doctrinal support and training for both psychological and unconventional warfare. The army school was moved from Fort Riley at the urging of the Psychological Warfare chief, Brigadier General Robert A. McClure, who ran the army's psywar unit during the Korean conflict as a joint operation with the Central Intelligence Agency. During the war, McClure had collaborated with Harrison on the Alsos mission.[7]

Since the Fort Bragg posting was less than six months, Evans was not eligible for base housing, but the couple found a charming cottage between Pinehurst and Southern Pines to rent. It was a respite after Fort Benning's austere housing. Owned by tobacco and textile heiress Ann Cannon Reynolds, the white-clapboard country cottage offered Evans a retreat in a natural setting after a day at Fort Bragg, about sixty miles away.

Psywar in Japan

Evans was assigned to Japan as chief, Plans and Policy, Psychological Warfare, AFFE/Eighth Army (rear). Evans just missed the Korean War. After three bloody years of battle with a million casualties, the conflict had turned into a stalemated ceasefire in late July 1953. Buttressed by their belligerent patron states, communist North Korea and democratic South Korea remained fiercely antagonistic. While the hot proxy war was over, the vicious Cold War between the United States and the communist bloc continued—particularly in covert operations and psywar.

Headquartered in the sprawling old Hardy Barracks building in central Tokyo's Roppongi district, Evans's psywar unit pulsed a steady stream of radio programs at North Korean and Chinese forces via thirteen radio stations and a host of short- and medium-wave transmitters. Each night MoRan, the psywar disc jockey, interspersed Korean pop music with propaganda delivered in her soft mellifluous voice. The news programs blared bulletins about North Korean uprisings and Stalinist purges. The psychological warfare unit's visual branch pumped out a blizzard of publications aggressively crafted to undermine North Korean public support. With the Korean War in uneasy abeyance, Evans's psywar unit was the only part of the U.S. Army still actively engaged in open operations against the communists.[8]

In the dark days of the Cold War, the Evanses shared the American public's determined opposition to international communism. "We were afraid communism could take over the world," Jan said. "Ben was taught we had to fight communism."[9] Psywar was Evans's weapon.

Psychological warfare was an ancient military art. Over two millennia ago, legendary Chinese strategist Sun Tzu prized psychological warfare, opining, "All warfare is based on deception." He counseled using artifice to defeat the enemy with minimal loss of blood and treasure. "To subdue the enemy without fighting is the supreme excellence," he wrote. Alexander the Great ordered his armorers to forge immense breastplates for (nonexistent) giants. Abandoning the armor when he tactically retreated, Alexander convinced his enemies they had narrowly avoided a certain defeat by gargantuan warriors. Surrender came soon after. Persian warriors marched on the Pharaoh's army with cats tied to their shields, routing the discombobulated Egyptian soldiers, who were encultured to revere cats as sacred. So it went down through the centuries, military leaders using psychological warfare to try to win strategic gains while keeping combat at a minimum.[10]

During World War I, the British waged an insidious psywar campaign against the Germans. Nazi propaganda minister Joseph Goebbels credited the British forces' "easy victory" in that war with their psywar dominance. The Nazis claimed the British psywar campaign was responsible for "the corruption of the German soul."[11] The Germans learned the lesson: Goebbels crowed in 1940 that "we have become political psychologists," as the brainwashed German population embraced Adolf Hitler and Nazi armies overran European democracies demoralized by his relentless propaganda machine.[12] The Nazis' psywar operations during the Czechoslovakia campaign undermined the will of the Czechoslovakians and their British and French allies to the point that the Nazis were able to occupy the country without a full-scale war.

Inspired by the Nazis' successful use of targeted propaganda and deceptive information operations, the Americans quickly ramped up psywar operations when they joined World War II in 1941. There were some remarkable successes. Prior to D-Day, Operation Fortitude convinced Hitler's generals that they were facing both an invasion of Norway and a cross-channel invasion of the Pas-de-Calais region to be spearheaded by General George S. Patton's chimerical First United States Army Group, which was comprised of ghost regiments, mock aircraft, dummy tanks made of rubber, and battalions of psychological warriors generating false radio traffic and misleading communiqués.[13]

Truth was negotiable. The cornerstone of psywar, according to the U.S. Army psychological warfare manual, was "truth," though it had to be "credibly presented" to convince target populations to "cease resistance or take actions favorable to friendly forces."[14] On the psywar battlefields, however, truth and credibility seldom marched together. As master propagandist Vladimir Ilyich Lenin put it, "A lie told often enough becomes the truth."[15] For generations of psychological warriors, particularly those with high ethical standards, the systemic dissembling and manipulation often created unresolvable moral quandaries.

Tokyo Life

"It was a whole new country," Jan recalled about Japan on their return five years after serving with the occupation forces.[16] The Korean War had revved up the Japanese economy with robust American resources, and the United States' support for reindustrialization and anticommunist purges cinched the deal. Japan was no longer economically supine.[17]

The Evanses first lived at Fourteenth and F Streets in a Tokyo residence owned by Americans, who had inexplicably stayed during the war. While the second-floor apartment reputedly had a view of Mount Fuji, sightings were rare through the Tokyo haze. Their second Tokyo residence was a two-story house in Washington Heights, the U. S. armed forces housing complex in the bustling Shibuya district. There were skiing trips to the Japanese Alps, State Department pool parties at the embassy, and nostalgic journeys to Fukui and Kyoto, where they visited with the Japanese servants who had cared for them during the occupation.

The Evanses joined the prestigious Tokyo Lawn Tennis Club. The club's rolls included members of the Japanese imperial family and a contingent of international members, including a young CIA couple, Donald and Meg Gregg, who befriended the Evanses.[18] In search of adventure, Donald had joined the CIA in 1951, at a time when the young agency's reputation far outweighed its capacities. "We had a great image," Gregg recalled, "but couldn't do shit."[19]

It was in Tokyo that the Evanses began to work out their marital relationship. Ben focused on his intelligence work, and Jan, with her family history of successful investing, managed the money. "In Japan, I took over," Jan said. "I put Ben on an allowance. He never cared about money. He gave away all of his money to the beggars."[20] So Jan managed the household while attending night classes at the Jesuit-run Sophia University, from which she graduated with a Japanese-script diploma. "I graduated from a university with a diploma I can't read," she laughed.

In Japan Evans quietly sidled away from his family's Methodism, joining his wife in Tokyo's new Episcopal church, Saint Alban. "Ben took a course to become an Episcopalian, and was confirmed an Episcopalian in Tokyo," Jan said. "I was an Episcopalian and it was convenient." Ben never told his parents of his conversion, staying on the Methodist rolls for trips back home to Indiana. "To them, Episcopalian was like marrying a Catholic," Jan said about her staunchly Methodist parents-in-law. "You don't need to tell your family about something like that if it would upset them."[21] It was a particularly delicate time for Ben's parents, his mother was dying of breast cancer. In order to visit with his mother in her final days, Ben finagled a mission to courier documents to the United States. Ruth Fraley Evans died after her son returned to his post in Japan.[22]

Evans concentrated on his highly classified psywar work—work he could not share with his wife. "He never talked much about work. I knew what he did was secret," Jan said. The daughter and stepdaughter of intelligence officers, she knew the protocols: "I was careful not to ask questions. It was hard. I am a naturally curious person. When I did ask questions, Ben would ask, 'Now, Jan, is that need-to-know?'"[23]

Evans's psywar accomplishments were garnering positive attention. With his West Point and Columbia degrees and recognized achievements in the field, his military future looked bright.[24] And his connection to army intelligence luminary Harrison, his wife's stepfather, did not hurt. Ben's nephew, Daniel Evans Jr., recalled, "He'd say, 'It's great to be married to the general's daughter. It's great for your career.' He'd laugh."[25]

The Split

Evans's next assignment was Chief, Political Intelligence, Eighth Army (Korea). During his duty in Korea, Evans hatched a big idea: U.S. psywar radio stations soon began blasting North Korea with a $250,000 offer to any fighter pilot who would fly a MiG to United Nation forces. There is no record that any defectors took advantage of Evans's offer.[26]

While Evans served in Korea, his wife was on the road, making her way around the globe. Unable to join her husband in Korea, and with the diploma in hand that she had promised her parents Jan decided to take the opportunity to see the world—over the objections of her mother and husband. Her wanderlust began years before when she heard officers swapping war stories with her stepfather. "Listening in at parties to these generals and colonels, talking about their times in Germany, in Africa—it opened windows to another world that I didn't know about; that I hadn't experienced," she said. "Listening to those World War II vets, it just lit me up. To hear all these tales, I decided I had to do that. I had to get it out of my system before I had children."[27]

With a redheaded *Stars and Stripes* journalist named Barbara Lambert as a traveling companion, Jan spent five and a half months making her way through twenty-four Asian and European countries, including stops in Hong Kong, Singapore, Thailand, Burma, Istanbul, Germany, and Great Britain.[28] While she was in a London post exchange in late 1956, Jan happened upon a *Stars and Stripes* article that named Captain Benjamin C. Evans on an "Outstanding List," denoting him for early promotion to major.[29]

Evans had been giving a lot of thought to his career—military and otherwise. In the spring of 1956 as Jan prepared for her around-the-world trip, he sent a letter from Tokyo to his father-in-law and mentor, Harrison.[30] Formatted as a military memo, Evans opened with a general statement: "This plan is designed to provide a frame of reference and delineate actions to be taken which will provide more effective utilization of B. C. Evans, Jr. & enhance his growing prosperity." Written to a trusted adviser, Evans's letter was a young husband's ruminations at a critical juncture in his life.

His wife's upcoming journey was on his mind. Assessing "Friendly Forces," Evans listed an understanding family, the army, banks, American Express, family friends in his wife's ports of call, and her mature traveling companion. Among "Enemy Forces," Evans listed his tropism toward security over "reasonable risks," his tendency to overestimate his own capacities, the allure of "greener grass," and "A depression." Being a new husband, he worried that his glamorous, globetrotting wife would become a "target of opportunity" without his presence. The last enemy force was "The Infantry Career Management Branch, Dept of Army," which controlled the trajectory of his military career.

Evans went on to enumerate the reasons why his military career was going to stall far short of general's stars. Chief among them was his lack of combat experience, "having missed two wars." He noted the infantry officer ranks were filled with combat-tested captains, majors, and lieutenant colonels. He saw his psywar work as another barrier to advancement: "in the long run I will be penalized for my interest and demonstrated ability in psychological warfare or a related assignment." However effective psywar might be, the army did not see it as equal to combat. Given the barriers to commanding rank, he concluded it best to resign his commission, sooner rather than later.

Musing on alternatives, Evans considered business opportunities that could utilize his West Point and Columbia education, as well as his psywar expertise. He thought about rewarding jobs in the government—"most likely the CIA, State," stating what he called his "do-gooder" objective: "to make the world a better place in which to live."

9

THE AGENCY

The Central Intelligence Agency was a phoenix that emerged from the ashes of the Office of Strategic Services, the first U.S. national intelligence service. Established by the Joint Chiefs of Staff in the early days of World War II, the OSS was charged with strategic intelligence analysis and coordinating espionage, subversion, and propaganda behind enemy lines.[1] General "Wild Bill" Donovan directed the OSS with a fierce élan.

Donovan recruited his spymasters from the social elites, calling them his "league of gentlemen." Wall Street bankers, corporate chieftains and attorneys, Ivy League professors, and Social Register adventurers gave the OSS its moniker, "Oh-So-Social."[2] Donovan's academics and strategists were soon joined by a motley crew of martial arts experts, stuntmen, safecrackers, burglars, public relations flacks, and dissident émigrés from dozens of countries. Their job was to defeat fascism by whatever means necessary.

While the OSS gathered intelligence on virtually every country on earth, the organization was barred from covert operations in Latin America and the Pacific. The Western Hemisphere was the Federal Bureau of Investigation's bailiwick thanks to J. Edgar Hoover's maneuvers, and General Douglas MacArthur claimed the Pacific theater as his exclusive turf. So, operating from forty overseas offices, the OSS confined its covert operations to Europe, Asia, and North Africa.

The OSS headquarters in Washington, DC, was housed at the far end of Foggy Bottom, atop a small bluff overlooking the Potomac River. The moldering masonry buildings were surrounded by an abandoned gasworks, a roller-skating rink, and the turreted-brick Heurich Brewery, owned by Jan King Evans's grandfather. The spies often wandered over to the brewery for beer breaks.[3]

In late 1944, with the Allied victory increasingly certain, Donovan began to lobby OSS supporter President Franklin D. Roosevelt for a postwar intelligence service. Donovan wrote to Roosevelt, "When our enemies are defeated, the demand will be equally pressing for information that will aid us in solving the problems of peace."[4] Beyond Roosevelt, the OSS had few supporters. It was an ad-hoc organization of amateurs, without powerful alumni to intercede in the halls of Washington. Donovan had preferred flying to far-flung field stations on clandestine missions to building an enduring Washington bureaucracy, so was ill-prepared for attacks by FBI and Pentagon officials who coveted the budgets and power of a national intelligence service.

When Roosevelt died in April 1945, Donovan knew it was probably the end of the OSS, nevertheless Donovan wrote to President Harry Truman that the United States "does not have a coordinated intelligence system. The defects and the dangers of this situation have generally been recognized."[5] Wary of Donovan, Truman ordered an internal review of the OSS. Written by army intelligence officer Colonel Richard Park Jr., the report was a scalding review of the OSS performance, both for fiscal waste and "badly conceived, overlapping and unauthorized activities."[6] Park wrote that Donovan's proposal for a global intelligence service had "all the earmarks of a Gestapo system." When the Park report was leaked to the press, OSS critics echoed warnings of an "American Gestapo."

With the cover he needed, Truman summarily disbanded the OSS on September 20, 1945, six weeks after dropping the atomic bombs on Japan. His executive order dissolved the OSS just ten days later. The research and analysis personnel went to the State Department, and the covert operations and other OSS functions were transferred to the War Department as the Strategic Services Unit. Most of the OSS personnel, including Donovan, were discharged.

In a mournful farewell ceremony held in the skating rink near the OSS headquarters, Donovan told the two thousand assembled OSS personnel, "We have come to the end of an unusual experiment." By way of congratulating them, Donovan said, "You should feel deeply gratified by President Truman's expression of the purpose of basing a coordinated intelligence service upon the techniques and resources you have initiated and developed." Offering the intelligence officer's eternal dream, Donovan concluded by saying, "You can go with the assurance that you have made a beginning in showing the people of America that only by decisions of national policy based upon accurate information can we have the chance of a peace that will endure."[7]

Donovan was right about the OSS's formative role. The agency's recruitment of social elites and tropism toward covert actions left a deep imprint on America's intelligence organizations. The OSS likewise influenced the U.S.

military's development of Special Forces, which used OSS-trained experts and materials at the Fort Bragg training center into the 1950s.[8] When Donovan visited the newly established Tenth Special Forces Group at Fort Bragg in 1953, he said, "You are the offspring of the OSS."[9]

Truman realized that he was getting both too much and too little intelligence and knew that he needed a centralized intelligence service—just not Donovan's OSS. Territorial bureaucracies were withholding crucial national security information from him. And he was being overwhelmed with uncoordinated, often redundant, intelligence from multiple agencies.[10]

Truman moved quickly. On October 22, 1945, Secretary of War Robert Patterson created the Lovett Committee, chaired by Wall Street banker and foreign affairs éminence grise Robert A. Lovett, to advise the government on the post-World War II organization of U.S. intelligence activities.[11] The committee, comprised of Lovett and six high-ranking military officers, held nine meetings and reviewed written reports from the full spectrum of U.S. military and civilian intelligence. Representing the Army Intelligence (G-2), General Eugene Harrison, Jan's stepfather, advised the Lovett Committee. Committee member General John Magruder, who had served in the OSS, said their work was for "the holy cause of central intelligence."[12]

Within a week of convening, the committee produced a preliminary report, which cited the chaotic state of U.S. intelligence during the war, when there was "a lack of harmony and cooperation," "overlapping functions and confusion and a failure to cover important fields," and "a feeling of jealousy and mistrust among the various intelligence organizations of the Government." The committee unanimously recommended the establishment of a centralized intelligence service, terming it the "Central Intelligence Agency." The committee members agreed that the agency would have an independent budget.[13]

Following the committee's recommendations, in January 1946 Truman established the Central Intelligence Group, which absorbed the short-lived SSU. And to oversee the new intelligence agency, Truman also established the National Intelligence Authority, comprised of the Secretaries of State, War, Navy, and a presidential representative. On January 24, 1946, Truman hosted a luncheon at the White House, where he presented the first Director of Central Intelligence, Rear Admiral Sidney Souers, with a black hat and cloak and a wooden dagger. Truman then proceeded to humorously outline the duties of the "Cloak and Dagger Group of Snoopers."[14]

In 1947 a Red Scare erupted, fanned by leaked inside information about

Soviet penetration into the U.S. government.[15] Truman responded to the public uproar with Executive Order 9835, which instituted the "Loyalty Order," requiring loyalty oaths and investigations of people suspected of antidemocratic affiliations. The House Un-American Activities Committee held explosive hearings, focusing on the high-profile Hollywood movie industry, which led to the notorious blacklisting of actors, writers, and directors. Truman also decided to enlarge the centralized intelligence service. The National Security Act of 1947 replaced the CIG and its watchdog NIA with the newly established National Security Council and the Central Intelligence Agency. The National Security Act was implemented on September 18, 1947, the birthday of the CIA.[16]

The CIA was a small, underfunded intelligence agency with vicious rivals and a legally ambiguous mandate. The National Security Act had directed the agency to correlate, analyze, and distribute information, and "other functions and duties related to intelligence affecting the national security." But there was no specific authority for covert overseas operations. The agency instead had to rely on a loophole of hazy language to justify hundreds of extralegal clandestine missions over the next years. From the beginning, there was an institutional tension between the patient accumulation of intelligence and the secret warfare that came to dominate the agency's resources.

By 1949 CIA leaders were intent on protecting covert operations from unwanted scrutiny. At their behest, Congress passed, without public debate, the Central Intelligence Act of 1949, which authorized the agency to use unvouchered funds, including secret funds transferred from other (mainly the Pentagon) departments, for overseas covert operations of a "confidential, extraordinary, or emergency nature."[17] Freed from standard governmental budgetary oversight, the secret covert operations budget was subject only to an annual approval by a small armed forces subcommittee, giving the CIA enormous latitude. As one of the subcommittee members, Richard Nixon, later said, "If it's secret, it's legal."[18] Added to the agency's unvouchered budgets was a secret skim from the Marshall Plan, which eventually funneled $685 million to the CIA.[19] The agency's resources were soon dominated by covert operations, which in 1951 received $400 million of the agency's $587 annual budget. When General Walter Bedell Smith became the CIA leader in 1950, he complained he had "inherited an unholy mess." While approving momentous coups and multitudes of covert actions, Smith attempted to direct more assets to research and analytical work, which he termed "the heart and soul of the CIA."[20]

Like the OSS, the CIA leadership was select. Allen Dulles, a Wall Streeter and OSS veteran, declared the CIA would be "directed by a relatively small but elite corps of men with a passion for anonymity." The top ranks of the CIG and early CIA were heavy with military men, especially from the military academies, but the CIA leaders such as Dulles demanded that military men divest themselves of rank to "take up the cloth of the intelligence service."[21]

The CIA in the early years did not do a great job, failing to foresee the Korean War and underestimating the odds of China's intervention.[22] Counterintelligence was porous. On the eve of the Korean War, a Soviet spy penetrated the agency's signals intelligence center and sabotaged the codebreakers' work. CIA analysts failed to predict the Soviet Union's atom bomb, detonated in 1953, and miscalculated the Soviets' intercontinental missiles, which were first launched in 1957, by a dozen years. The agency had virtually no human assets behind the Iron Curtain and there were few credible agents in Asia. The ability to gather intelligence in Asia was "almost negligible," one of Smith's deputies concluded in 1952 after inspecting the CIA Asian stations.[23]

With a shortage of experienced intelligence officers, the CIA was learning by doing—and often not very well.[24] The officers nonetheless pursued clandestine operations around the globe, organizing a coup in Iran in 1953, and in Guatemala the following year. During the Dwight Eisenhower administration, the CIA undertook 170 covert political, paramilitary, and psychological warfare operations in forty-eight nations in Europe, Asia, the Middle East, Africa, and Latin America.[25] Donald Gregg, served as CIA station chief in South Korea, as well as U.S. ambassador to South Korea. He termed the 1950s and 1960s as the CIA's "wild and wooly days," a period when "the Agency's image was far better than its actual capacities."[26] Referring to the often-hapless covert missions, he said, "It was swashbuckling of the worst kind."[27]

The Dinner Party

Benjamin C. Evans Jr. wanted in the CIA, where he envisioned a solid career while making a difference in the world. He wrote Harrison that his mission was "To create a happy family and establish a substantial home through making a living in such a way that offers advancement with merit and contributes to a lasting peace."[28] Jan said, "By this point, he was trying to prevent war. He thought with the CIA he could prevent war."[29]

Soon after returning from Korea, Evans resigned from the army, with the intent of quickly joining the CIA. He was an experienced psychological warfare officer, he knew the culture of intelligence, and he came from the right kind of people who had the right connections. He was a shoo-in. But the CIA was in a hiring freeze in 1956.[30] So the couple hunkered down for six months in the basement apartment at Lady Norma Lewis's Georgetown mansion. In the interim, Evans turned down opportunities in business and other government agencies that his friends and social connections offered.[31] "The CIA was the only thing he ever pursued," Jan said.[32]

The Evanses began marshaling family resources. As a longtime Washington grande dame, Lady Lewis had a host of influential friends in the government. Former CIA director Walter Bedell Smith was an old friend.[33] Members of CIA executive Richard Helms's family were part of the Evanses' Washington social milieu.[34] A well-connected family friend eventually insured Evans's path into the agency.

Colonel Donald H. Galloway was Harrison's West Point classmate and best friend. Graduating in 1923, Galloway and Harrison were cavalrymen at a time when that was the most prestigious branch of the army. "Back in that day," Jan said, "the cavalry were the top dogs." Both men served as intelligence officers in World War II. In 1947, after a stint in CIG operations, Galloway joined the newly formed CIA, which was then led by fellow West Pointer, General Hoyt Vanderberg.[35] "There's a bond that the military academy graduates have—much more than universities," Jan said. "You speak a language that no one else understands."[36] Under Vanderberg, Galloway was given the position of assistant director for special operations. Tall, imposing, and used to command, Galloway communicated at the CIA with a parade-ground voice, characteristically barking orders with the addendum, "On the double, *please*."[37] Jan recalled that "Colonel Galloway was someone who could get something done if he put his mind to it."[38] And Galloway decided his best friend's son-in-law needed a position in the agency. So he held a dinner party.

"All the top CIA people were there," Jan said about the party at Galloway's home in Spring Valley, an affluent northwest Washington neighborhood of movers and shakers.[39] She remembered there were five couples—"All CIA." Among them was James Jesus Angleton, the CIA's legendary head of counterintelligence, whose spy-catching mania eventually contorted the agency's operations.[40] "He was full of himself," Jan said.[41] According to Jan the evening went well and "Colonel Galloway gave Ben his blessing—he was in," Jan continued, "I guess I got passing marks [too]."[42]

10

TRADECRAFT

At the Farm, the Central Intelligence Agency's high-security, nine-thousand-acre training facility on the York River near Williamsburg, Virginia, Benjamin C. Evans Jr. was taught the tradecraft of covert operations: lock picking and clandestine materials drops, learning to surreptitiously open letters, case a location, and evade pursuers.[1] "I don't think he was very good at any of it," Jan King Evans said, claiming he could not even get them in the locked house if they forgot their keys. "I didn't see anything useful out of that."[2]

What was useful was his CIA training in the dark arts of espionage: personality evaluation and manipulation, subterfuge, and misinformation. It was the con man's bag of tricks that the CIA had codified in the service of national security.[3] Already a socially sophisticated psy warrior, Evans honed his listening skills and absorbed the intricacies of mind games, stealth, misdirection, and deception.

Evans entered federal service from Indiana in August 1957.[4] After his training, the CIA assigned him to the Western Hemisphere Division, which had intelligence responsibilities for twenty-one independent countries from Canada to the tip of South America, as well as the Caribbean nations of Haiti, the Dominican Republic, and Cuba. In the 1950s the Western Hemisphere Division also covered seven dependencies, including Alaska, Jamaica, and French Guiana.[5] The CIA was beefing up Western Hemisphere Division, particularly in the Latin American region.[6] Serving in staff and line positions, Evans's specialties were political and paramilitary operations.[7]

The 1950s were a time of bold action for the agency. When Walter Bedell Smith moved to the State Department after President Dwight Eisenhower's 1952 election, Allen Dulles took over as the CIA director. Covert operations, Dulles's specialty, became an important element of Eisenhower's "New Look" national security policy, formulated to combat the perceived existential Soviet threat. General James H. Doolittle's 1954 report to Eisenhower on covert operations stated the case frankly: "It is now clear that we are facing an implacable enemy whose avowed objective is world domination by whatever means and at whatever costs. If the U.S. is to survive, long-standing American concepts of 'fair play' must be reconsidered. We must learn to subvert, sabotage, and destroy our enemies by cleverer, more sophisticated, and more effective methods than those used against us. It may become necessary that the American people become acquainted with, understand, and support this fundamentally repugnant philosophy."[8] Dulles oversaw Operation Ajax, the 1953 coup in Iran that overthrew democratically elected president Mohammad Mossadegh, replacing him with the pliable Mohammad Reza Pahlavi, Shah of Iran. In 1954 the CIA's Operation PBSUCCESS toppled Guatemalan president Jacobo Arbenz Guzman, the democratically elected reformer whom U.S. officials saw as a threat to American business interests, especially those of the United Fruit Company.

In 1956 Eisenhower established the President's Board of Consultants on Foreign Activities to advise him on intelligence matters. Soon after, the board enlisted Robert A. Lovett, who had headed the Lovett Committee, and David K. E. Bruce, OSS officer and diplomat, to examine the CIA's covert operations. The Bruce-Lovett Report castigated the agency's meddling in other countries' internal affairs without oversight or coordination—sometimes without even notifying the impacted country's American ambassador. The report ridiculed the hubris of the agency's top covert officials: "The CIA, busy, moneyed, and privileged, likes its 'King Making' responsibility. The intrigue is fascinating—considerable self-satisfaction, sometimes with applause, derives from 'successes'—no charge is made for 'failures'—and the whole business is very much simpler than collecting covert intelligence on the USSR through the usual CIA methods!"[9] In early 1957 the board informed Eisenhower that covert operations were absorbing about 80 percent of the CIA budget, and were operating for the most part on "an autonomous and free-wheeling basis in highly critical areas."[10]

On October 4, 1957, a few months after Evans joined the CIA, the Soviet Union launched its *Sputnik* satellite. For Americans watching the tiny shining orb arc across the sky, it was an ominous sight, illustrating both the Soviet Union's technological prowess and capacity to attack the United States with nuclear weapons and intercontinental missiles. The media blared reports that the decolonizing countries of Africa and Southeast Asia were ripe for communist takeover, as was restive, underdeveloped Latin America. Therefore, the CIA had a mission: to aggressively gather information and to disrupt the communist movements with covert operations.[11] Fed by the electorate's fears of global communism, the CIA had growing governmental resources to do the job.

When Evans joined the CIA, the agency had offices in forty locations across Washington. There was the CIA's Foggy Bottom headquarters, where the OSS was housed during World War II. The nearby Heurich Brewery, being a good neighbor, erected a bus shelter for the CIA employees.[12] At midday CIA employees would cross over to the brewery's Hospitality Hall, where they could get complimentary beers to wash down their bagged lunches. "The brewery knew a lot of the people were spies," Jan said.[13] Some CIA operatives were housed in ratty old temporary buildings—"the tempos"—along the National Mall. But the CIA had other plans. In October 1957 the agency started clearing ground for a mammoth new complex at Langley, across the Potomac River in Virginia. When completed in 1963, the eight-story headquarters building of more than a million square feet had a parking lot for three thousand cars, and a cafeteria that seated 1,400 people.[14] For seventh-floor CIA executives responsible for administration, the building was a logistical headache.

Family Man

Evans's desire to be a good family man came to fruition. The couple's first child, Karla, was born at George Washington University Hospital on October 6, 1958. Having only recently become part of the clandestine service, the couple did not yet have their covert cover in sync. When asked by a nurse, Jan King Evans said her husband worked for the State Department. When the baby's birth certificate came to her to review, she realized that Ben had told the office that he worked in real estate. "We didn't have our stories straight," she laughed.[15]

The baby's christening was held at the National Cathedral's tiny Children's Chapel, attended by close family and friends, including Mary Smith, the wife of Walter Bedell Smith.[16] The Evanses were living in the imposing family home at 3033 Woodland Drive. During World War II, family patriarch Christian Heurich bought the classical-styled four-story brick residence for his daughter, Karla Heurich King Harrison. It was the family home for Karla and Charles King before his death in Normandy in 1944. After Karla remarried, she, her children, and General Eugene Harrison made it their Washington residence. Following the general's retirement, the Harrisons moved to a home in Clearwater Beach, Florida. After Jan and Ben Evans returned to Washington to take his CIA position, they moved into the family house. Claiming her grandfather's purchase price of $32,000 was "way too much," Jan purchased the house from her mother for $25,000.[17]

After the baby was born, Karla came up to DC to help. "Mother realized Ben was doing all the work—the cooking and the cleaning. So mother left money so I could have help forever," Jan recalled.[18] From that point on, the Evans family had live-in help, who resided in the basement apartment.

After training, Evans was off every morning to his new job, working out of various CIA offices, including one near the Sixteenth Street hotels.[19] As he acquired working knowledge of his Western Hemisphere Division job, the CIA utilized Evans as a spokesman, sending him out to give speeches and recruit at universities. Jan was busy with their new baby, and her many Washington friends from her Cathedral High School years. With her nurse's training acquired at Fort Benning, she volunteered as a nurse's aide in Washington hospitals, including Walter Reed.

In 1959 Evans was posted to Havana, Cuba, where he would covertly work out of the embassy. As with many CIA overseas operatives, his cover was as a State Department official, the Second Business Secretary in the Foreign Service Reserve. His CIA title was Chief Political Action Officer.[20] The Havana assignment excited the Evanses. "We were going to be there for four years, and it was going to be idyllic," Jan said.[21] She organized the move, packing up the four floors of their furniture and belongings, including the family silver. As an ostensible diplomat's wife, she took an etiquette and protocol course that the State Department taught in Virginia and at the Italian embassy. "I had to learn the protocol: wear a hat; to make calls on all the women above me; the women below me had to call on me. Be ready to receive two days a week," she recalled. "Where to sit according to my position; always on the left of my husband—he was higher ranking. I had to order calling cards; learn which corner to turn down. Of course, I knew a lot of that already from my grandmother [Lady Norma Lewis]."[22]

Through 1957 and 1958, the CIA officials in the Western Hemisphere Division had been watching the rebellion against Cuban dictator Fulgencio Batista unfold. Led by firebrand Fidel Castro, the revolutionaries had been waging a successful insurgency. In March 1958 the United States had suspended arms shipments to Batista's forces, and by August Castro's troops were winning the fight. On January 1, 1959, Batista flew to exile in Miami, and Castro's hirsute rebels took Havana and with it control of the Cuban government.

The U.S. government response to Castro's revolutionary movement was ambivalent.[23] On the one hand, analysts thought that Castro would need to make a deal with the U.S. government and American business interests to prop up his shaky regime. But there were also concerns about the communistic rhetoric espoused by Castro and members of his inner circle. The CIA decided to pursue a hydra-headed strategy. In late December 1958 the CIA's Havana station cabled a proposal to reach out to Castro through intermediaries to make a deal. The cable read, "An operation this nature could pay big future dividends if fully qualified person could be found for job and dispatched quickly. Regardless how we may feel about Castro and his movement, both will be important political forces for a long time to come." At about the same time, the Western Hemisphere Division tasked the CIA's Paramilitary Division to organize airdrops of arms and "locate dissidents who were both anti-Castro and anti-Batista."[24] Handling covert agents became Evans's job in Havana.

11

CUBA AND THE REVOLUTION

Benjamin C. Evans Jr. met his agent in a Havana restaurant, not too far from the U.S. embassy.[1] Oscar Echevarria was perfectly positioned to be a Central Intelligence Agency asset. "I was inside the government," Echevarria said, speaking of his work as an economist in Fidel Castro's revolutionary government. The stories he had heard about Castro's draconian style of leadership while commanding the rebels deeply troubled Echevarria. "Castro was very totalitarian," he said.[2] Determined to do what he could to overthrow the new dictator, Echevarria reached out to the CIA.

Echevarria had a circuitous path to becoming a CIA asset. A son of a wealthy Cuban family, Echevarria had a privileged boyhood of a Jesuit education, equestrian pursuits, and international travel. After graduating with a degree from the Saint Thomas de Villanova University, a Roman Catholic institution that instilled U.S.-democratic ideals in its students, he joined his father's large publishing company, which printed the Catholic workers' newspaper, advertising, and commissioned books written by university professors.[3] Echevarria's family ideologically averred dictatorships.[4] The family was anti-Batista after the dictator detained its patriarch to shake him down. Castro's dictatorial proclivities likewise concerned them.

In February 1959, just a few months after Castro took power, one of his father's authors, economist Raul Cepero Bonilla, asked Echevarria to serve as his undersecretary in the Castro regime's Department of Commerce. Echevarria was soon appointed to be the Assistant Secretary for Prices and Supplies, which provided unfettered access to inside information on the Cuban economy. As an adviser for governmental technical appointments, he recruited fellow members of the Agrupación Católica Universitaria, a prestigious Marian congregation of Catholic professionals and university students. Echevarria was forming a brain trust of like-minded potential counterrevolutionaries, who could funnel information to him.

About the same time, two influential men, Raul Maestri and Ken Crosby, introduced Echevarria to Jim Noel, the CIA Station Chief in Havana. Maestri was a distinguished University of Havana economics professor and well-connected television host on Cuba's *Meet the Press*, on which Echevarria had appeared. Crosby was Merrill Lynch's man in Havana. A colorful ex-Federal Bureau of Investigation agent, Crosby had been undercover as a Merrill Lynch executive in Latin America during World War II, when the FBI was responsible for anti-Nazi operations there.[5] With Castro's political intentions still unclear, Noel quickly realized Echevarria could provide the CIA valuable information. "This was a typical case of being in the right place at the right time," Echevarria wrote.[6]

Noel also realized that Echevarria and his soon-to-arrive covert officer Evans had something in common to provide cover: They both attended Culver Military Academy, where they were both summer Black Horse Troop captains. In the phraseology of covert tradecraft, their shared Hoosier experience gave them a "plausibly deniable" reason to meet.[7]

Cuba, Pearl of the Antilles

When Evans met Echeverria to discuss counterrevolution, the six-story U.S. embassy on Havana's Malecón waterfront was the largest in the world. Approximately sixty U.S. diplomats and spies worked there, serving the interests of American capitalism and tourism. U.S. business interests dominated the Cuban economy in the 1950s. American capital had flooded into the country following World War II, eventually reaching almost a billion dollars, which ranked Cuba third among nations for direct U.S. investment. By the late 1950s, U.S. financial interests included 90 percent of Cuban mines, 80 percent of its public utilities, 50 percent of its railways, 40 percent of its sugar production, and 25 percent of its bank deposits.[8]

In the 1950s Cuba was also the hedonistic destination for carousing celebrities, politicians, executives, and sybaritic tourists of all stripes. Frank Sinatra crooned at the Hotel Nacional casino and Ernest Hemingway, Ava Gardner, Spencer Tracy, and Marlene Dietrich downed daiquiris at El Floridita. Young senator John F. Kennedy came down with his fellow senator George Smathers for a licentious romp.[9] Each year, hundreds of thousands of American middle-class junketeers signed on for fifty-dollar, all-expenses-paid tours to exotic tropical Havana—the majority lured by the gambling, horse tracks, nightclubs, bordellos, and sultry Afro-Cuban rhythms.

Castro's victory changed all that. The day after Batista's flight into exile, Cubans ravaged the casinos. At the Plaza Hotel's casino, people dragged gaming tables into the street and set them on fire. U.S. tourism plummeted. The year after Castro took power, only four thousand Americans straggled into the Pearl of the Antilles.

But among the Cuban people, Castro maintained resounding popular support. In February 1959, when Echevarria began meeting with the CIA, the influential Cuban magazine *Bohemia* published a survey that indicated Castro had the support of 95 percent of the people, who were eager for change after decades of the corrupt Batista regime. With Castro's policies unclear at that point, many groups, including Cuban and U.S. powerbrokers, thought they could influence the direction of the government, perhaps toward tempered reform rather than revolution.

Castro began to institute popular policies, such as lowering rent, phone, and electric rates, and in May 1959 the Agrarian Reform Law, which redistributed confiscated land, roiled the Cuban and American elites. Castro followed with policies that improved Cubans' standard of living, such as salary increases for the sugar industry.[10] Even six months later, when the Cuban public could see Castro's increasingly radical moves had alienated the United States, he still retained a 90 percent approval rating.[11] In a dispatch to Washington, Noel reported the revolutionary leader was "the idol of the masses," while also stating that "Castro's popularity was very low among the middle and upper classes."[12]

Even before Evans arrived in Cuba, he was gathering information on the revolution. In late July 1959 Evans was at a hotel in Tampa, Florida, checking in as a State Department employee, "Ben Elliot." He and a CIA colleague were there to interview a Cuban informant, Jose Marcos Diaz, who gave a detailed report on the state of the Cuban security forces, including force readiness, supply levels, and summations of commanders and instructors.[13]

Through 1959 Castro was finessing his political moves with a smokescreen of anticommunist messaging. The U.S. government, still hoping to make a deal, remained ambivalent. The CIA continued its bifurcated policy of seeking "rapprochement with present government" while contingency planning for paramilitary action if the Cuban government proved to be communist dominated.[14] Cubans such as Echevarria had already decided their government's new laws portended more radical policies; Castro needed to be overthrown.

The House

Evans and Echevarria became friends, bonding as they talked about their Culver experiences, particularly their long summer horse treks across the northern Indiana countryside with their Black Horse Troops. "It was very pleasant," Echevarria said about their conversations, which mentally transported them from revolutionary Havana to the Culver of their boyhoods. Culver's equestrian program had long attracted wealthy Cubans, imbued with the Latin love of horsemanship. When Echevarria attended Culver in the summers of 1952 and 1953, there were six Cubans in the program. During Culver's winter semesters, there were even more Cuban cadets, including dictator Fulgencia Batista's sons.[15]

Evans taught Echevarria the tradecraft of espionage. Echevarria wrote, "The rules are simple: 'Nome de guerre,' 'compartmentalization,' 'need to know,' 'cover,' and 'plausible denial.'" Evans's nom de guerre was "Colonel Whitney," memorializing the long-serving head of Culver's cavalry program during both of their student days.

In return Echevarria educated Evans about Castro's socialist direction and the dire implications for relations with the United States. Echevarria introduced Evans to newspaperman and politician Angel Fernandez Varela, a fellow member of Agrupación Católica Universitaria. Varela, who was also opposed to Castro's regime, was another important intelligence source for Evans. As the editor of the important *Información* newspaper, Varela could provide breaking inside news. Varela also had unique insights into Castro's thinking, as Varela had taught the dictator *Moral y Cívica* when he attended El Colegia de Belén, the Jesuit boarding school in Havana.

Informed by their shared worldview, Evans soon came to trust the information that Echevarria and his fellow counterrevolutionaries provided about Castro's trajectory toward communism. Sooner than many of his CIA and State Department colleagues, Evans realized that the Cuban-American political relationship was going to devolve very fast. And he needed to tell his wife.

After they had arrived in Havana in early September 1959, the Evanses had rented a gracious apartment on the Malecón, the city's elegant seaside esplanade.[16] In Jan's mind, it was temporary housing. She had brought their four floors of furniture from Washington to outfit a home that would befit a young family of means. As she made her obligatory calls on the other diplomats' wives in the fashionable neighborhoods of Havana, she was scouting for their new home. Her husband's news came as a shock. "Three weeks after we arrived," Jan said, "Ben came and said we're not staying. Things are much worse than we thought. Things are not what they appear to be." He told her that they were not going to get a house. They would stay in the Malacón apartment until they returned to the Unites States—whenever that might be. "Well, I cried," she said. "We never argued. I just cried and got my way."[17]

Later in 1959, Ben, Jan, and Karla, moved to the tony Miramar neighborhood, where they rented a spacious white stucco villa at 4407 5A-A Avenue from Ambassador Carrillo.[18] "It was a beautiful home," Jan said. There was room for their furnishings, and she embarked on a decorating spree, arranging for workmen to repaint the house and install lighting fixtures from Miami. The gardener maintained the manicured grounds that included an elaborate backyard children's playhouse with toilet facilities. The Cuban maid did the housekeeping, helped with baby Karla and cooked meals from the offerings of an itinerant vendor who arrived in a horse-drawn wagon.

The Evanses' social life centered on the embassy and the staff stationed there. During her obligatory diplomatic calls on the fifty embassy wives, Jan learned about Havana life.[19] The Evanses belonged to the Havana Country Club, where wealthy expats and Cubans golfed and mingled. Some months after moving in, the Evanses celebrated their new home with a big party, attended by the entire diplomatic list, including Ambassador Philip W. Bonsal and his wife. Beyond the perennially calling of diplomatic wives, there were regular visitors, including their new Cuban friends, Echevarria and Varela, and Americans Noel, Crosby and David Phillips—all connected to the CIA.

Phillips was a longtime CIA spy in Latin America, who had worked on the 1954 Guatemalan coup. After a covert stint in Cuba and then the Middle East, he resigned and returned to Havana on the cusp of Batista's flight with the intent of making a fortune as a Castro-connected public-relations man. But after Castro brought all public relations under the government, David A. Phillips Associates fell on hard times. So, Phillips returned to his true calling: that of a CIA spy.[20] Another friend was William T. Heagney, First National Bank of Boston's longtime lead banker in Havana and the father of one of Jan's Connecticut College classmates. With his inside knowledge of commercial dealings, Heagney became one of Evans's covert sources.[21] While the Evanses were stationed in Havana, none of their family members came for a visit. Because of the political instability, Evans strongly discouraged stateside friends and family from coming to Cuba.

The Evanses had good relations with their upscale Miramar neighbors, who were likewise unsettled by the revolutionary government. "Whenever Castro got on the radio and screamed for hours," Jan said, "the neighbors came over to apologize." The Evanses' Cuban neighbors in affluent Miramar were in the minority. In January 1960 five hundred thousand Cubans attended a Havana rally to hear Castro speak about the revolution. The U.S. embassy reported that during Castro's almost five-hour speech, he asked the crowd, in the name of "revolutionary justice," whether they approved the "shooting of the assassins." The report indicated, "All the hands were raised to the accompaniment of a 'vengeful roar.'"[22] Through 1959 and into 1960, hundreds of Batista officials and informers, including some Americans, were being led to "el paradón" (the wall) for execution by firing squads.[23]

Visitors to the Evanses' villa sometimes encountered a surprising sight. Karla had spotted a large bearded and khaki-uniformed Castro doll in a shop. Smitten with the doll, Karla insisted that she had to have it. So as CIA spy Evans plotted to overthrow the Cuban dictator, his daughter toddled through the house with her beloved Castro doll.[24]

The Counterrevolution

Soon after meeting Echevarria, Evans began organizing his agents and enablers.[25] He enlisted a young, redheaded Vassar graduate who worked in the embassy. She agreed to let the conspirators meet in her apartment in the nearby Vedado neighborhood. He arranged for Jimmy O'Malley, a CIA operative who also was the principal of the private Saint George School in Vedado, to serve as a courier.

Evans also recruited Elena Falla, Echevarria's girlfriend who worked in the embassy. Falla's father, the president of the world's largest sugar company, had insisted she get a job, so she took an embassy filing-clerk position. She wrote that Evans approached her desk and told her he worked with her boyfriend. "This gentleman would appreciate, if I was willing to serve as a courier when needed, it involved no risk as it would be oral communication," Falla wrote. She agreed.[26] "He had the most beautiful blue eyes in the world," she said. "You could melt. You could see his soul through his eyes. He was a really beautiful man."[27] Evans transferred Falla into the embassy's diplomatic visa section, where she could expedite visas for the counterrevolutionaries, including Cubans traveling to Guatemala for CIA paramilitary training. Later she loaned Echevarria her British Riley automobile so he could drive incognito to Evans's Miramar house for clandestine meetings. The venerable Havana restaurant, El Carmelo, became another rendezvous point. "Ben would say, 'Go meet Oscar and give him this.' It was just little bits of paper. I could eat them if I got stopped. It wasn't scary. It was just fun to get out of the embassy," said Falla.[28]

But in actuality, Evans was dispatching Falla on delicate missions—"hairy" in the spook argot.

Evans recognized that Castro's broad popular support precluded a frontal propaganda attack, so he recommended they initially discredit communism by framing it as an anathema to the Cuban revolution's ideals. The band of counterrevolutionaries printed tens of thousands of copies of *Batista Father of Communism*, a subversive booklet written by a young Jesuit seminarian, at the Echevarria publishing company. The booklets were financed jointly with CIA funds provided by Evans and money contributed by an influential sugar mill executive, Melchor Gaston. The conservative Catholic ACU distributed the booklets. By October 1959 the conspirators had printed more than five hundred thousand counterrevolutionary booklets, including the *Batista* title and *What the Communists Hide, Communism and Dictatorship, Careful with Certain People, and Was Marti Communist?* At the time, there were only about 1.5 million Cuban families, comprising a population of not quite seven million. It was a massive propaganda program—far too big to be secret, particularly at a time when Castro's security forces were tightening the screws.[29]

In Washington, the CIA secretly formalized its Cuban policy. In a December 11, 1959, memorandum, Western Hemisphere Division Chief J. C. King stated the objective: "The overthrow of Castro within one year," replacing him with a junta friendly to the United States. The CIA program included psywar propaganda operations, including invasive actions against Cuban media, radio attacks on Cuba from nearby countries, and the formation of pro-U.S. opposition groups, with the goal of militarily establishing a counterrevolutionary enclave in Cuba.[30]

In Havana the propaganda campaign was already in high gear. On December 14, 1959, the printers were running another hundred thousand Batista booklets, when the Cuban intelligence service, Dirección General de Inteligencia, known as G2, raided the plant. Echevarria's uncle and three employees were arrested.

After getting the news, Echevarria warned Evans, so he could protect the other members of the group. Echevarria then reached out to his boss, Secretary of Commerce Raul Cepero Bonilla, to intercede with a personal note to the feared head of G2, Major Ramiro Valdes—"The Commandant." Armed with the letter, young Echevarria went to the G2 headquarters in Miramar "to try to solve the situation." He managed to spring his uncle and the printers from custody. As Echevarria waited on a terrace to speak with "The Commandant," a Cuban captain sat beside him on the bench. The captain mentioned he came from the notorious La Cabaña fortress, where the firing squads had been executing enemies of the revolution. He told Echevarria that they had just jailed a man for publishing antigovernment propaganda. And that is what happened to Echevarria.

At midnight, the G2 officers incarcerated Echevarria, and in the morning his interrogation began. His interrogator was a captain, a Spanish psychiatrist who had honed his skills during the Spanish Civil War, when he was a leftist major in the Republican army. It was a long, nerve-wracking day of interrogation and psychological intimidation, but about 3:00 p.m. Echevarria was released—by order of Raul Castro, Fidel's brother. Raul Cepero Bonilla's efforts had worked.

Echevarria and Evans were undeterred by their brush with the Cuban intelligence service, and they, along with Varela became crucial players in the anti-Castro program being crafted in Langley. On January 18, 1960, the Western Hemisphere Division organized Branch 4, a task force to run the Cuba counterrevolutionary operations. The task force initially had a staff of forty, including eighteen at the Langley headquarters, two in Santiago, and twenty, including Evans, at the Havana Station.[31]

At a Washington press conference in January 1960 Ambassador Bonsal decried Castro: "He is an extreme Leftist and is strongly anti-American."[32] In February 1960 a Soviet trade delegation arrived in Havana with great fanfare. The subsequent Soviet-Cuban pact included a massive Cuban-sugar-for-Soviet-oil agreement, as well as a low-interest loan for Soviet-bloc imports. The pact clearly signaled the Cuban government's socialist direction. The East German trade delegation followed with another trade deal. A few weeks later, the Soviet Union and Cuba resumed diplomatic relations, which had been suspended since 1952. Washington was seething.

On March 17, 1960, President Dwight Eisenhower met with his national security leadership and approved the CIA plan, "A Program of Covert Action Against the Castro Regime," which called for four primary courses of action: 1. form a moderate opposition group in exile whose slogan will be to restore the revolution that Castro betrayed; 2. create a medium-wave radio station to broadcast into Cuba, probably on Swan Island, south of Cuba; 3. create a covert intelligence and action organization within Cuba responsive to the orders and directions of the exile opposition; 4. begin training a paramilitary force outside Cuba, and also train elite paramilitary cadres for immediate deployment into Cuba to organize, train, and lead an anti-Castro resistance. "There is no better plan," Eisenhower said at the meeting. But worried about leaks and security breaches, he told the national security team to be prepared to deny the plan's existence. And for operational security and plausible deniability, Eisenhower insisted only two or three U.S. officials should have contact with the Cuban counterrevolutionaries, agitating them to do most of the dirty work.[33]

In late March 1960 Echevarria, Varela, and José Ignacio Rasco, a conservative Catholic who had been a classmate of Fidel Castro, joined Evans and other CIA agents in a secure apartment at the Presidential Gardens in the Arlandria section of Alexandria, Virginia.[34] The goal of the four-day meeting was to organize the Frente Revolucionario Democrático, an organization designed to aggregate the disparate Cuban counterrevolutionary groups and to provide cover and legitimacy for the American anti-Castro policies. Echevarria wrote that Evans was calm and collected, interested in hearing diverse opinions before voicing his own course of action.[35] With the intention of reversing the revolutionary legislation and organizing a paramilitary force, the FRD proved to be the catalyst for the creation of other Cuban opposition groups, also typically comprised of moneyed Cubans who had suffered losses under the new regime.[36] On the last night of the planning session, March 29, 1960, the conspirators celebrated at the landmark Occidental Restaurant, fabled for Washington deal making.[37] Colonel J. C. King, head of the Western Hemisphere Division, joined the party as an emissary of CIA director Allen Dulles.[38]

The counterinsurgency fervor was increasing. In January 1960 Cuba began to experience widespread acts of sabotage, primarily directed against the sugar industry, including aerial incendiary bombings of sugar fields, some by planes with U.S. markings. In early March 1960 saboteurs destroyed *La Coubre*, a French ship carrying arms for Castro's forces that was moored in Havana harbor. About a hundred people died and hundreds were wounded. At the funerals for the victims, Castro blamed the United States, comparing *La Coubre* to the sinking of the American battleship *Maine*. The same month FRD leaders discussed ratcheting up psywar to encourage armed resistance and sabotage, and to demoralize the military with a campaign "based in terror."[39]

Assassination was not yet part of the CIA's anti-Castro plan—though that decision was not without debate within the agency. In his December 1959 memorandum, King also suggested: "Thorough consideration be given to the elimination of Fidel Castro. . . . Many informed people believe that the disappearance of Fidel would greatly accelerate the fall of the present government."⁴⁰ But the CIA leadership realized that Castro's "mesmeric appeal" would cause the Cuban people to "react violently" if U.S-connected forces eliminated him. In a January 13, 1960, meeting on Cuba, Dulles "emphasized that we do not have in mind a quick elimination of Castro, but rather actions to enable responsible opposition leaders to get a foothold."⁴¹ Evans focused his cell of Cuban counterrevolutionaries on organization and psychological warfare. Echevarria said, "Ben was not a violent man."⁴²

In May 1960 the FRD leadership and CIA officers met in Miami, where they hammered out the details of their partnership. CIA money was not unexpectedly part of the arrangement. Frank Bender, the lead CIA officer on the operation, later bragged that he "carried the counterrevolution in his checkbook."⁴³

Eisenhower's March 17, 1960, directive to establish an anti-Castro radio station on Swan Island, a small island of guano off the coast of Honduras, initiated swift action. In late March U.S. Navy Seabees were given an urgent order to construct a radio station with two 220-foot radio transmission towers, a landing strip, and living and office facilities on the near-deserted island, which did not even have a loading pier. A week later, navy ships were disgorging materials on the island and the Seabees began a crash construction project. On May 17, 1960, the CIA's Radio Swan began beaming a strong signal to Cuba and much of the Western Hemisphere.⁴⁴ The Spanish-language programming of music, news, religion, and soap operas was heavy with anti-Castro polemics. The station became a major element of Evans's CIA psywar campaign against the Cuban government. It must have had some impact. Radio Mambi, a Cuban government station, denounced Radio Swan, telling its listeners that it wasn't a station, it was "a cage of hysterical parrots."⁴⁵

Radio Swan's signal was so strong, advertisers clamored to take advantage of the station's powerful transmission, forcing the CIA to accept advertising to maintain its cover.⁴⁶ But Radio Swan's paper-thin cover didn't last long. The island was purportedly owned by Gibraltar Steamship Corporation, a CIA proprietary that owned no steamships. Radio Habana, the Cuban government station, soon pinpointed the station location and the ruse, exposing Radio Swan as a CIA propaganda machine.⁴⁷

It was a turbulent time for U.S.-Soviet relations. On May 1, 1960, the Soviets shot down a CIA U-2 spy plane over Soviet airspace. At the Paris summit a few weeks later, Soviet premier Nikita Khrushchev lashed out at Eisenhower, who was furious about the public denunciation. Soviet oil tankers had begun arriving in Havana a few weeks prior. The Cuban government ordered the foreign-owned Standard Oil, Texaco, and British-Dutch Shell refineries to refine the Soviet crude. At the direction of U.S. government officials, the refineries refused. Three weeks later the Cubans nationalized foreign refineries, offering Cuban government bonds as recompense for the expropriations, an offer that Washington summarily dismissed.[48]

The pressure continued to build. In July Eisenhower retaliated by cutting Cuban sugar imports by seven hundred thousand tons, which U.S. officials thought would bring the young government to heel. But the Soviet Union quickly agreed to purchase the amount cut by the United States, and then Communist China announced it would purchase a half-million tons of Cuban sugar. With most of the payments in barter, Cuba was now locked into a communist orbit. Castro threatened to nationalize all the American-owned property in Cuba, "We'll take and take until not even the nails in their shoes are left. We will take American investments penny by penny until nothing is left."[49]

The Last Ferry

"Cuba was difficult," Jan said. "Ben always had a plan to get Karla and I out. He always had plane tickets for us. Ben would be a worry-wart for his family." And the family was soon to be bigger, as Jan was pregnant with their second child, who was due in September.

Jan was ambivalent about leaving Havana. She had moved all their possessions from Washington; they were in a great house, with ample domestic help. "We were going to be there for four years, and it would be idyllic," she said about their initial outlook. "We did not expect what was going to happen."[50] But there were other serious issues to consider: "I couldn't have my baby there. All the good doctors had left. And the hospitals were not in good shape." As the Cuban revolution lurched leftward, tens of thousands of educated Cubans, including many of the best doctors and medical professionals, had fled the island. And Evans knew the conflict between Washington and Havana was going to get much worse.

There was a long-standing embassy plan to evacuate the diplomatic staff and their families. They would gather at the Havana Country Club for exfiltration by aircraft. But then Castro expropriated the country club for a workers' recreation center, closing off that contingency plan.

With U.S.-Cuban relations deteriorating by the day, Evans announced it was time for his wife and daughter to leave Cuba. "I knew he knew a lot more than I did. So I went when he said," Jan indicated. Evans booked passage for the family on the SS *City of Havana*, the largest passenger ship operating between Cuba and Florida. They booked tickets on the last ferry that transported cars.[51] Wary of nationalization, the U.S.-owned West India Fruit and Steamship Company was shutting down its service between Havana and Key West.[52] Not wanting to tip off Cuban intelligence, the embassy refused to ship the Evanses' furniture back to the United States, so Jan had to decide what to take with them in the car. "I spent a week packing that car," she said. Working secretly in the hot garage, Jan packed and repacked their Pontiac station wagon, until it was stuffed with their family photos and silver, essential clothes, and baby things.

As a CIA controller of intelligence assets, Evans cared about his string of agents. Echevarria wrote, "Ben always advised me that we should not take extreme risks even if that would compromise success. He always put my safety and that off [sic] my associates at par with the functional interest of his post." Echevarria wrote that Evans "never took a party line defending all U.S. government actions. When mistake[s] were made he called as he saw them."[53] Evans warned his Cuban counterrevolutionaries to be very careful. At some point he told his banker-informant, Heagney, "Get out of Cuba as soon as you can."[54]

On July 14, 1960, the Evans family drove their car onto the *City of Havana*. Ben's agent, Falla, was coincidentally on the same ferry, accompanying her mother, nephews, and their nanny. While they were ostensibly going on holiday to the United States, they brought the family dog, a parrot, and fifty-seven canaries in seven cages, all crammed into one of the ship's staterooms. Soon the Evanses and Falla were up on deck, watching El Morro castle and the Malacón recede as the ferry churned seaward through the muddy harbor. Falla recalled, "They called my name and wanted me to go to the bridge." She flashed on loaning Echievarria her car for his CIA meetings, and feared Cuban intelligence officers were going to detain her. "My heart was beating really hard; my knees were knocking." Evans was discretely watching. "His hand was right at my elbow—kind of hard. He said, 'You're going to go up the stairs, you're going to smile, and you're going to ask them what they want,'" Falla remembered Evans telling her. "When I got to the bridge, the captain said, 'Your mother has so many animals, we're going to give you another stateroom.'"[55] Soon they were looking north. The United States was only ninety miles away.

12

CRISIS

Benjamin C. Evans Jr. returned to Havana, Cuba, flying from Miami on one of the few flights still bound for the island, spending only a few days in Florida. Cuban had become a malestrom.[1] As he drove the Havana streets patrolled by bearded young militiamen, political graffiti proclaimed revolutionary ardor: "Cuba, Si, Yanqui No!"; "Patrio o Meurte!"; and "Paredón!"—"Against the Wall!"

Through the summer of 1960 Fidel Castro's nationalization of U.S. property was accelerating—with overwhelming popular support. On August 6, 1960, tens of thousands of Cubans packed the Cerro Stadium to hear Castro announce a new revolutionary law. It was an emotionally charged event, replete with a rousing Cuban national anthem and a plea by Raul Castro for quiet so they could hear Fidel read Law Number 851, the Nationalization Law. Fidel told the crowd his regime passed the law because of the U.S. government's "constant aggression against the fundamental interests of the Cuban economy." The Nationalization Law expropriated the businesses and properties of twenty-six American-controlled companies, including the national telephone and electric companies, Texaco, Esso, and Sinclair oil companies, and a long list of sugar mills owned by U.S. corporations. As Fidel Castro read the name of each nationalized U.S. corporation, a roar of Cuban voices thundered, "It was called!"[2]

Evans flew back to a city that was a clandestine cat-and-mouse game. With Havana now the epicenter of Cold War conflict, spies of a dozen political persuasions plotted intrigues across the city, from the cobbled warrens of Habana Vieja to the palm-lined avenues of Miramar. Central Intelligence Agency case officers, often glassy-eyed with fatigue, met with their Cuban counterrevolutionary agents at all hours of the day and night.[3] In mid-June 1960 Cuban G2 agents had arrested U.S. diplomats Edwin L. Sweet and William G. Friedman during a meeting with counterrevolutionaries. The Cubans charged Sweet and Friedman with financing subversive publications, granting political asylum, and encouraging terrorist acts and expeditiously expelled them.[4] Of course, Evans was doing the same work. With communist counterintelligence units combing the city through the summer of 1960, Evans continued to handle his string of Frente Revolucionario Democrático conspirators, including Oscar Echevarria and Angel Varela, who were actively recruiting agents from the conservative Catholic Agrupación Católica Universitaria.[5]

In early July 1960 the CIA transferred Cuban exiles to Guatemala for paramilitary training. The plan was to prepare them for guerilla warfare with two- and three-man units. Cuban militias in the provinces were already fighting a low-grade anti-Castro insurgency, capturing 112 contras on August 5, 1960. CIA officers were beginning to plot extreme actions against the Castro regime, including a plan to assassinate Raul. Through August 1960, however, the CIA was still not planning to assassinate Fidel—though there was the nefarious scheme to sprinkle his boots with a depilatory to cause his macho beard to fall out.

The CIA, realizing that Castro had consolidated control, lost confidence that a guerilla insurgency would ignite a popular uprising, especially given the Western Hemisphere Division was having trouble finding Cuban volunteers to be anti-Castro agents. A CIA memo in June 1960 stated, "Many of the Agents who were proposed by other WH Stations for use in Cuba were either found to be unacceptable, or did not want such an assignment."[6] The CIA strategists began to reconceptualize the anti-Castro offensive, which morphed from guerrilla infiltrators to a full-scale amphibious invasion by approximately 1,500 infantry with tanks and air cover. The newly hatched CIA plan was to establish an "entrenchment," a redoubt where the counterrevolutionary government could foment a long civil war. It was, as a CIA historian termed it, "a complete and radical shift."[7] On August 18, 1960, President Dwight Eisenhower approved $13 million for covert anti-Castro operations, which could include the use of U.S. military personnel and equipment. CIA staffing requirements for the dramatically larger mission increased, even though the agency was already having trouble finding qualified officers for the Cuban operations.[8]

In mid-September 1960 Evans learned his Cuban agents were in danger. Cuban G2 had arrested three CIA technicians in the process of bugging the New China News Agency office in the twenty-three-story Edificio Seguro Medico building in Vedado. The CIA quickly cabled the bad news to Washington. The arrests presented a very big problem: G2 had arrested the CIA equivalent of James Bond's "M," a high-level Office of Technical Services officer, who was a top surveillance gadget developer with inside knowledge of every CIA bugging operation and audio technician in the world. The technicians had "thin covers," but no one could predict how long they would hold up under Cuban interrogation—or even worse, Russian interrogation. It was a disaster.[9]

Evans quickly dispatched his liaison, Jimmy O'Malley, to warn Echevarria that he "should seek diplomatic asylum immediately."[10] Evans hoped that Cuban G2 might be waiting to arrest Echevarria until after Castro made his major address at the United Nations in New York on September 26, 1960, thus giving Echevarria a brief window to seek safety. Echevarria rejected political asylum; he wanted to be able to return to Cuba. But he knew it was time to go.

Concerned G2 might arrest Echevarria at the airport, Evans needed to learn if his agent was under surveillance. The men employed a classic spy technique. The next day at noon, Echevarria began following a prearranged route, shadowed by CIA officers checking for Cuban intelligence. Echevarria had an alert escort. He wrote, "Much to my surprise, at the segment at the Hotel Nacional it was Ben doing the counter surveillance." Evans and his men did not detect any tails. And CIA agents in the Dirección General de Inteligencia reported there was no immediate threat to Echevarria's counterrevolutionary cell. The coast was clear. On September 21, 1960, Echevarria boarded a flight at Rancho-Boyeros Airport and flew to Miami, where he joined the counterrevolutionaries working with Radio Swan. "Ben said, 'You are needed on the political side,'" Echevarria remembered. Flying on small planes out of Florida down to Swan Island multiple times, Echevarria helped beam the anti-Castro émigré message to the communist-controlled island. "There was no editorial second-guessing by the CIA," Echevarria said.[11]

Echevarria was joining a vast wave of Cubans fleeing the Castro regime. In 1959 a total of 285,967 Cubans received passports. Through 1960 crowds of Cubans, many well-educated, thronged the U.S. embassy in hopes of snagging one of the two hundred visas the overworked consular staff processed each day. The anxious applicants had often waited months for their visa appointment. More than 60,000 Cubans left in 1960.[12] In all, 250,000 Cubans emigrated to the United States between 1959 and 1962.[13] Among the refugees were children of counterrevolutionaries, who feared the communist government would hold their children hostage or indoctrinate them.

Instigated by the CIA, the Cuban children's international escape organization came to be known as Operation Pedro Pan.[14] The CIA psywar officers and Cuban counterrevolutionaries had a clever plan. It started with spreading rumors about a new Cuban law that would impact families. Then it went on the air. On October 26, 1960, the powerful CIA-controlled radio station on Swan Island began broadcasting stories about an impending Cuban law that would remove children from their parents for communist indoctrination. Radio Swan reported the Cuban counterrevolutionary underground had a copy of the forthcoming law, trumpeting, "Cuban mothers, don't let them take your children away! The Revolutionary Government will take them away from you when they turn five and keep them until they are eighteen. By that time they will be materialistic monsters."[15] On December 13, 1960, Costa Rica's La Republica headlined a story: "The State in Cuba Will Assume Guardianship Shortly," reporting children were being trained to inform on their families.[16] It was CIA disinformation. There was no such law. Designed to destabilize Castro's communist government, the CIA's psychological warfare had its intended effect. Cuban parents, particularly conservative anti-Castro parents, were terrified and quickly began to seek ways to get their children off the island, even if they could not leave themselves.

It was a time of rumors in Cuba. With Castro's government expanding its nationalization and expropriation policies, jailing increasing numbers of political dissidents, and consolidating control, the Cubans were primed for fake news. And as with most successful psywar operations, the planted "truth" was plausible.[17]

An organization to handle young Cuban refugees quickly coalesced into being. Operation Pedro Pan, the brainchild of James Baker, an American private-school headmaster in Havana, and Father Bryan O. Walsh, a thirty-year-old Catholic priest in Miami, was initially designed to handle a few hundred Cuban children. Under the auspices of his organization, the Catholic Welfare Bureau, Walsh arranged with the U.S. State Department, which authorized him to issue visa waivers to Cuban children six to sixteen, if his charity agreed to support them. The first young emigres began disembarking in Miami in December 1960. Thousands more followed. Many of the generally affluent children were housed with relatives in the Miami area, but eventually thousands were scattered across the country, sometimes in difficult conditions.

One such example occurred in Evans's home state of Indiana. Dozens of uprooted Cuban children were sent to Saint Vincent Orphanage in Vincennes, Indiana, where authoritarian Catholic nuns demanded the cossetted children of the Cuban upper classes adhere to a Spartan regime. Almost overnight the children went from wealthy Latin homes with doting domestic help to a grim orphanage, where they were expected to scrub the bathrooms and clean the communal kitchen. It was traumatic for the Cuban children, already stressed by separation from home and parents.[18]

Before Operation Peter Pan ended in 1962, 14,048 unaccompanied Cuban children were sent to the United States.[19] It was the largest exodus of unaccompanied children in the history of the Western Hemisphere.

The Family

After the SS *City of Havana* docked at Key West, Jan and Karla's journey did not get any easier. When Jan King Evans drove their station wagon off the ferry, the customs official demanded she unload everything from the jam-packed car for inspection. She was hot, agitated, tired—and very, very pregnant. In no uncertain terms, she let the official know that she was not going to unpack that car: "I told him, 'Let us go through—or I'll call your boss General Joseph Swing.'" Swing, who had served with Jan's stepfather, General Eugene Harrison, in occupied Japan, was the Commissioner of the Bureau of Immigration and Naturalization. Jan fumed, "We'd been serving our country; we had diplomatic plates—and this was our welcome home."[20] The official wisely let them pass. Jan drove the station wagon four hundred miles north to the Harrisons' gracious seafront home in Clearwater Beach, Florida, on the gulf coast. Soon after their arrival, a hurricane evacuation order drove them from the beach into an inland hotel, where Jan's precautionary taping of the windows brought the manager around.[21]

Louise Evans was born on October 13, 1960. Her father was there, flying back from increasingly turbulent Cuba. He stayed for a week or so, and then returned to Havana. Jan settled in with her daughters and the Harrisons. They were all ensconced in a comfortable home with ample domestic help. Not long after Louise was born, a reporter from the *Clearwater Sun* called, wanting to learn more about the diplomatic refugees living in the area. She interviewed Jan and Mrs. Allen Turner, whose husband was also a foreign service officer in Havana. The Turners had met in in Shanghai after the 1949 communist victory. Having also had to flee Red China, Turner was an experienced evacuee when she precipitously left Havana with her four children.

The two diplomatic wives were circumspect. The journalist wrote, "Because of their husbands' now sensitive positions in the Havana Embassy, neither wife is free to comment on Castro, Cuba, or communism, but both report that their Cuban acquaintances 'couldn't have been nicer.'" The women concurred they'd be in Clearwater until "the men came out or they can go back." Jan added, "Which we don't really anticipate any time soon."[22]

The Embassy

In the waning days of the Eisenhower administration, communist Cuba remained a thorny issue. Clandestine CIA operations were not panning out. Although counterrevolutionary bombings and shootings were plaguing Havana, the uprising was not spreading. Cuban militias were hunting down rebel guerrillas and airdropped CIA supplies were going astray. Cuban G2 was successfully ferreting out counterrevolutionary and American spies. The Castro government technicians were jamming the Radio Swan signals, and Cubans were beginning to mistrust the propaganda broadcasts.[23] On his second trip to the United States as leader of the Cuban government, Castro traveled to New York in September 1960. At the UN General Assembly on September 26, he raged against Radio Swan, charging the United States with putting the powerful transmitter in the hands of "war criminals." Emboldened by international support, Castro nationalized another 382 businesses on October 12, 1960.

Castro's belligerence incensed Eisenhower, who was already under pressure from U.S. corporate leaders to do something about Cuba. There was also political pressure. Amid a stalemated presidential race, Democratic candidate John F. Kennedy made Cuba a campaign issue. Though CIA director Allen Dulles had briefed Kennedy about covert operations, the candidate made political hay by claiming the Cuban counterrevolutionaries "have had virtually no support from our government." Eisenhower was ready to do something. On October 19, 1960, the president signed a partial embargo of exports (excluding food and medicine) to Cuba. The next day a U.S. State Department spokesman announced the recall of Ambassador Philip Bonsal for an indefinite period, with no plans to replace him. Castro countered by nationalizing another 166 businesses.[24]

Though October and November the CIA ramped up the large-scale amphibious invasion. Eisenhower signed off on the CIA invasion plan, but remarked, "I'm going along with you boys, but I want to be sure the damned thing works."[25] He remained concerned that the secret American role in the Cuban invasion was going to be unveiled. The State Department informed the president that the operation was already common knowledge in Latin America. Through the last part of 1960, the CIA marched forward. Landing crafts were purchased, freighters and pilots hired, and soldiers trained. Psywar continued. On December 12, 1960, planes from the United States dropped anti-Castro leaflets over several Cuban cities. The economic war also continued. On December 14 the White House announced that Eisenhower was prohibiting the import of eight hundred thousand tons of Cuban sugar.

The signs were clear to Castro. In a speech on December 31, 1960, he denounced the "imperialist plan" to invade Cuba. Warning an invasion would "not be a military cakewalk," he stated casualties would be heavier than Normandy and Okinawa. In a televised four-hour speech a few days later, Castro announced the total number of personnel in the U.S. embassy and consulate could not exceed eleven, the same number allowed at the Cuban embassy in Washington. At 1:20 a.m. on January 3, 1961, the Cuban Ministry of Foreign Relations sent a telegram to the U.S. Charge d'Affairs in Havana informing the embassy that all U.S. government personnel more than eleven must leave Cuba within forty-eight hours.

The next morning Eisenhower met with his advisers. They reviewed the military plan, assessed Castro's reportedly waning popular support, and discussed the appropriate response to Castro's expulsion of the embassy personnel. That evening at 8:30 the State Department sent a note to the Cuban Charge d'Affairs in Washington advising him that the U.S. government was breaking diplomatic relations with Cuba, and demanding all Cuban embassy personnel withdraw as soon as possible. Eisenhower also announced that the Havana embassy would be closed. "There is a limit to what the United States in self respect can endure. That limit has now been reached," Eisenhower said.[26]

Castro's precipitous move caught the Havana Station CIA officers off guard. The station was short staffed, its ranks having been winnowed by Cuban G2's recent unmasking of a number of important officers.[27] Soon after learning of the decision, Havana Station chief Jim Noel gathered seven key personnel, including Evans, to devise an action plan. Noel emphasized, "It is necessary to insure at all costs the link with our principal agents."[28] Case officers began alerting their strings of agents, insuring that their links were secured. There were frantic contacts made with Cuban agents still being trained in Panama to handle the main counterrevolutionary groups. Officers began secreting caches of radios, arms, and money to support the agents left behind.[29] The CIA's new incinerator incessantly burned. After packing as much gear as the time allowed, the communications officers began destroying what remained. On January 7, 1961, they transmitted the following: "This is last msg from HAVA station. All files and crypto material destroyed . . . on evening Jan 6 Swiss amb placed 'Carte de Proteccion' notices on emb doors minimizing takeover of building by GOC."[30]

Evans was among the last Americans to leave the embassy. A news photo captured him walking out of the embassy, a tall man in a khaki raincoat, carrying a valise in each hand.[31] With a confident smile on his face, he headed to the ferry, ready for his next assignment.

13

THE BOMB

Benjamin C. Evans Jr's next Central Intelligence Agency assignment was Chile, another fraught Latin American posting for a covert officer with a family. Chile was quasi-colonialized by American business interests, particularly in the mining industry. And like Cuba, Chile was convulsed with strife, fueled in part by the competing Cold War powers. The CIA had launched Chilean operations early in the 1950s, when officers began secretly buying political influence and financing propaganda. After the Korean War, President Dwight Eisenhower decided that land reform was essential to a stable Chile. He ordered U.S. diplomats to pressure the conservative Chilean elites to reform or suffer the withdrawal of American aid. Eisenhower also ordered the CIA to secretly forge alliances with the Jesuits, who were organizing anti-Marxist reform movements in Chile. The new John Kennedy administration, intent on more liberal policies in Latin America, likewise wanted reform. The CIA accordingly ramped up clandestine operations in Chile, funneling support to political parties with the organizational heft to carry out a reform agenda.[1]

However, Evans and his family did not go to Santiago. Evans knew he did not want to subject his family to another dangerous posting and passed on the Chile assignment. After he closed the Havana embassy, he headed to the Covert Actions Division in Washington, DC.

Fiasco

Cuba still had Evans's attention—though higher-ups had removed him from the Cuba desk when he returned to Washington. It was a frustrating time for him. His family was still living with Jan King Evans's mother and stepfather in Clearwater Beach, Florida, and Evans was batching it at Lady Norma Lewis's Georgetown mansion as the Cuban invasion raced forward without him. "He was upset," Jan said. "He was not on the Cuba desk, he wasn't involved; didn't know what was going on. He was not informed. He couldn't understand—he knew more about Cuba than anyone."[2]

In the waning days of his administration, Eisenhower had encumbered

Kennedy with the CIA's ambitious invasion plan, which came with a vanguard of passionate, combat-trained Cubans eager to fight Fidel Castro. Kennedy was ambivalent about the operation. Though he had run for president as a resolute anticommunist, Kennedy had criticized Eisenhower's Cuba policy, which he contended used governmental power on behalf of the U.S. corporations dominating the island's resources, instead of helping Cubans free themselves of Fulgencio Batista's repressive dictatorship and progress economically. In a speech in Cincinnati, Ohio, in October 1960, candidate Kennedy said, "We let Batista put the U.S. on the side of tyranny, and we did nothing to convince the people of Cuba and Latin America that we wanted to be on the side of freedom."[3] Like Eisenhower, Kennedy was concerned that the CIA's secret role in the Cuban invasion would explode on the world stage, creating a foreign relations disaster.

Despite Kennedy's wariness, the CIA was raring to go. Knowing that Kennedy's anticommunist rhetoric had helped him squeak out a narrow victory over Richard Nixon, the CIA had the new president politically boxed in. Kennedy nonetheless tried to shut down Cuban paramilitary training, arguing U.S. involvement would be obvious once the counterrevolutionaries stormed the beaches. But the CIA officials countered they could not have hundreds of CIA-trained Cuban fighters loose in Miami's restive émigré community as the dirty secret would be out in no time—though the "secret" was already common knowledge.

Despite Kennedy's nervous misgivings, preparations for the invasion of Cuba continued inexorably through the winter and spring of 1961. The CIA officers had a complicated plan involving pinpoint air strikes to take out Castro's air power, a duplicitous story about Cuban defector pilots, an amphibious landing in a perfunctorily reconnoitered bay, and faith in a spontaneous popular uprising. As the operation moved toward D-Day, the CIA officers were still trying to organize the squabbling Cuban exile leadership into a cohesive counterrevolutionary government-in-exile. The CIA was counting on flawless subterfuge, a wildly successful military operation igniting widespread rebellion, and the naive acceptance of an implausible cover story. In addition, the counterrevolutionary conspirators shared the belief that Kennedy would order U.S. military intervention if the invasion went awry. Many CIA insiders were not cognizant to the plan, and those who were had divergent opinions. Chief of Clandestine Operations Richard Helms, a longtime spy and later CIA director, termed the plan "harebrained," and had nothing to do with it.

On April 17, 1961, approximately 1,400 U.S.-trained Cuban counterrevolutionaries and a handful of CIA officers landed on the beaches of the Bahia de Cochinos—the Bay of Pigs.

From the beginning, the invasion was a fiasco. The initial air strike, which had been dramatically downsized to hide CIA involvement, failed to take out all of Castro's air force, which began strafing and bombarding the invaders. As the beaches became killing zones, Radio Swan blasted disinformation: "The invaders are advancing on every front. Throughout all of Cuba, people are joining forces with the underground rebels fighting Fidel Castro. Castro's forces are surrendering in droves." The reality was much different. Over the next three days, Castro's forces pounded the invaders. Hoping for a "quiet failure" over a "noisy success" that would trigger international opprobrium, Kennedy withheld U.S. air or naval support.[4] The final radio dispatch from Brigade 2506 leader Pepe San Ramon told the tale of abandonment: "Am destroying all equipment and communications. Tanks are in sight. Am taking to woods. I cannot repeat cannot wait for you." And to the CIA officer who hadn't responded to his calls for aid, he radioed: "And you, sir . . . are a son of a bitch."[5]

The after-action reports indicated that 114 Cuban counterrevolutionaries died at the Bay of Pigs and 1,189 were captured, including three of Elena Falla's cousins and Culver Military Academy graduates Tito Reyes and brothers Felipe and Mario Silvas.[6] Culver student Gustavo Villoldo also took part in the Bay of Pigs operation, copiloting a B-26 dropping napalm.[7] During the prisoners' trials, Castro's prosecutors contended that the invaders were predominantly members of Cuba's upper-middle class, who were fighting to recover 852,000 acres of land, 9,666 residential buildings, 70 factories, 12 nightclubs, 10 sugar mills, 5 mines, and 3 commercial banks.[8] A few months after the invasion, Che Guevara chatted with White House adviser Richard Goodwin at an international conference in Uruguay. Goodwin reported that Guevara said, "he wanted to thank us [the United States] very much for the invasion—that it had been a great political victory for them—enabled them to consolidate—and transformed them from an aggrieved little country to an equal."[9] A year and a half after the invasion, the U.S. government traded more than $50 million worth of food and medical supplies for the Brigade 2506 prisoners' release.

There was hell to pay in the wake of the Bay of Pigs invasion.[10] Multiple postmortems, including an internal CIA inspector general investigation and the Taylor Committee's scathing Cuba Study Group report, cited multiple failures of intelligence, organization, and execution. Kennedy called in intelligence guru Robert A. Lovett for advice. Lovett pronounced the CIA to be disorganized, amateurish, and costly, and recommended the president empower civilian oversight with the Foreign Advisory Board of Consultants and redefine the agency's legal mandate. With National Security Action memorandums 55 and 57, Kennedy moved many of the Cuban paramilitary operations to the Pentagon.[11] By early 1962 CIA Director Allen Dulles, Deputy Director Charles Cabell, and Deputy Director for Plans Richard Bissell, who had championed the invasion, were all forced out of the agency.

Despite his deep involvement in the Cuban operations, Evans was still in the CIA's Covert Action Division after the Bay of Pigs. It was somewhat surprising. "If anyone was involved with the Bay of Pigs," Jan said, "they were toxic."[12] Evans's organizational distance from the Cuba desk and the failed invasion probably saved his career. And connections might have helped.[13]

While he was not officially on the Cuba desk after he returned from Havana, Evans had gleaned that Kennedy's support for the invasion was vacillating. He had accordingly warned his friend Oscar Echevarria not to join Brigade 2506—the United States might not have the Cubans' back.

And that proved to be the case. A few weeks after the disastrous Bay of Pigs invasion, Evans convened a small postmortem at the Shoreham Hotel in Washington. There he and a very weary David Phillips met with Echevarria and Angel Fernandez Varela. "We learned why it failed," Echevarria said. "The whole plan of the CIA was predicated on total control of the air."[14] The CIA officers also warned that the Cuban counterrevolution was in trouble. Echevarria wrote, "They emphasized that while the U.S. continued to oppose the Castro regime there were great uncertainties if that work would lead to his fall in the near future."[15]

The Family and the Bomb

Jan and her daughters made their way back to Washington in the winter of 1961. For a while the family lived at the Alban Towers, the six-story Gothic Revival apartment building on Massachusetts Avenue near the National Cathedral. When their furniture at last arrived from Cuba, the Evanses moved back to their commodious Woodland Drive residence. But it was not exactly calm there either. With the Cold War heating up in 1961, Washington was a prime target for Soviet intercontinental ballistic missiles.

Berlin was the epicenter of conflict between Moscow and Washington. On January 6, 1961, just a few days after Evans helped close the Havana embassy, Soviet Premier Nikita Khrushchev announced his country's support for national wars of liberation and demanded the Western powers end their occupation of West Berlin. The Allies refused to withdraw from West Berlin. In the summer of 1961, as thousands of East Germans fled to the West, Khrushchev threatened nuclear war if the United States pushed too hard. At the June 1961 Vienna summit, the Soviets judged Kennedy to be indecisive and weak, so began hardening their positions, particularly in Berlin. Around midnight on August 13, 1961, East German soldiers abruptly began unrolling miles of barbed wire around the perimeter of West Berlin and across the center of the city. Soldiers stood guard every few yards. Within a few hours, West Berlin was isolated. Two days later, masons began constructing the Berlin Wall.

On August 18, 1961, U.S. troop reinforcements commanded by General Lucius D. Clay, the hero of the Berlin airlift, arrived in West Berlin. The East German border police began harassing Western military and diplomats moving between the zones of occupation. The Soviet Army moved three divisions closer to Berlin. Kennedy ordered 148,000 National Guard and Reserve soldiers to active duty. The thrust and parry climaxed at Checkpoint Charlie in October 1961, when the U.S. military began escorting American diplomats into the eastern sector. The military initially used jeeps to escort the diplomats, but on October 27, 1961, Clay ordered ten M-48 tanks to the checkpoint to assert American prerogatives. Not to be intimidated, Soviet leaders dispatched ten T-55 tanks to the crossing. And the confrontation began. For sixteen hours while the world held its breath, the battle-ready tanks faced off a hundred yards apart.[16]

As television coverage beamed footage of the military confrontation to America, Washingtonians began preparing for nuclear war. It was a time of backyard and basement fallout shelters filled with enough water, food, and supplies to survive a nuclear holocaust. Washington parents tried to play it cool. "It's a weird dichotomy, wanting to set the tone—not scare the kids," Karla Evans said. "I could feel more anxiety from my father. He'd get tight-lipped."[17] Jan and her friends prepared for the worst. "For all the younger people, it was a question of protecting your kids," said Sandra McElwaine, a longtime friend of Jan's. "We had an agreement," McElwaine said, "If Ben said things were bad, we'd grab our children and flee down to Jan's uncle's farm in

Virginia. My station wagon was parked in the driveway with military cans of gasoline, water and medical supplies. It was scary and we took it seriously." For two days as the tank commanders in Berlin stared at each other over open gun sights, Kennedy and his brother Robert used a back-channel contact in the KGB Washington Rezidenz to negotiate a mutual stand-down. There were sighs of relief when the tanks slowly rumbled away from the border. "I later realized how down to the wire it was," McElwaine said. "Of course, Ben, being an honorable person, never told us how bad it was."[18]

14

WORLD OF SPIES

"Ben was such a do-gooder," Jan King Evans said.[1] So his assignment to the Central Intelligence Agency's Branch Two of the Covert Action Staff was a good fit. Responsible for psywar and paramilitary operations that effected other countries, Covert Action officers developed propaganda and disinformation campaigns, and bought influence with political parties, labor unions, media, and international organizations. Paramilitary operations were generally sequestered in the Covert Action Staff's Special Operations Division.

The Covert Action Staff was part of the largest of the CIA's four directorates, the Directorate of Plans, or Clandestine Service. The Clandestine Service was divided into three staffs: Foreign Intelligence, Counterintelligence, and Covert Action.[2] Two out of three of the Clandestine Service's officers and clerical staff focused on general intelligence: liaison, espionage, and counterespionage. Though the Covert Action Staff had the smallest number of personnel, it ate up half as much of the budget as spying and counterspying combined. Interventions in the internal affairs of other countries cost big bucks.[3]

Benjamin C. Evans Jr. was assigned to Branch Two of the Covert Action Staff, CA/2. He was working with one of the CIA's "proprietaries," ostensibly independent institutions and businesses that were actually funded and directed by the agency. Radio Swan was a proprietary, as were Radio Free Europe and Radio Liberty, which pulsed propaganda toward communist countries behind the Iron Curtain. The proprietaries typically had a board of directors made up of important Americans, who provided a convenient cover behind which CIA officers directed the operations.[4]

The Covert Action officers also subsidized a galaxy of publications, from tiny Eastern European émigré newsletters to substantive book publishers, such as Frederick A. Praeger. The agency supported a vast array of newspapers and magazines, including *Bohemia* in Cuba, *Prevves* in France, and *Argumentem* in Sweden, as well as the literary bellwether, *The Paris Review*.[5] At its peak, the agency had more than eight hundred news and information organizations and individuals on its Propaganda Assets Inventory.[6] For a number of years the CIA subsidized the U.S. Communist Party's organ, *The Daily Worker*, by secretly buying thousands of bogus subscriptions in hopes of convincing policymakers that the communist threat was alive and thriving in America. The CIA supported hundreds, perhaps thousands, of professors and university administrators—so many the agency literally lost count.[7]

The Covert Action officers who worked with propaganda and influence peddling had a softer reputation in the agency. One CIA official called them "the do-gooders of the clandestine business."[8] The Covert Action branch that worked with academic, cultural, and publishing organizations was called "the enlightened wing of the CIA."[9]

Evans worked with the agency's second-largest proprietary, The Asia Foundation.[10] The Asia Foundation's primary mission was to shape public opinion with pro-American ideas, particularly by currying the favor of influential thought leaders. The agency accordingly funded conferences, scholarly research, and exchange programs sponsored by TAF.[11] In both Asia and the United States, TAF pounded out a steady drumbeat of anticommunist propaganda aimed at besmirching Communist China, North Vietnam, and North Korea. While TAF's activities were primarily legitimate, its international operations gave cover for Covert Action officers to recruit agents with deep connections to their home countries. The Asia Foundtation was keystone of the CIA's larger strategy to extend clandestine operations into academic, cultural, and civic institutions, the CIA's funding for TAF eventually reached $88 million annually.

The CIA and TAF both had good reasons to hide their connection, and they did so assiduously with multiple layers of misinformation, beginning with lying about the year that the CIA established the foundation. The foundation long insisted it began in 1954, but the CIA established the organization in 1951 under the name of the Committee for a Free Asia.[12] The CIA cryptonym for the operation was DTPILLAR. A secret CIA fact sheet stated, "CIA created The Asia Foundation (TAF) shortly after the Korean War in response to a demonstrated need for an ostensibly private organizational asset through which the United States Government could counter communist initiatives and cope with rising nationalism and economic insufficiency, in ways not open to U.S. official attention."[13]

Funded in great part by covert CIA funding, TAF's public mission was to promote academic and public interest in Asia. Its clandestine purpose was to fight communism and rising Third World nationalism in close accord with the CIA. The CIA designed TAF to be both "an instrument of psychological warfare" and "a vehicle for covert operations," including agent recruitment and support for CIA-backed paramilitary groups.

The foundation claimed "forward thinking citizens" founded the organization. In reality, the CIA selected the leadership, who were made "witting," in the spook phrase, of the CIA interest and controlling authority over policy. At the direction of the domestic-based foundation executives and the agency, TAF staffers overseas were expected to coordinate with the U.S. embassies and CIA station chiefs. The CIA had direct control over the foundation leadership, including vetting and approving all key staffers and trustees, who were typically prominent Americans, including author James A. Michener, industrialist and Ambassador to Italy James D. Zellerbach, and Columbia University president (and former State Department security analyst) Grayson Kirk.[14]

The foundation president was both selected by the CIA and on its payroll. Robert Blum, a veteran of the OSS and the CIA, was TAF's first president.[15] While there were supposed to be boundaries between the U.S. government and the purportedly independent foundation, Blum secretly remained on the government payroll as a contract agent until his presidency ended in 1962.[16]

In 1964 Hayden Williams took over as TAF president. Before joining TAF Williams had taught at the Fletcher School of Law and Diplomacy and the University of Washington, serving as associate dean at both institutions. He had lectured at the National War College and Naval War College, served as President Dwight Eisenhower's Deputy Assistant Secretary of Defense for National Security Council Affairs, and President John Kennedy's Deputy Assistant Secretary for International Security Affairs.[17] Williams was an establishmentarian, comfortable with murky power politics. He was perfect to lead TAF with its secret connections to the CIA, especially when he bonded with his CIA liaison, Evans, who shared the same worldview.[18]

Evans was also a born and bred establishmentarian. "Ben was a Republican and conservative," Jan said.[19] A campaign finance report from Richard Nixon's 1962 race for California governor listed B. C. Evans as a contributor.[20] Given that Evans's conservative political views coincided with the former vice president's militant anticommunism, support for Nixon's comeback campaign would not be unlikely—especially given Evans's criticism of Kennedy's refusal to commit U.S. troops to the Bay of Pigs operation.

Together, Evans and Williams forged a partnership to battle communism and postcolonial nationalism with culture, persuasion, and money. The Asian Foundation programs blossomed in thirteen major Asian countries from Japan through Afghanistan: American advisers in Cambodia and Laos, Chinese-language textbooks in Hong Kong, a ten-year contract to produce textbooks for Afghanistan, Foreign Service Institutes in Korea and Vietnam, congressional and Harvard fellowships for promising Asian student leaders, credit unions in Taiwan, counseling centers in Japan, rural reconstruction projects in the Philippines, support for Buddhist conferences in India, and widespread dissemination of millions of U.S. friendly books and journals. A secret CIA document reported Williams's zeal for his work, both public and covert: "Since becoming TAF president in January 1964, Dr. F. Hayden Williams has demonstrated a lively interest in keeping TAF programs on target and has shown a great readiness to work closely with CIA. Under his leadership, good TAF-CIA working relationships should continue, and operational objectives of the project should be enhanced."[21]

Williams briefed CIA Director John McCone and other top agency executives on the foundation's burgeoning work. A secret report on the briefing noted that CIA officers conducted seminars and training programs for TAF, "to better inform and integrate the TAF staff into the Agency and U.S. Governmental operational efforts in Asia."[22] Thanks in part to the close friendship between Williams and Evans, the foundation and the agency worked shoulder to shoulder.

It was the age of spies. The Joe McCarthy-era spy trials of Alger Hiss and the Soviet spy couple Julius and Ethel Rosenberg heightened public paranoia, as did the unmasking of the British Portland and Cambridge Five Soviet spy rings. Britain's intelligence scandal bled into America in 1963, when headlines revealed that high-ranking British intelligence official and double-agent Kim Philby had fled to the Soviet Union. Philby had been the chief British intelligence representative in Washington, where he became drinking buddies with the CIA's obsessive counterintelligence spook, James Jesus Angleton.[23] The Profumo Affair in 1963 added the salacious details of British Secretary of State for War John Profumo having an affair with swinger Christine Keeler, who was also having sex with Soviet spy Yevgeny Ivanov. The resulting scandal threatened to topple Prime Minister Harold MacMillan's government. Sex and spies really grabbed the public's attention.

Popular culture became suffused with espionage. James Bond held thrall in the bookstores and movie theaters. Adolescents smirked at Mad magazine's

"Spy vs. Spy" cartoons and clueless television spook Maxwell Smart. Beyond the pulp fiction and snarky satires, the Cold War adversaries were devoting enormous resources to discover their adversaries' strengths and weaknesses. The Cuban Missile Crisis revealed how effective intelligence gathering had become. The two nuclear powers knew quite a lot about each other—intelligence voraciously gleaned from both open-source material and covert espionage through organizations such as TAF.[24]

The World

In late January 1964 Evans departed Baltimore-Washington Friendship Airport, the sole first-class passenger on Pan Am Flight 118. He was headed around the world on CIA business. His first scheduled stop was Paris, where he was booked into the posh Saint James Albany Hotel near the Louvre for three days of meetings in the city. But bad weather forced his plane to land in Rome, where he stayed at the five-star Hotel Excelsior near the Spanish Steps. The flight cancellations afforded Evans an unexpected three-day holiday in "this beautiful sunny city," the tourist-spy gleefully wrote his wife. "Am taking an American Express tour this PM of the city, and going on an all day tour tomorrow of Hadrian's Villa, Vill d'este, and Tivoli."

Touring alone did not bother him. He gloried in his solitary travel on the flight and in his late-night transit when he arrived in Rome. "Since I am a bit of a 'loner' myself, I really have enjoyed just going alone," he wrote his family. He walked the streets of the Eternal City, admiring the ancient Colosseum, regretting the Vatican's rococo excess, watching Romans engage in the sidewalk cafés, and buying an Italian doll for his daughters—an American midwesterner guilelessly touring the old world. And a family man missing his girls, signing off with, "My how I miss you and the girls. Wish you were here and again ROME IS BEAUTIFUL."

Jan passed on his letter to the Evans family with an addendum. She confessed to being "green with envy," lamenting that her daughters' young age prevented her from going along. She assured the Evans family in Indiana that the taxpayers did not pay for Ben's first-class seat, writing, "he was authorized tourist on this section of his jaunt but decided he had to go first class—which almost caused a divorce in our family!"[25]

A two-day layover in Athens provided Evans more eye-opening experiences, from his tour of the Acropolis to dinner at a taverna: "They don't serve dinner here until 9:30 PM—can you believe it?" Midnight found him in the rooftop bar, where a Parisian duo played fiddle and harp. Jan forwarded her galivanting husband's missive on to his family with a terse addendum about her daughter being in the kitchen rolling cookies.

On January 27 Evans flew into the restive eastern Mediterranean. He reported about his stop in Cyprus: "Heard no shooting but guess it is a trouble spot these days." It was on to Beirut, "the Paris of the Middle East." Staying at the modernist Hotel Phoeonicia overlooking the seaside corniche, Evans caught the floorshow. He wrote his wife, "Strip tease is against the law here, as is the twist, so it wasn't as bad as you might expect." Touring interspersed with work: a trip to Sidon and a Turkish castle; time at the American embassy to "visit for a while with others," as Evans, ever conscious of operational security, discretely wrote his wife. A few days later he wrote about meeting with Dr. Charles Malik, a Lebanese diplomat and academic then teaching at the American University. As Lebanon's foreign minister a few years prior, Malik had persuaded the American government to dispatch U.S. troops to suppress riots against the pro-Western Chamoun government. Evans reported that pro-American Malik, who had also served as the United Nations General Assembly president, was "especially interested in the American political scene and hoped the Republicans would not take a defeatist attitude."[26]

At home in Washington, Jan juggled mothering five-year-old Karla and three-year-old Louise with her charity work. Her active social life took her to a Connecticut College benefit, a National Geographic Society lecture, Washington's exclusive Sulgrave Club for events, and a merry-go-round of engagements with family and friends.

Evans had flown from Beirut to Karachi, Pakistan's throbbing main port and financial hub. The Asia Foundation had been running programs in Pakistan since 1954, when its staffers began advising the young country's leaders on economic, educational, social, and cultural development. As was the TAF-CIA modus operandi, there was a focus on influencing Pakistani leaders with exchange and education programs.[27]

Evans soon moved on to Peshawar, the dusty frontier town that was the gateway to the Kyber Pass and the wild Pashtun tribal borderlands. He wrote from Peshawar's venerable Dean's Hotel, the preferred lodging for generations of British officers and agents, who perennially tried to pacify the bellicose Afghan tribesmen. Evans wrote that Dean's Hotel was "very modest if not primitive," a far cry from his luxury European accommodations. "This is an old historic city," he wrote. "Full of camels, tribesmen roaming the streets in various costumes." He bought an ancient Buddha head for $8.50—"fairly disfigured (that's why it's cheap)." At a park, he watched "children of these strange people playing and acting like children anyplace in the world."

After booking a bus ticket to Kabul, Evans managed to cadge a ride with a friend. Winding through the Kyber Pass past plodding camel caravans, they drove to the Afghan capital in about five hours. "Kabul is different," he emphatically wrote. "Many Russians here and the city about as it was 500 years ago."

The central Asian country had become a Cold War set piece as the U.S. and the Soviet Union maneuvered for hegemony. With their long experience with the Great Game competition between the British Raj and the Czar's Russian Empire, the Afghans deftly milked both the capitalists and communists for all they were worth. Down in the south, the United States was pumping millions into massive development projects, such as the Helmand and Arghandab Valley Authority, a Tennessee Valley Authority-scaled hydroelectric and irrigation project that was intended to develop a vast swath of arid Helmand Province. The Soviets were equally ambitious in the north. Soviet highway construction projects included the Salang Highway with its spectacular tunnel beneath the Hindu Kush, which provided the first motor link between Afghanistan and the Soviet Union's communist republics. Both adversaries vied for influence in Kabul, with competing cultural centers and Soviet and American "advisors" jostling one another as they made their way to Afghan ministries and officials.

The fiercely independent Afghans had fended off empires—and central governance—for centuries and influencing them was a tough assignment.[28] A secret CIA 1964 report on Afghanistan and its twelve million tribal peoples stated, "Most individuals place their own welfare and that of their tribe or village above the interests of the central government. The general population traditionally ignores the law of the land, especially if personal gain is at stake. They see little sense in laws that have been made 'down in the city,' by city people, and for the benefit of the government—laws that work real or imagined hardships on the country man." The report noted that "a relatively few politically conscious persons" were responsible for "a shaky national unity."[29]

The Asian Foundation had begun programming in Afghanistan in 1954. In Kabul Evans met several "friends" and "other people," as well as the American ambassador to Afghanistan, John M. Steeves, a career diplomat, who had served in a World War II psywar unit in the China-Burma-India theater. Continuing his international shopping quest for Karla and Louise, Evans purchased an Afghan doll. And for himself, he ordered a karakul hat made of the curly pelts of fetal sheep. "I got the best quality," he reported.

A few days later Evans was in Lahore, Pakistan, the ancient Punjabi city that was one of the British Raj's major seats of power. "This hotel is quite nice," he wrote from the classic colonial-era Hotel Faletti, "and the city is quite attractive." The next day he left for New Delhi, India, for three days of meetings with "friends" and colleagues at the embassy. He talked with a fellow 1946 West Point graduate, Amos A. "Joe" Jordan, who was special assistant to the American ambassador to India, Chester Bowles. Jordan, later a brigadier general, graduated third in his class at West Point, as well as being a top intercollegiate boxer. After studying as a Rhodes Scholar at Oxford University, he earned a Columbia University doctorate in international relations. It was the early 1960s, when the focus of U.S. foreign policy was pivoting to the postcolonial world. Jordan's dissertation, published as *Foreign Aid and the Defense of Southeast Asia*, articulated a comprehensive strategy for the application of American financial and military power in less-developed countries, particularly in Asia. Returning to West Point as a professor, Jordan was among U.S. foreign policy advisers pushing for broad-spectrum interventions in Asia. In 1964 when Evans met with him, Jordan was advising Bowles on the Indian defense budget, the Soviet political strategy on the subcontinent, and the U.S. response, which included military aid to the Indian government.[30] Jordan and Evans had a lot to discuss.

Through American Express, Evans booked a side trip though the Indian countryside to the Taj Mahal in Agra. "India depresses me," he wrote. "Never really want to see any of it again. Why all these people with all this land haven't cut out a better life for themselves is beyond me." With time to muse about the pros and cons of international experience, he wrote his wife that they should save their money so they could take their daughters on a round-the-world trip. But solid Hoosier Evans was not ready to go native. He went on to write, "I really do not like the ideal of their going to school in Europe. There's not one thing (except language) that would be gained." Evans wrote his father, "I have been no place where I would want to live. Washington looks mighty good to me."

Evans wrote his thrifty wife, "You would have been real proud of me last night in Delhi," as he had vacated his room at midnight to save a day's charges, even though he did not need to leave for the airport until 3:00 a.m. He was on his way to Bangkok, in the epicenter of American anticommunist operations in Southeast Asia. Flying over Calcutta—"understand that's the only way to see it"—and Rangoon, the capital of Burma, his plane flew through jungle mountain passes to the capital of Thailand.

Once again, Evans chose the best, in this case the Oriental Hotel, the luxury Siamese accommodations on the banks of the bustling Chao Phraya River. After opening in 1876 the hotel had established itself as an outpost of Western-style luxury in the East. During World War II the Japanese Imperial Army commandeered the Oriental for officer quarters. After the war, Thai and Western investors, including American Office of Strategic Service veterans John Webster and Jim Thompson, bought the then-derelict property. When Evans arrived, the hotel had regained its status as one of the world's greatest.

Evans hit the ground running, scheduling meetings for breakfast, lunch, and dinner. Then it was a tour of the floating markets of Bangkok. As his tour boat negotiated the small tributaries, he reveled in the multiplicity of Thai orchids and birdlife, perhaps triggering memories of his grandfather's gardens in Crawfordsville. He wrote his father, "It's probably a poor commentary on my intellect and cultural level, but I think the most enjoyable thing I've done on this trip is to take a river trip in Bangkok and see wild orchids, peacocks and jungle in the raw." Referencing the cast of Americans he had encountered traveling in Asia, Evans wrote, "American tourists are sure an 'odd lot'—you do meet nice people—but on the whole the people that seem to have $ to spend for travel are a bunch of characters."

After three days, Evans flew on to Kuala Lumpur, Malaysia. It was Chinese New Year, an important Malaysian holiday. With a large Chinese population, the city was essentially shut down for business. He had dinner with unidentified "friends" in an old mansion owned by wealthy Chinese who lived on the top floor. The next day he went to the U.S. embassy. "Thinking about you so often and get your pictures out and have practically worn them out," he wrote his wife. "Golly that is a cute picture of Karla and Louise. You just have to smile when you look at it. I also have a very beautiful wife you know . . . or do you?"

Evans stopped in Singapore, staying at the Goodwood Hotel, another colonial-era hotel with manicured gardens and obsequious service. Beside his meetings with "friends," he wiled away his free hours with long walks in the Botanic Garden, where he fed the wild monkeys and admired the orchids. On February 21, 1964, almost a month after he left Washington, Evans wrote his wife, "I sorta feel like 'I'm on my way home now' and it's a good feeling." Vietnam was next on his itinerary.

A few days later, Evans wrote from Saigon's Hotel Caravelle, a redoubt of Western modernity plunked down in the midst of wartime Indochina:

"All Americans here are most concerned, i.e. plain scared—due to the recent bombings of Americans, first at a baseball game and then again on Sunday at the American theatre where 3 Americans were killed, one US M.P. shot, and 49 Americans injured. Very heavy American patrols around the commissary and American dependents school today. A pretty sorry mess here." Vietnam soon got a lot sorrier.[31]

When Evans arrived in Vietnam, there were about 23,000 U.S. soldiers, most advising the South Vietnamese army's fight against the communist Viet Cong insurgency. CIA officers based out of Saigon Station were primarily engaged in intelligence gathering and organizing Montagnard tribes into paramilitary units.[32] However, things were changing fast. Only a few months before Evans arrived, South Vietnamese army officers, tacitly encouraged by U.S. officials, had revolted against the corrupt government of President Ngô Đình Diêm.[33] Some Washington policymakers, who had decided Diêm was ineffectual against the growing Viet Cong movement, instigated the coup with a diplomatic dispatch, an infamous bureaucratic end-run known as Cable 243. Though CIA analysts had been jiggering intelligence reports to reflect the Kennedy administration hawks' optimistic assessment of the war, CIA director John McCone vociferously opposed the U.S. plans to depose Diêm, arguing that there was not an adequate replacement for him.[34] In the course of the November 1963 coup, soldiers executed Diêm and his despotic brother, Ngô Dình Nhu. One of the junta's generals, Dương Văn Minh, popularly known as Big Minh, was ruling the country—the first of a succession of military rulers, as one coup quickly followed another.

It soon became clear the Diêm coup was a disaster. The United Sates was widely blamed for instigating Diêm's murder, the CIA was smeared for being part of the plot (though McCone had opposed it), and the military juntas that followed were far more feckless than Diêm and Nhu.[35] As South Vietnam spiraled toward governmental entropy and a communist victory, the American leadership suddenly had to consider a greatly expanded U.S. military intervention.

Evans was on the last leg of his journey, making his way home. He flew to Hong Kong for meetings with "friends." A brunch with one group, tea with another, lunch with others, and meetings at the consulate. In the lobby of the Peninsula Hotel where he was staying, Evans spotted Chin Yi, a Chinese colleague from his Tokyo psywar days. A wealthy Chinese Nationalist, Yi took Evans to dinner and then out shopping in antique shops. Evans had already availed himself of Hong Kong's celebrated tailors, ordering a summer tuxedo made of burgundy silk and purchasing a pair of handmade Italian golf shoes. And a doll for the girls, adding to the half dozen he was already carrying in his luggage. And jewelry and antiques for his wife. "It's terribly hard to 'keep your wants down' here," he wrote.

Evans had a couple of days in Tokyo, the last stop on his round-the-world junket. He revisited the old Tokyo haunts from his time as a young married officer. He stopped by their old apartments, talked to expat American and Japanese friends, and walked through Meji Park. "Went to St. Albans and said a little prayer," he wrote to his wife about their Tokyo church. "Tokyo has changed a great deal. Traffic is just plain horrible—but understand countryside is unchanged." While he was trying to stay engaged, his mind was elsewhere: "Really anxious to get home but am having a most interesting trip. I love you all so."

15

LIMITED HANGOUT

Revelations about the Central Intelligence Agency's proprietaries exploded in February 1967 when *Ramparts,* a leftwing Catholic magazine, exposed the CIA's longtime financial support of the National Student Association.[1] The article detailed the way the agency used national security confidentiality agreements to make student organization leaders "witty" about CIA support. The oaths bound the students to secrecy, ensnaring them in the agency's covert operation. "So intimately was the CIA involved in NSA's international program," the *Ramparts* article read, "that it treated NSA as an arm of U.S. foreign policy." The muckraking journalists followed CIA money through the "conduits" of agency-controlled front foundations, which funneled tens of millions of dollars to the NSA. The *Ramparts* list of front organizations included The Asia Foundation.

In 1967 the war was raging in Vietnam. With enormous draft call-ups, more than 485,000 U.S. troops were fighting and dying there—approximately 10,000 American deaths in 1967 alone.[2] President Lyndon Johnson's massive escalation had ignited a nationwide protest movement—campuses were in revolt, antiwar demonstrations roiled Washington, congressional hawks and doves sparred on Capitol Hill, and inner cities were aflame. The media covered a nation at war with itself. The establishment was under siege.

The counterintelligence officers in the Directorate of Plans knew the NSA article was coming, alerted by informants planted inside *Ramparts*. The CIA's propagandists had been smearing the magazine for its anti-Vietnam War coverage, and covert officers had secretly investigated hundreds of Americans connected to the magazine.[3] The counterintelligence officers quickly developed a damage control plan to counter the article. The CIA decided the NSA would hold a preemptive press conference, where its student leadership would partially reveal the CIA relationship and claim it had independently decided to terminate it. In spook speak, it was a limited hangout, which the Covert Action Staff devised to make the *Ramparts* article old news. But when the magazine's executive editor Warren Hinkle got wind of the ploy, he bought full-page ads in the *Washington Post* and *New York Times* announcing the upcoming revelations. On February 13, 1967, the night before the articles were to appear, CIA, State Department, and White House officials were in a tizzy. Then an NSA leader disregarded his security oath to go on record confirming the NSA-CIA links. Hinkle said, "It is a rare thing in this business when you say bang and somebody says I'm dead."[4]

To mitigate adverse congressional reactions, CIA director Richard Helms led agency efforts to quickly brief intelligence subcommittees, which were previously unwitting about CIA subsidies and control of the NSA, The Asia Foundation, and other like-minded organizations. Nonetheless, there was a furor on the Hill. Eight influential Democratic congressmen wrote a protest letter to Johnson, stating they were "appalled" to learn the CIA funded the NSA for over a decade. The congressmen wrote the CIA program "represents an unconscionable extension of power by an agency of government over institutions outside its jurisdiction."[5] Republican governor George Romney of Michigan declared that the covert relationships "smacks of a secret government in our society."[6] There was intense media coverage of covert CIA money going to at least 135 organizations, which included foundations, labor organizations, and businesses.[7] Surprising names popped up: the National Council of Churches, AFL-CIO, and Young Women's Christian Association, among them. A confidential State Department telegram to worldwide diplomatic posts on February 25, 1967, reported the spectrum of reactions: "Disillusionment, disappointment, cynicism, some moralizing characterize many reactions, but sympathetic understanding Cold War problems also expressed."[8]

The public criticism alarmed Johnson, already under siege for his rapid troop escalation and bombing in Vietnam. Two days after the *Ramparts* article appeared, Johnson appointed a three-person committee—Undersecretary of State Nicholas Katzenbach; Health, Education, and Welfare Secretary John W. Gardner; and Helms—to investigate the relationship between the agency and voluntary American organizations operating internationally.

The Family

Beyond their work relationship, Benjamin C. Evans Jr. and Hayden Williams became fast friends. Managing TAF relationship was Evans's full-time job. He and Williams talked on the phone daily, often multiple times, coordinating operations across a vast swath of Asia. Williams also became a family friend, going out to dinner with the Evanses when he was in Washington. "We were very active," Jan King Evans said.[9]

Family life was brisk at the Woodland Drive home as Karla and Louise Evans entered Cathedral School. Ben would leave in the morning for his drive to "the office," as he termed the CIA, returning in the evening, most often for a quiet dinner at home. Ever a car buff, he drove a beige Lincoln Continental sedan, a status symbol in 1960s Washington. At some point, the Lincoln gave way to a Checker cab, utilitarian but nonetheless an eye-catcher in the CIA parking lot. On Sundays the family attended Saint Alban Episcopal Church on the heights above Washington. Jan was engaged with the Junior League, Red Cross, and other charity work. With Washington residents at last able to vote in national elections, Jan became active in the Republican Party. There were family trips to visit Lady Norma Lewis and the Heurichs in their respective Washington mansions. The Heurich name was further burnished in 1965 when the family donated a portion of the brewery land along the Potomac River for the construction of the John F. Kennedy Performing Arts Center.[10]

Each year there were trips to Florida to visit Jan's mother and stepfather for two weeks. Ben could not fly with his family on commercial flights to Florida; he had to take a train.[11] With the threat of being "skyjacked" to Cuba, the CIA proscribed their spook from flying on any airliner headed South. He was able to fly to Florida with his family when Marjorie Merriweather Post, good friends with Lady Lewis, loaned them her private plane for a holiday at Mar-a-Lago, her lavish estate and 126-room mansion in Palm Beach.

In 1963 the Evanses wangled their way into the exclusive Chevy Chase Club with the help of Colonel Donald H. Galloway, who had facilitated Ben's recruitment into the CIA. Ben was more than thirty-five, the cut-off age for legacy memberships, which was through Jan's father, Charles B. King, who had received a membership as a West Point graduation present. Galloway convinced the board to use Jan's age as the metric—the first time the board used a woman's age as the marker. "Colonel Galloway, he was always so helpful," Jan said. With his assistance, the Evanses joined the exclusive Maryland country club that dated back to the 1890s. It was an elite place at the leafy northwest verge of the capital, where Washington's movers and shakers could commingle with their elevated peers and gambol on the golf course, tennis courts, and other sports facilities. The Chevy Chase membership list included a former president, Supreme Court justices, senior government officials, celebrity media people, corporate leaders, prominent attorneys, and financiers. It was heady company for the Evans family. When they were in grade school, the Evans daughters joined the Chevy Chase youth sports clubs, Karla excelling at swimming (the butterfly) and Louise at tennis.

Shadow Life

At some point when the girls were little, Evans had a crisis.[12] According to family lore, he broke down at his desk at CIA headquarters, vomited in the wastebasket, and had to take a month's medical leave. "He was asked to do something immoral. Something he couldn't do," Jan recalled. She conjectured that he was asked to organize an assassination for someone he knew—perhaps a West Point classmate who had run afoul of the agency.[13]

The clandestine service demanded a life of moral ambiguity.[14] An eternal teeter-totter between idealism and realism; means and ends.[15] A life that most often could not be shared; a life of ethical tension—a shadow life. CIA director and family friend Walter Bedell Smith said that running the CIA required leaving your moral scruples at the door, but then added, "you'd better well remember where you left them."[16]

Evans lived with the conundrums of an honorable man encultured to follow orders. He was an Eagle Scout; a West Pointer imbued with "Duty, Honor, Country;" and a military officer sworn to uphold the Constitution. He was also an intelligence officer charged with dissimulating to both the enemies of the United States and the American populace and their elected representatives.[17] Jan said her husband hated to lie, so refused to attend West Point reunions so he would not have to deceive his classmates about his work.[18] "To live a life so covert," she mused, "when you are so open."[19]

During his career as a covert officer, Evans engaged in psychological warfare, generally far removed from the violent work of special operations.[20] Evans's West Point classmate, Major General Calvert Benedict, termed him "a true and gentle man."[21] His CIA colleague and friend, Ambassador Donald Gregg, judged Evans to be temperamentally suited to be an administrator, rather than in operations, plotting "wet work."[22] Jan's conjecture that her husband was ordered to organize an assassination of someone he knew would accordingly present a grave emotional quandary. The gap between opposing moral imperatives could prove unbridgeable.

"He was home for a month, couldn't work or do anything. Had to go to a psychiatrist," Jan said. Emotional distress and breakdowns were part and parcel of CIA life. The agency's Office of Medical Services doctors, the "spooks in white," were always ready to assist troubled officers and staff. Sometimes the help was a few sessions in the OMS office, sometimes it was outside counseling, and sometimes changes in assignment. "People had a range of problems that would threaten or impair their work. We would help them," said Dr. Barney Malloy, CIA psychiatrist for over three decades and an Evans family friend.[23] Malloy said Evans handled pressure well—"with equanimity." Stressing the psychological toll of intelligence work, Malloy said, "For an individual, there are the confusions and qualms you've got to deal with. There's this weight to operate efficiently. There's a great deal of pressure to conform; there's a lot of competitiveness in the groups. The clandestine cloak over everything ups the ante in every respect. When there is secrecy involved, the consequences can be more drastic."

Overseas, the CIA assistance extended to the families. Compartmentalization meant the wife often didn't know anything about her spouse's work. If someone saw the wife was depressed, it would cause concern. "So we would prop up and help the family. They were out overseas in strange environments. Back then the husband might have been trained in Chinese, but the wife was just plopped down," Malloy said. "It was more a problem in the early days when the wife was often a tagalong." As time went on the CIA realized the value in sending out "tandem" couples, with both spouses being CIA officers.

The OMS had a list of CIA-vetted psychiatrists for clandestine officers to consult. "These were people we knew," Malloy said. "They had to sign confidentiality agreements. They also wouldn't be delving into covert matters." So once a week, Evans would leave the Woodland Drive house for his appointment with a CIA-approved psychiatrist in northwest Washington.

After a month of medical leave, Evans was judged fit to return to work. Each weekday morning, he'd again climb in the car for his drive to "the office," continuing his covert management of TAF. To a certain extent, Evans could thank the CIA's paternalistic culture for his return to duty after his crisis. With his social and military connections, he had benefactors and protectors to ease his passage back. And in the 1960s, the CIA still accepted divergent ways of thinking about special operations. "You could have a sense of revulsion about an assassination, and still be respected," Gregg said.[24]

The Termination

Though the February 1967 *Ramparts* article and subsequent *New York Times* story had only hazily mentioned TAF as a conduit for covert funds, Evans and Williams knew their cover was blown. The CIA and the foundation had been preparing to deal with exposure for over a year. With antiestablishment fervor building, investigative reporters were digging for dirt in every corner. And a story about collusion between the clandestine intelligence agency and the supposedly squeaky-clean foundation was bound to come out sooner or later. In May 1966 the Chief of the Covert Action Support Group wrote a memorandum about efforts being made to "firm-up cover for the Asia Foundation by means of a credible source of income." The memo also noted that TAF wanted the CIA to sign over various assets to the foundation. The chief stated, "we are repeatedly bombarded by this Foundation about this proposal."[25] In September 1966, the CIA leadership was determined to carry on with the foundation. A CIA memo noted the secret 303 Committee of high-level U.S. officials had concurred: "TAF's effectiveness and value to the U.S. Government were strongly reaffirmed and the Agency was authorized to undertake a number of measures to shore up TAF's ostensible private image"[26]

By early 1967 the agency was concerned *Ramparts* and the *New York Times* were on to its connection to the foundation. Then after the *Ramparts* NSA article, the Katzenbach Commission became a ticking bomb. Better to get ahead of the story with some carefully crafted disinformation. On March 21, 1967, TAF commenced its limited hangout with a carefully scripted narrative that the CIA helped write. The statement was "plausible," though far from the full, more damaging truth. A UPI news story datelined San Francisco stated, "The prestigious Asia Foundation, a private group which spends more than $4 million annually in strengthening U.S.-Far East relations, has acknowledged receiving financial support through the Central Intelligence Agency. But a spokesman for the foundation yesterday stressed that the funds 'in no way affected' its policies and programs." Beyond misinformation regarding the budget, which was actually almost double the reported amount, the TAF statement claimed that a broad range of corporations, institutions, and individuals funded the foundation—though in truth the CIA provided the bulk of the funding.[27] Williams cabled the overseas foundation staffers to deny they "have any knowledge whatsoever of any USG [U.S. Government] relationships or funding arrangements."[28] No one could predict if the media would buy TAF's limited hangout. The next day at the CIA executive morning meeting, the

Deputy Director of Plans reported that his briefing on counterinsurgency with Vice President Hubert Humphrey had been postponed, and instead talked about the press reaction to TAF's tainted confession.[29]

In June 1967 the Katzenbach Committee recommended a prohibition of covert funding to any U.S. educational institution or private organization for overseas activities. Johnson approved the recommendations and required that the CIA terminate funding for TAF and other voluntary organizations by the end of 1967. On June 6, 1967, the deputy director of plans sent a memo to the CIA director entitled "Liquidation of CA Staff Proprietary Project DTPILLAR." The memo laid out plans for a "terminal Agency grant" of $8.5 million, which was "to be funded through covert channels."

Spotting a legal loophole, the CIA borrowed from its following year's funding to provide a surge of money to tide TAF over until alternate financing was arranged. A secret memorandum recorded that a CIA officer delivered the final increment of the terminal funds on August 10, 1968, to a Wells Fargo Bank in San Francisco. The memorandum noted that the funds were in "U.S. Treasury Bonds and Notes in Bearer Form," which were placed in a safety deposit box.[30] According to Jan, Ben was the bagman, flying to San Francisco with millions of dollars in a suitcase.[31]

16

THE SEVENTH FLOOR

Benjamin C. Evans Jr. had a new assignment—help run the agency—with an office on the seventh floor, the executive aerie atop the Central Intelligence Agency's headquarters in Langley, Virginia. It was a good time for Evans to join the executive staff.

In the aftermath of the exposés of CIA improprieties, the Covert Action Staff was on a short leash for the first time in the agency's history.[1] In September 1967, after decades of unfettered operations, CIA director Richard Helms ordered station chiefs around the world to be very cautious with clandestine operations, especially those that were "politically sensitive." In a time of international anti-American sentiment and domestic antiwar protests that made most covert actions suspect, the great river of psychological warfare money that had long flowed to proprietaries, political parties, periodicals, foreign agents, and propaganda operations began to slow.[2]

As covert action declined, the CIA executive leadership's reputation was conversely rising. After Helms had correctly predicted Israel's preemptive launch of the Six-Day War on Egypt, Syria, and Jordan in June 1967, President Lyndon Johnson saw intelligence in a positive new light. Helms said about Johnson's volte-face, "This was the first time that he was really sort of jarred by the fact that 'those intelligence fellows had some insight that these other fellows don't have.'"[3] Helms's accurate forecast of the war got him a seat at the table—a very powerful table. Johnson invited Helms to his Tuesday lunch, where Helms shared the agency perspective with the president, secretary of state, secretary of defense, and the chairman of the joint chiefs of staff. Helms said he was in "the magic inner circle."

While Helms had the ear of the president, Evans could help do what needed to be done on the seventh floor. Evans earned his operational stripes in Cuba, and proved his organizational mettle managing The Asia Foundation. He was "smooth," as his friend and longtime spy Donald Gregg termed him—socially adept, infallibly discrete, and facile in the ways of power.[4]

In the Room

Evans was now working with remarkable people at the apex of a powerful global organization. From his inner sanctum behind the seventh-floor door numbered 75706, Helms was at the top of the pyramid, not only running the CIA but serving as the chairman of the board of the entire U.S. intelligence community, which also included the Defense Intelligence Agency, the National Security Agency, the military and State Department branches of intelligence, the Federal Bureau of Investigation, and the Atomic Energy Commission.

Coming from a privileged East Coast background, Helms became a journalist right out of Williams College, where he had excelled. He joined the United Press for a stint in Europe, where he snagged an exclusive interview with Adolf Hitler. Helms then joined the *Indianapolis Times* advertising department, becoming the national advertising manager. While living in Indiana, Helms married Julie Bretzman Shields, a wealthy Indianapolis artist with two children from a previous marriage.[5] During World War II, Helms served with the Office of Strategic Services. After the war, he joined the elite cadre of former OSS officers who filled important CIA positions during the Cold War. Tall, dapper, with carefully slicked hair, Helms served in the clandestine division.[6] After opposing the Bay of Pigs invasion, he served as director of operations, and then as Deputy Director of Central Intelligence under Director William Raborn, a former naval officer who had directed the Polaris ballistic missile submarine system.[7] In June 1966 Helms took over from Raborn, who had an unhappy fourteen-month tenure. The first DCI to come up through the agency ranks, Helms's "Little Ivy" and OSS pedigree cheered the old guard. He was running an agency that had about twenty thousand employees with a $1 billion budget.[8] With the CIA's clandestine operations mostly hidden from the rest of the U.S. government, Helms was one of the very few, perhaps the only one, who knew the entire covert picture. He had secrets to keep.

When Evans arrived on the seventh floor, Rufus L. Taylor was the deputy director of intelligence, the second in command. At the time, Taylor was wrestling with two controversies. Yuri Nosenko was a Soviet KGB officer who had defected in 1964. Nosenko claimed he had information about the John F. Kennedy assassination. CIA counterintelligence officers, led by an increasingly paranoid James Jesus Angleton, decided Nosenko was a double agent. Angleton's CIA cadres seized Nosenko in 1964 and held him in solitary confinement in a safe house in Clinton, Maryland, for three years, during which time he was allegedly subjected to sensory deprivation and psychedelic drugs.[9] Cadaver-thin in his Saville Row suits, Angleton was a spectral figure stalking the seventh floor on unending mole hunts. Angleton's cohorts and countervailing CIA officers fought it out. Was Nosenko a double agent or an honest (by spy standards) defector? The fight grew so vicious, Helms eventually had to tell Taylor to sort it out. In 1969 the CIA formally acknowledged Nosenko as a real defector and released him with compensation to live under an assumed name, and Angleton lost his prize prisoner.

The Vietnam War was also creating a headache for Taylor. A midlevel CIA analyst, Sam Adams, was insisting that U.S. military intelligence had grossly underestimated the number of Viet Cong and North Vietnamese combatants by hundreds of thousands. In 1967 Adams demanded the CIA correct troop levels in the U.S. Order of Battle, which policymakers used to make decisions about the war. Military intelligence insisted on using the lower Viet Cong numbers so the war could appear winnable. Bowing to pressure from the U.S. Army, the CIA used the military's intelligence numbers. But after uncounted hundreds of thousands of Vietnamese insurgents launched the Tet Offensive in early 1968, Adams's numbers were quietly included in the Order of Battle. Claiming that the CIA had abrogated its responsibility by kowtowing to army intelligence, Adams filed suit against Helms.

Colonel Lawrence K. "Red" White was executive director/comptroller, the number-three man at the CIA. Appointed to the position by Raborn in 1964, White was the day-to-day manager of the agency, responsible for devising and implementing agency policies and programs as directed by the DCI and his subordinate deputy directors and mission-support leaders. White was Evans's boss.

Born in Tennessee, White was a 1933 West Point graduate. During World War II, he served with distinction in the Pacific, where he earned a Distinguished Service Cross, a Silver Star, two Legions of Merit, three Bronze Stars, and other commendations. Grievously wounded in the Philippines in April 1945, he spent almost two years recovering in military hospitals before joining the CIA. His initial post in operations was running the Foreign Broadcast Information Branch, which handled all covert collection operations. White quickly whipped "an unruly and troublesome organization" into shape, which caught the attention of his superiors. When he became director, Walter Bedell Smith was given the charge to reorganize the CIA, so in 1950 he established the Directorate of Administration to centralize the agency's then-chaotic management. "When 'Beetle' Smith came, he really shook that place up," White said.[10] The following year, Smith tapped White to take an executive position in

DA, where he worked closely with then-Deputy Director Allen Dulles. When Dulles was named director, he assigned White to run DA. During his tenure in administration, White helped Dulles develop the colossal new CIA headquarters in Langley.[11] Important to the spook community, White also facilitated critical legislation that created CIA career development and benefit packages.[12]

After White moved to the seventh floor, Raborn and Helms both wanted him to focus on the agency administration and management so the officers could better do their intelligence work. "It is an administrative job, or was, when I was there, in that I didn't get into intelligence. I didn't interfere with clandestine operations, except to the extent that I had to approve their budgets," White told a CIA interviewer. "I dealt in all the non-intelligence."[13] White became celebrated as the "Father of Integrated Support," later credited by Helms for "the conception, establishment, and direction of the complex structure that supports world-wide intelligence operations."[14]

Evans was brought on board to help with the massive undertaking: conceptualize and implement a comprehensive decision-making process that would control the agency's resources and manpower.[15] During 1968 and 1969, Evans developed planning tools that projected intelligence collection and analysis requirements and identified the resources required to do the work. White subsequently assigned Evans to the comptroller's procurement policy board to develop a resource planning staff.[16]

Evans came up with a concept: the Management Advisory Group, which the DCI formally established in June 1969. The MAG was comprised of fourteen of the CIA's most promising midlevel officers—a "deep select"—who served one-year terms. During the weekly dinner meetings, the young officers gained a greater understanding of other divisions, which were often stovepiped from one another. After hashing out ideas, the group would make broad-spectrum recommendations to the DCI. A March 1971 report about the MAG stated the officers had recently addressed agency issues that included the CIA image, personnel promotion and retirement policies, the need for better communication between top management and all employees, and the problem of functional duplication between directorates.[17] The MAG provided the DCI with fresh new ideas from younger officers, while affording upper-level executives an opportunity to assess the up and comers. "It was his baby," Shirley Cornett said, calling the MAG "quite successful."[18]

By 1970 Evans was on the Executive Director-Comptroller's staff. A few years later, as William J. Casey prepared to take over as director, Evans was sitting in a makeshift office amidst the hurly-burly of passersby, working on a new project: the establishment of an Executive Secretariat. "I can still see him calmly and carefully drawing up the organizational charts for the Executive Secretariat meshing it effectively with the other offices in the Agency," an officer remembered.[19] And the secretariat meant a much bigger job: Evans was slated to serve as the Executive Secretary to the Director and Deputy Director of Central Intelligence, as well as the Executive Secretary of the CIA. Evans was in the room.

Overt

For the first time in his CIA career, Evans was not undercover and in a top executive position at the agency. "I thought it was very prestigious when Ben was named executive secretary of the CIA," Jan King Evans said.[20] At last his family could tell people where he worked. Though that did not always go well. Karla Evans said, "I still remember the first time I said my father worked for the CIA. A fourth-grade teacher asked where our fathers worked. When I said my father works at the CIA, the teacher said, 'Shhh—You can't say that.'" That evening she asked her father if it was OK to say where he worked. Evans assured his daughter she could indeed tell people. "We could say where he worked, but almost never did," she said.[21]

Evans wanted a piece of countryside where he could be in nature, a retreat akin to his grandfather's Indiana idyll. After two years of family forays into the rural areas around Washington, DC, the Evanses finally found a place. It was a farm in Middleburg, Virginia, amid Loudoun County's horse-and-hunting country. "Ben fell in love with our farm because it had an albino deer. Not the best reason to buy a piece of land," Jan said. "I think that's a lousy reason to buy a piece of property—the deer can walk off; the deer can die." She laughed, "You can see the yin and yang of us."[22] In April 1970 the Evans family purchased Groveton Farm, a 500-acre dairy farm that included three houses and a stone barn.[23]

"Goofing off," Evans called it, unwinding from the office with manual labor, mucking out the big stone barn, maintaining the horse trails, and mowing the fields. "Ben used to joke about going home to mow the lower forty," his deputy, Tom Cormack said.[24]

"Daddy loved it out here," Karla Evans said. Louise Evans Turner remembered "getting lost" on the farm for hours with her father, dressed in his old corduroys and Barbour jacket, always with a hat and pipe. There would be breakfasts at the Coach Stop, a mom-and-pop restaurant in Middleburg. Though their clientele included Jackie Onassis, Elizabeth Taylor, and Paul and Bunny Mellon, the Coach Stop owners would fondly call Evans "chairman of the board." On to the hardware store to chat with Mr. Leach, and Billy at the Exxon station. "That was all the society he needed," Louise wrote.[25]

"It was his refuge; his utopia," Jan said. "Ben never showed he was under stress—but I know he was. The farm, the animals, provided a respite."

The family members were part of the farm crew. "We were all sort of slave laborers," Karla said, talking of creosoting and building stone walls. As the years went on, there was Honey, the golden retriever, and Softie, the cat. Even before they had the farm, the family had Lucky, the trick horse. The Evanses encountered Lucky on a visit to Indianapolis. "The girls fell in love with Lucky. He could kneel down; shake hands," Jan said. "So we came home with a horse." Lucky was boarded at Pegasus Stables in Maryland, not far from the Chevy Chase Club. "We said we bought the farm because we couldn't afford the board at Pegasus anymore," Jan said. She decided to raise sheep with the aid of local farm help. Though there was some family dissention after the hands butchered the lambs Moe and Joe—which Karla and Louise adamantly refused to eat. "They were not farm girls," Jan said.[26]

The first Saturday of each November when the Middleburg Hunt had its opening meet at the Evans family home, Groveton Farm became the focus of the local gentry. Sixty fox hunters, dressed to the nines in their formal frock coats and breeches, arrived early in the morning to prepare for their chase across the Virginia countryside. Mounted on their tall horses, some women sidesaddle, the riders were each served a stirrup cup of sherry and a snack, often a feather-light ham biscuit. The Master of the Hunt formally thanked Mrs. Evans, and then the hunters cantered away to the sound of the huntsman's horn, the baying hounds, and thunder of hundreds of hooves.[27]

For Evans, the hunt gave him an excuse to be outdoors in nature, clearing the trails for the hounds and horses. He sometimes worked together with Melissa Cantacuzene, one of the Middleburg Hunt leaders. "Ben was very enthusiastic, very interested in the hunt," Cantacuzene said. "The trails have been there forever. Middleburg's been going on for over a hundred years." Ever self-effacing, Evans never told the horsewoman about his past glory as the captain of the Culver Black Horse Troop. And of course, he did not talk about his work. "I never thought Ben was in the CIA," Cantacuzene said. "I thought he was with the army or something."[28]

While the Evanses seldom took part in the hunt, the opening meet became a social event. "I would invite our best friends for breakfast after the hunt went off," Jan said. Up to fifty West Point classmates and friends gathered on the autumn mornings to relish the pageantry before sitting down to an elegant morning repast. Later in the fall, there were Thanksgiving dinners at the farm, with Ben singing at the piano in the living room. "Back Home Again in Indiana" was his favorite song.[29] In the summer, the Evans family hosted picnic cookouts around the pool for CIA staffers and their wives. Shirley Cornett said, "It was relaxing for him. He always preferred the Middleburg life to the high-society Washington life."

The Office

Evans called CIA headquarters "the office." Most floors of the CIA headquarters were like any standard postwar office building, anonymous hallways lined with closed doors painted in bland midcentury colors—albeit hiding hives of intelligence work. The seventh floor was different, it had a clubby environment with hardwood-paneled executive suites and an elegant dining room with an abundance of waiters and refined silverware of a telling heft. Evans often ate in the executive dining room. "He had pie every day," Jan said. "I paid the bills. I knew what he was eating every day."[30]

Evans had a demanding job. A top-secret CIA job description stated: "The executive secretary, CIA, carries chief administrative responsibility for CIA interaction with the White House, Cabinet and all other departments and agencies. He reports directly to the Director of Central Intelligence and insures the successful completion of staff work for the Director and his Deputy."[31] A more extensive CIA position description noted the executive secretary received "little or no supervision," and was expected "to identify his own tasks and accomplish the same." The lengthy list of administrative and liaison tasks included, "reviewing and assigning appropriate action within the CIA to the thousands of incoming inquiries, requirements and tasks." The description stated, "It is a position requiring extraordinary skill, judgment and diplomacy. . . . The Executive Secretary is a key senior officer; the DCI and DDCI rely heavily upon him."[32]

"He's pretty much a traffic manager," said Tom Cormack. A fellow West Point graduate, Cormack began serving as Evans's deputy in 1973. Cormack said about the executive secretary, "He kept the plumbing going. Everything that came to the director, came through the executive secretary. You had to be on your toes and do things correctly."

The executive director and secretariat office was right across from the DCI office. The floor-to-ceiling windows looked out to a courtyard and the greenery beyond. Evans and Cormack had an office adjacent to an anteroom shared by three secretaries.[33] Cornett joined the CIA in 1962, right out of high school, where she was a typing whiz. She rose through the secretarial-stenographer ranks to the executive director-comptroller suites. In 1975 she began working with Evans as his staff assistant. "He was into himself a lot," Cornett said, "walking down the hall, lost in thought, one hand in his pocket. People said he wouldn't talk. He said some of his best ideas came when he was walking." She remembered he never had any cash. "He never had a dollar in his pocket—he'd have to borrow money for tobacco. 'I'll pay you back tomorrow,' and he always did."

The executive secretary's business day started with the 9:00 a.m. meeting, attended by a dozen top CIA executives, including the heads of the directorates. By 1970 Evans was taking the meeting minutes, later dictating them to Cornett. "How he ever took those notes without shorthand skills, I'll never know," she said. She was responsible for typing them into draft form. "I always hoped for short meetings," she said.

Evans was also generating detailed Action Items that encompassed the agency's global operations. For example, one of Evans's top-secret Morning Meeting Action Items from June 1970 summarized CIA analysts' deduction that the absence of Cambodian diplomats at a Soviet-sponsored reception in Hanoi augured a change in Soviet-Chinese Communist relations. A CIA department head started a "lengthy discussion" about relations between the communist powers. When another department head noted there were numerous reports that the Soviets were putting out word that the North Vietnamese were "fatigued," it led to the Action Item: Pull together all of the reports on the Soviet scuttlebutt about Hanoi's state of mind and study them—"the Director says that is the very least we should do," the Action Item concluded.[34]

Cormack said, "Mail would come in; the phone would ring. There'd be direct tasking here and there." The staff would process a succession of in-boxes, prioritized by urgency. But it was orderly—"a very calm environment," he said. Evans would say, "There's comfort in creating order."[35] It was a workaday world, 8:00 a.m. to 6:00 p.m., five days a week. No weekend work, even during crises. "I never felt a sense of panic," Cormack said, "nor did Ben, I'm sure."[36]

However, there were plenty of controversies swirling though the seventh floor in the years 1968 through 1973.[37] Despite President Richard Nixon's pledge to end the war, Vietnam had become the quagmire. CIA analysts continued to joust over the state of the war. In 1968 the CIA launched the secret Operation Phoenix, which the agency described as "a set of programs that sought to attack and destroy the political infrastructure of the Viet Cong."[38] Using paramilitary counterterrorism, capture, interrogation, and assassination tactics, Phoenix was intended to "neutralize" the Viet Cong leadership down to grassroots levels. By 1970, after tens of thousands of Vietnamese had been "neutralized" with little impact on the downward spiral of the war, Congress began investigative hearings. The CIA eventually judged Operation Phoenix, riddled by corruption and faulty intelligence, to be a failure and withdrew its support.[39]

As American antiwar and black-power movements grew exponentially through the late 1960s, the White House became obsessed with proving the communists were behind them. Johnson turned to the CIA for intelligence on American activists' links with unfriendly foreign powers. Although the agency found no communist sponsors, the domestic surveillance operation continued. When Nixon took office the agency's domestic surveillance continued under the codename Chaos, which eventually compiled an index of more than 300,000 American individuals and organizations, with extensive files on more than 7,200 citizens. There was widespread disagreement inside the agency about the illegal domestic spying—one wing wanted expanded surveillance and another faction wanted Chaos shut down. In March 1971 Management Advisory Group officers sent a memorandum to the DCI, stating, "MAG is seriously concerned about possible repercussions which may arise as the result of CIA's covert domestic activities." The officers wrote that revelations about domestic spying could trigger adverse consequences: "It is MAG's fear that such a negative reaction could seriously damage our Congressional relations, effect our work against priority foreign targets and have a significant impact on the viability of the CIA."[40] By the summer of 1972, Nixon was pushing hard for more CIA operations against his domestic enemies.[41]

The agency continued to focus on Latin America, including ongoing plots against Fidel Castro. Chile, with large U.S. corporate investments and a powerful leftwing movement, received outsized CIA attention. The agency pumped $3 million into the 1964 Chilean election to swing the presidential vote to pro-American Eduardo Frei for a six-year term. In September 1970, with leftist Salvador Allende leading presidential polls as the country headed for elections, Nixon and National Security Advisor (later Secretary of State) Henry Kissinger authorized another salvo of CIA political warfare in Chile.

The grave fear was that Latin America would become "a red sandwich," with Castro's Communist Cuba at one end, and Allende's Socialist Chile at the other. This time CIA propaganda failed and Allende won a narrow victory. An avowed leftist determined to nationalize U.S. business interests was about to take power. But the United States was not done yet. Rejecting State Department concerns about interfering in another country's democratic election, Kissinger snapped, "I don't see why we have to let a country go Marxist just because its people are irresponsible."[42] The CIA got extra funding for covert operations against Allende and his incoming government. With Cuba psywar veteran David Phillips at the head of a task force, the CIA attempted to get the Chilean Senate to block Allende's confirmation. The strategy was to apply maximum political and economic pressure, sweetened with massive bribes; it failed to work.

There was Track Two: a military coup. However, there was a problem. Chile was the only country in Latin America that had never had a military coup. Its officer corps was solidly behind democratic civilian rule. Behind the back of the U.S. ambassador, the agency's spies began trolling for Chilean officers who might be willing to overthrow Allende, and they found a few disgruntled former officers who liked the idea of CIA-financed power. Soon the CIA was smuggling arms to the conspirators, who were plotting to kidnap the democratically minded commander in chief of the Chilean army, General Rene Schneider. A few days before Allende was to be confirmed, gunmen ambushed Schneider. They botched the kidnapping, and Schneider died of his wounds a few days later. Phillips was relieved to learn the CIA weapons were not part of the assassination, although the agency had certainly encouraged the conspirators. Despite the CIA's best efforts, Allende was confirmed by the Chilean congress just a few hours before Schneider died.

The White House was livid that the CIA failed to stop Allende from taking power. General Alexander Haig, who was Kissinger's trusted aide, claimed that the Chilean operation failed because liberal-minded CIA officers had let their political leanings "flavor their final assessment and their proposals for remedial action in the covert area." Haig urged a purge of "the key left-wing dominated slots under Helms." When Kissinger concurred, Nixon demanded that Helms dismiss many in his leadership team.[43] "The CIA isn't worth a damn," Nixon fulminated.[44] Trying to avoid draconian cuts to the agency's budgets, Helms fired four of his six deputies, but Nixon continued to make threats to drastically cut CIA budgets for the next two years.[45]

As Nixon's purge of the agency continued through the early 1970s, Evans's seventh-floor position was safe. His political conservatism and Latin American anticommunist bona fides were unimpeachable; he had a West Point bond of trust with his boss, White, and, if nothing else, his well-bred bearing and sartorial mien mirrored that of Helms.[46]

17

FAMILY JEWELS

The nation's capital was in tumult in the early 1970s. The anti-Vietnam War movement was wracking the country; the media was in revolt against President Richard Nixon's White House. It climaxed on Sunday morning June 13, 1971, when the *New York Times* published a front-page article about what came to be known as the Pentagon Papers. Officially titled *Report of the Office of the Secretary of Defense Vietnam Task Force*, a trove of thousands of secret U.S. government documents about the Vietnam War from 1945 to 1967 revealed that the Lyndon Johnson administration had lied to both Congress and the American public.

The documents detailed the secret escalation of the Southeast Asia war with bombings in Cambodia and Laos, as well as previously undisclosed raids and attacks. The Pentagon Papers also unveiled the fights within the government about the war, which many officials privately assessed to be unwinnable, even as draft calls were shipping hundreds of thousands of American soldiers to Vietnam.[1] When the Pentagon Papers fueled a firestorm of protest, Nixon and his staffers decided to take measures—and enlisted the Central Intelligence Agency in their plans.

A dissident Rand Corporation analyst, Daniel Ellsberg, had leaked a copy of the top-secret report to the *Times*. In response to disclosures by Ellsberg and other officials, Nixon staffers formed a covert action team of experienced CIA-trained operatives, the so-called White House Plumbers, to plug leaks and discredit Ellsberg. Presidential adviser John Ehrlichman asked the CIA to help E. Howard Hunt Jr., James McCord, and Eugenio Martinez, an active CIA official, with their clandestine domestic mission. The agency accordingly gave Hunt spy gear, including a red wig, a miniature Tessina camera hidden in a tobacco pouch, fake documents, a tape recorder, and a voice-alteration device.

On September 3, 1971, three White House Plumbers, including Hunt and G. Gordon Liddy, broke into Ellsberg's Beverly Hills psychoanalyst's office looking for dirt.[2] Richard Helms subsequently ordered CIA officers to prepare two psychiatric profiles on Ellsberg as part of the campaign to damage his credibility. The CIA's domestic activities were, of course, illegal. The disclosure of the covert CIA domestic operations could devastate the agency's effectiveness, as the Management Advisory Group officers had warned in their memo to the head of the agency, Helms.[3]

It happened. On the night of June 17, 1972, Helms got a phone call at home. The head of CIA security told him that the District of Columbia police just arrested five men burglarizing the Democratic Party National Headquarters at the Watergate complex. They had been caught bugging the Democratic offices. The burglars included four Cubans from Miami and McCord. Helms learned that another of Nixon's plumbers, Hunt, was involved with the wiretapping. All the men were CIA veterans.[4] The men were connected to Nixon's political organization, the Committee to Re-elect the President.[5]

The next Monday, June 19, 1972, Helms disclosed the arrests at the 9:00 a.m. senior staff executive meeting on the seventh floor. Executive Director-Comptroller William Colby, who had replaced Lawrence K. "Red" White as Benjamin C. Evans Jr.'s boss, recalled the meeting: "We were all sitting around saying, 'Here is this story about the break-in; apparently they have arrested several former CIAs. Do any of you guys know anything about this?' No. Nobody knows anything. Helms's position was: we are going to catch a lot of hell, because these [men] are formers"—former CIA operatives. And Helms reminded the group that the CIA knew the men were working for the White House.[6] A classified CIA memo noted the executive meeting on June 19, 1972, when the senior staff discussed the Watergate break-in two days before and the burglars' CIA links. There was an Action Item: "The Executive Director was asked to review this topic and report to the Director." Watergate got tossed into Evans's office.[7]

Nixon's staffers were soon trying to enlist the CIA in the cover-up. Nixon's take-no-prisoners chief of staff, H. R. Haldeman, called Helms and General Vernon Walters to the White House. Haldeman ordered them, ostensibly in the interests of national security, to stop the Federal Bureau of Investigation from investigating the Watergate break-in. Helms told FBI director L. Patrick Gray to roll up the investigation. "I was being set up by the President of the United States to take a fall," Helms concluded.[8] Then some days later, Nixon's attorney John Dean demanded that Walters procure $1 million in hush money to pay the six incarcerated plumbers for their silence. Although the CIA had almost unlimited amounts of untraceable cash to distribute globally, Helms and Walters refused. Helms later stated that if the CIA had paid the hush money, "the end result could have been the end of the Agency."[9]

Watergate and Home

Privy to the republic's blackest secrets at the office, Evans focused on family when at home. It was extreme compartmentalization. Though he knew about the re-election committee's links to Watergate and the White House cover-up that was imploding on the evening news, Evans was tightlipped at home. The need for discretion was essential: One of the Indiana nephews, Daniel F. Evans Jr., was living with the family while working in Washington for the re-election committee. "I was 22 years old, hired to analyze poll results for President Nixon," Dan Evans recalled. Given Nixon's cakewalk of a campaign against Democratic candidate George McGovern, he reported, "It wasn't a very tough job." A 1971 Indiana University economics and political science graduate, Dan had served as a summer intern for then-Indianapolis mayor Richard Lugar, which whetted his appetite for politics. His job with Nixon's re-election organization offered national experience. While Nixon won a landslide election victory, the president's legal and political woes were mounting. "After the Watergate break-in, I could tell the change in atmosphere around there," Dan remembered. "Things were tense at best. I had the good sense to get out of there and left Washington in January of '73."[10] While Evans took his nephew to the CIA several times, and occasionally his daughters visited headquarters, work and family seldom mingled.[11]

Despite Evans's shadowy work, Woodland Drive was a conventional 1970s household, albeit an affluent one. It was an orderly home, as Evans preferred. After a half-hour commute along the Potomac River, Evans arrived home about 6:00 in the evening. A Scotch in his favorite chair, perhaps a pipe, and then family dinner of baked chicken and fish sticks and frozen TV dinners prepared by Woodsy, the Evans's governess-cook. "It was simple food—Army-Navy food," Jan King Evans said. "Plain food; Ben had a big appetite."[12] He loved liver and onions and dashed his salads with Tabasco sauce. On the weekends Evans would cook his go-to dinners: spaghetti, salad, and garlic bread, alternating with steak, baked potato, and asparagus; sometimes artichokes with hollandaise sauce. There were also dinner outings to the Chevy Chase Club. Evans periodically crossed the bridge to the Adams Morgan neighborhood for Caribbean-style black beans and rice at the old-school Cuban restaurant, Omega.

Evans had other Cuban affinities. His covert agent in Havana, Oscar Echevarria, moved to Washington in 1963 to attend Georgetown University. "I became part of the family," Echevarria wrote, "and they were an integral part of all my important events."[13] Evans counseled his Cuban friend to excel academically at Georgetown, where Echevarria was elected to Phi Beta Kappa at a ceremony attended by Evans. After graduation, Echevarria took a job with the Inter-American Development Bank in Washington, where he and Evans periodically lunched in the Army and Navy Club's paneled, high-ceilinged dining room. One lunch in 1968 was a shared celebration: Evans was the witness when Echevarria became a U.S. citizen in Alexandria, Virginia. Their friendship deepened with regular visits to the Evanses' homes in Washington and Middleburg. Echevarria married fellow agent Elena Falla in the Heurich House. In 1972 the Echevarrias moved to Venezuela. Three years later, Echevarria formed EISCA, an international consulting firm, a joint venture with Boston-based Arthur D. Little, which afforded him the opportunity for visits to Washington. Though the years, Echevarria and Evans were able to maintain their close friendship—unusual for agents and case officers. Karla Evans said, "They were like brothers, really."[14]

Evans was a warm and attentive father. In the summers, there were swimming meets for Karla Evans and Louise Evans Turner, with Evans holding up three fingers at the end of pool as his daughters thrashed for the finish line. It was his personal code: three fingers meant, "I love you." Snowy winters meant long slides down Woodland Drive on the family sled, the girls taking turns riding on their father's back. He would descend to the basement to play the Steinway piano down there. "Daddy would every evening sit in the hallway and tell us stories of his childhood in Indiana," Louise remembered.[15]

Jan and Ben had an active social life, including an abundance of benefit dinners. "As a child it seemed to me that my parents went out to a lot of parties," Louise wrote. "It didn't seem like dad wanted to go as enthusiastically as mother wanted. I would sit in their bedroom and watch them get dressed and thought they were both beautiful. I adored when my father wore black tie and when he shaved before going out I would sit on the closed toilet seat and watch him brush the shaving cream on and shave with an old fashion blade."[16] Louise said her father was a reluctant partier: "Dad was a foreigner to Washington society. . . . He put up with it. He knew how to act."[17]

At dinner, the handsome and solicitous Evans was a preferred tablemate. "Women loved to sit next to him," Jan said.[18] Family friend Norma Richards agreed: "He was one of the most physically handsome men in Washington at that time. He was very charming, very warm."[19] Evans found it easy to dodge questions about his work. "Just ask people to talk about themselves," he told his wife. "Everyone always likes to talk about themselves." Karla said, "He was clearly versed in understanding other people's emotions," reflecting both his natural inclinations and the CIA's black-arts training that taught him to parse other people's personalities.[20]

An elite Washington Cave Dweller, Jan served on numerous boards, including the American Red Cross, the Young Women's Christian Association, the National Child Research Center, the Junior League, and the National Cathedral Building Committee. She also got involved in Republican politics, beginning as a precinct committeewoman in 1964, the first year that Washingtonians could vote in presidential elections. Through the 1970s, she rose in the national party hierarchy, lobbying on behalf of strong environmental policies, pro-choice women's issues, and fiscal conservatism. Beyond developing the Heurich family holdings in Washington, Jan continued to purchase Loudon County property.[21]

Despite the agency pressures, Evans remained healthy—though his September 7, 1973, medical examination did note he had experienced "left chest palpitation and left anticubital tingling" three months before while carrying a marble table. He was seventy-four and a half inches tall and weighed 181 pounds, with a blood pressure reading of 130/80.[22] A robust specimen, all considered. But mortality lurked. A few weeks after his exam, Evans's father, Benjamin C. Evans Sr., unexpectedly died in Los Angeles, where he had been living since 1957 after marrying his second wife, Beatrice McMahan. He was buried in Oak Hill Cemetery in Crawfordsville, Indiana.[23]

Smoking Gun

After Helms refused to wholeheartedly join the Watergate cover-up, his relationship with Nixon was doomed. When it became obvious that Nixon was going to fire him, Helms asked for the ambassadorship of Iran, which the president granted. In his stead, Nixon appointed tweedy, professorial James Schlesinger to be Director of Central Intelligence. Schlesinger was going to be on the hot seat. By 1973 the media had connected the White House to Watergate. Acting on tips from associate director of the FBI, Mark Felt, later famous as Deep Throat, *Washington Post* reporter Bob Woodward was investigating the links between one of the burglars, Hunt, and presidential aide Charles Colson. As Nixon was inaugurated for his second term in January 1973, the cover-up was already beginning to unravel—and the CIA troubles were just beginning.

Unbeknownst to Evans as he went about his work on the seventh floor, he was close to the CIA's darkest secrets. They were compiled in a CIA Inspector General 133-page report that detailed the agency's assassination operations—

Executive Actions in the agency argot. The report, ordered by Helms in 1967, included the assassination plots against foreign officials, along with other extralegal actions, such as the CIA's domestic mail-interception program.[24] It was dangerous knowledge. Disclosure would have a devastating impact on the agency. Helms kept the only remaining copy locked in his office safe.

As he was leaving office in January 1973, Helms had a problem with his secrets, not only the revealing Inspector General report, but also thousands of transcript pages of recordings made in his office. Time was short: Nixon was prematurely terminating his tenure as director. Incoming DCI Schlesinger was already in the building, looking through Helms's papers. U.S. Senator Mike Mansfield had sent Helms a letter, informing him that the Senate was going to investigate "campaign activities"—as in Watergate. Mansfield asked Helms to preserve relevant CIA documents. Helms knew how to adhere to the letter of the law, while protecting CIA prerogatives. He instructed his secretary to go through the sequestered papers in his safe and preserve anything relating to Watergate—and to destroy everything else. When she was done, not one page was left.[25]

Schlesinger arrived in the DCI's office with a mandate to change "the gentlemen's club" that had run the CIA since its beginning. He first focused on the clandestine directorate, pushing out the old guard with relentless pressure and wholesale early retirements. The new DCI was so unpopular a bodyguard sat outside his seventh-floor office. A closed-circuit security camera was trained on Schlesinger's official portrait to discourage irate employees from defacing it.

Incensed to learn the plumbers' agency connections, Schlesinger wanted to know the CIA's dirty secrets. Colby remembered Schlesinger's ire: "He was sore as hell; he said, 'I thought we were supposed to get everything from Watergate together. Goddamn it, let's find out where these time bombs are.'"[26] On May 9, 1973, Schlesinger issued a directive to every CIA employee to report any action that may have exceeded the limits of the CIA's charter. In May 1973 Nixon was shuffling his remaining senior executives as indictments, resignations, and terminations were thinning the ranks. The same day Schlesinger ordered the reports, Nixon named him to be Secretary of Defense, less than six months after he became the DCI. Nixon asked Colby to replace Schlesinger as the director.

The executive scramble was another episode in a season of Washington scandals. In late February Gray had revealed during his congressional confirmation hearing that he complied with Dean's order to provide daily updates on the Watergate investigation, and stated that Dean "probably lied" to FBI investigators. A few weeks later, convicted Watergate burglar McCord confessed that he perjured himself during his testimony, writing that Watergate was not a CIA operation, pointing investigators toward the White House. Dean flipped a few weeks later, telling investigators he discussed the cover-up with Nixon at least thirty-five times. Senior White House officials, including Ehrlichman and Haldeman, resigned in late April 1973. Two weeks later, the Senate Watergate Committee began nationally televised hearings, appointing special prosecutor Archibald Cox. In mid-July 1973, Nixon's former appointments secretary disclosed that all conversations and phone calls in the Oval Office had been taped since 1971, precipitating a flurry of legal actions to get the recordings. Serial indictments and convictions of White House insiders became daily news fodder. Nixon was increasingly beleaguered. In late July 1974 the House Judiciary Committee passed Articles of Impeachment. A few weeks later, the White House released a June 23, 1972, Oval Office recording that captured Nixon and Haldeman conspiring to use the CIA to block the Watergate investigations.[27] The recording became known as the "smoking gun" tape. Nixon's last Republican senatorial defenders stepped back. On August 9, 1974, Nixon resigned from the presidency.

In the aftermath of Watergate, the agency's association with the plumbers and Helms's short-term collusion with the cover-up tarnished the CIA's reputation. But given the political and legal devastation experienced by the Nixon administration, the agency escaped major damage. While the top echelon of the agency clearly knew who was organizing the cover-up, none of the CIA officials blabbed as Nixon's top advisers had done. The CIA officials clung to the defense that they had adhered to the letter of the law. And they argued somewhat successfully that they were doing the best they could in an impossible situation.

The Secrets We Keep

"Ben never told me anything, Jan said. "And I never asked. And if I did, he'd ask, 'Now Jan, is that on a need-to-know basis?' For someone who has a natural curiosity, I compliment myself as being a good CIA wife."[28] She was not alone. Tom Cormack, Evans's deputy, said, "My dear wife would say I never knew what you were doing."[29] Domestic reserve was deeply encoded into the culture of CIA families. Biographer David Talbot wrote about CIA avatar Allen Dulles, "Dulles was a guest in his own family home—amiable but detached." Dulles's daughter Joan said the family paid a "price" for never "talking in the home about your life and your politics and what's going on." Talbot termed it "emotional anesthesia."[30]

"I didn't know what my father did," Louise said. "I kind of knew he did something, but I didn't know about the CIA." In lieu of knowledge, she conjectured he was a postman. "You have to pretend your father is someone he is not." She recalled going to the CIA for lunch with her father when she was sixteen. "There were long institutional hallways. "It was like a hospital," she said, "but every door was a different color—'70s colors, pink and purple. Hallways of really ugly doors." They ate lunch in the agency dining room. "That was normal," she said, "but when I had to go to the rest room, dad had to escort me. I thought, 'I can't even walk down the hallway without an escort.'" When she got on the elevator, she suddenly recognized a friend's mother. Her father told her, "You can't say that woman was in the elevator with us."[31]

"Breaking cover," telling children about their parents' CIA connections, was a rite of passage. "It's like telling your kids about Santa Claus or the facts of life," CIA official and ambassador Donald Gregg said. When he learned his father was in the CIA, the Greggs' son felt betrayed. "John was outraged," Donald said.[32] A CIA official herself, Meg Gregg said, "It is not an easy life for an agency family. There's a lot of dissembling. You have to be pretty nimble."[33] Timing is crucial. CIA official Jack Devine wrote, "You want to catch them when they are old enough to handle it responsibly, but not after they have developed hardened misperceptions about the intelligence world. I tried to tell them in their early teens and while on assignment in the United States, where they were not likely to spread the news to their classmates the next day." When he told his sixteen-year-old daughter, she shrieked, "You're an assassin?"[34]

It became the Evans family's shared secret.[35] "We were not supposed to send Christmas cards or do anything that connected you to anyone in the CIA," Jan said.[36] "We were taught not to question," Karla said. "There were roles to play. There was a public life and a private life. And in D.C., there is a lot of public life."[37] The Evans family circle of friends was comprised of others in the intelligence world, often with a military background.[38] Jan said her husband's occupation impacted the family's social standing in the Washington hierarchy: "We were never social because of the CIA. People never knew where he worked. The CIA was not a status position."[39] She spoke of joining Washington's elite International Club that included members of the diplomatic community: "When I was proposed for the International Club and they found out Ben was at the CIA, they didn't want to put that in the directory. It would scare off the international members."⁴⁰

The Secretariat

Colby had a new administrative organization to assist him. On July 12, 1973, Evans's Executive Secretariat was officially established.⁴¹ Reporting to the DCI from across the hall in Room 7D6015, Evans had two staff assistants and two secretary-stenographers working under him.⁴² He also had mammoth responsibilities: review and distribute all incoming and intra-agency correspondence sent to the DCI and DDCI; flag the critical messages; assign tentative actions and suspense dates to the appropriate directorate heads; record all the decision making, whether in writing or by phone; periodically update the senior staff on the evolution of "particularly sensitive topics"; organize, index and most importantly, compartmentalize sensitive material; develop meeting agendas and take meeting minutes; monitor the scheduling of "all major intelligence production tasks"; approve the DCI office expenditures, including the Executive Dining Room billings; approve cable dissemination requests made by staff; review all cable and electronic transmissions and keep DCI and DDCI in the loop; act as a Career Service Approving Officer for all officers below grade GS-16; and, finally, "Perform other functions as assigned by the Director." Cleaning the Augean stables looked like child's play in comparison.

Each day Evans's work ranged across the CIA global operations. Sometimes there were matters closer to home. A May 30, 1973, memo sent to Evans noted that CIA actions against whistleblower Ellsberg in 1970, and threats by the radical Weathermen against CIA officers, warning senior officers to vary their route to work, and "report any peculiar telephone calls or unusual events around their residences." The memo included a classified chronology that documented the plumbers' connection to the agency and to Nixon's senior staff in the White House and the Committee to Re-elect the President.⁴³

Then there were his myriad administrative tasks. For example, in 1973 Evans was preparing recommendations on Superior Accomplishment Promotions for the DCI to consider, and delineating elaborate protocols for the executive dining room—"I need to clarify the operative ground rules under which my colleagues should operate with respect to a fairly delicate topic: official entertainment of U.S. government employees."⁴⁴ There were lengthy memos on CIA interns, job applicants, stationery use, and the ticklish issue of authorized first-class travel.⁴⁵ It was the work of a consummate organization man, operating at the peak of his powers in a vast bureaucracy.

The Family Jewels

In 1973 Washington was in a constitutional crisis—the Nixon administration was fighting for its political life and the CIA was facing an existential threat. "Needless to say, things here at the office are occasionally confused but each day is different," Evans wrote his father-in-law and mentor Gene Harrison. "I am sure you agree with me that this town has 'gone bananas.'"⁴⁶

As the Senate Watergate Committee began its hearings in May 1973, reports from CIA employees of illegal activities began to pour into Colby's office, to be later collated by the Inspector General. The Inspector General's initial twenty-six-page summary for Colby was titled "Potential Flap Activities." That was an understatement. The loose-leaf collection of reports, which eventually totaled 693 pages, included the domestic spying operations, the mail interception program, the secret psychotropic drug-testing programs, the illegal training of local police departments, the plumbers' CIA connection, and a summary of the suppressed 1967 report on assassinations. The explosive reports later became known as "The Family Jewels."⁴⁷

Colby, a covert man of action for most of his adult life, was also a devout Roman Catholic. He believed in heaven and hell, and the eternal consequences of mortal sin. The revelations of illicit assassination plots, involuntary drug experiments, and secret prisons deeply unsettled his sense of spy morality. But he was not a naïve altar boy. A pragmatic career intelligence officer, Colby understood that "skeletons in the closet" could destroy the CIA.⁴⁸ He called them "bad secrets." As with Watergate, Evans knew all about the Family Jewels. A July 10, 1973, memo indicated, "I talked with Ben Evans after the meeting today about the skeletons assignment mentioned yesterday morning by Mr. Colby."⁴⁹

The CIA's darkest secrets were suddenly thrust into the bright light. On December 22, 1974, the *Times* published revelations by investigative journalist Seymour Hersh about the agency's enormous domestic spying operations.⁵⁰ The CIA knew a year before that Hersh was nosing around the domestic covert operations, interviewing retirees, seeking out leakers, and piecing together a very intricate puzzle. He also had an inside source: Colby, who owed him a favor. At Colby's request, Hersh had earlier spiked a juicy story about the CIA's *Glomar Explorer*, a deep-sea drilling ship that was part of a top-secret operation to recover a sunken Soviet submarine. Colby said, "I thought I owed him a lot on that one, because he had worked on it and could have gone on, as he did later."

Earlier in December 1974, Hersh had asked Colby for an interview about the domestic programs. Colby agreed, thinking he could again talk him out of publishing, or at least diminish the story's importance. That did not work. When Hersh confronted him with the domestic wiretaps, surveillance, and mail openings, Colby admitted, "There are some little things that happened." That was confirmation to Hersh, who ran with the story. That was the beginning of the CIA's "Black December."

It was a combustible moment. Already raw from the Vietnam War and Watergate, Americans were deeply distrustful about their government. The press was eager for conflagration. An iconoclastic band of members of Congress who had been elected in post-Watergate 1974 were intent on disrupting the Hill's cozy relationship with the intelligence agencies and to push back against critics who claimed that the congressional oversight committees were "blind and toothless watchdogs." Soon the CIA was facing investigations by the Church Committee in the Senate and the Pike Committee in the House.

When he ran the domestic spying story, Hersh did not know about the assassination programs. That knowledge came from a January 16, 1975, off-the-record meeting between President Gerald Ford and top journalists from the *Times*. Ford mentioned that Colby had told him about CIA assassination plots. Given it was an off-the-record interview, the *Times* did not use it. But someone did gossip to CBS journalist Daniel Schorr, who asked Colby about assassinations. Surprised by the question, Colby blurted out, "Not in this country." The president's ill-considered disclosure about CIA assassination programs was the lit match. "That blew the roof off," Colby said.[51]

When Ford had learned the rough outlines of the Family Jewels, he told his top advisers that if the secrets got out, the "CIA would be destroyed." To preemptively head off disaster, Ford established a commission headed by Vice President Nelson Rockefeller. The Rockefeller Commission was charged with investigating the domestic activities, in the hopes it might deflect public attention from even more scandalous foreign activities. Even though it was damage control with a tight area of purview, the commission was bound to unearth other ugly secrets. Helms warned the president, "A lot of dead cats will come out."[52]

Colby was a cooperative witness, so much so that Rockefeller pulled him aside to ask, "Bill, do you really have to present all this material to us? We realize there are secrets you fellows need to keep and so nobody is going to take it amiss if you feel that there are some questions you can't answer quite a fully as you seem to feel you have to."[53] Discomfited by Colby's disclosures, Henry Kissinger told him, "The trouble with you, Bill, is that whenever you go up on the Hill, you think you're going to confession."[54] In one year, Colby testified thirty-two times to Congress, and "loaned" tens of thousands of secret CIA documents to Congressional investigators.[55] As the committees unveiled decades of CIA misdeeds, there was a fair amount of grandstanding by the members. At a press conference in July 1975, U.S. Senator Frank Church, the chair of the Senate committee, hyperbolically stated, "The agency may have been behaving like a rogue elephant on the rampage."[56] Colby said in the midst of the probes, "I do fear the result could be a farce or tragedy, or both."[57]

Colby thought candor was the CIA's only hope. He later told CIA historians, "In the context of the time, we'd just had Watergate, you really weren't going to get away with stonewalling them. It just wasn't going to work. On the other hand, if you go to a committee which starts out with a prosecuting mission and give them the whole view of American intelligence, which is a very good story, then these become rather small against that larger picture. In order to do that you've got to tell them quite a lot, but you don't tell them names."[58]

But then the names did start coming out. In August 1975 *Playboy* magazine published excerpts of former CIA officer Phillip Agee's tell-all memoir, *Inside the Company*. Initially published in Britain, the book identified 250 alleged CIA officers, agents, and front companies. When the book was published in the United States six months later, it became an instant bestseller. The exposure of covert officers and agents appalled Evans. "I remember how distressed he was when CIA undercover operatives overseas were discovered," his nephew, Daniel Evans Jr., remembered.[59]

There were many in the CIA who opposed Colby cooperating with the congressional investigators, Helms among them.[60] "I think he was wrong," Helms said, noting that during his administration the CIA had not sent one document to Congress. James Jesus Angleton spoke for many spooks when he said in 1976, "The congressional investigations were like being pillaged by a foreign power, only we have been occupied by the Congress with our files rifled, our officials humiliated and our agents exposed."[61] The CIA officers called the congressional investigations of 1975 and 1976, "The Time of Troubles." Evans was among those questioning Colby's strategy. It was a worrisome time for him. "In Washington, at Woodland Drive, he would often take a walk around the block, to clear his head, he never spoke of work; I never asked," Louise wrote.[62] "My father was aching," she said.[63] At some point during the Family Jewels controversy, Evans went to Colby's house in northwest Washington to discuss his concerns.[64] He had never gone to any previous director's home on agency business, but Colby's disclosures deeply troubled him. "Ben did not like that. He did not like it when people talked too much," Jan said.[65]

The investigations put an enormous strain on the Executive Secretariat. In late November 1974 Evans estimated that his staff had expended six thousand man-hours in support of the Rockefeller and congressional investigations. He wrote, "Two officers, myself and [redacted] were interviewed by the Rockefeller Commission staff, and I have had one session with a Senate Select Committee staffer."[66]

The CIA survived the investigations, but not without a price. The agency's effectiveness was impaired overseas. "It created an awful lot of trouble abroad—people saying how can we deal with you, you guys put all of your stuff in the newspapers all the time," Colby said. The agency's covert use of journalists, professors, and other experts was sharply curtailed. The big change was serious congressional oversight of the agency by the Senate Select Committee on Intelligence and the House Permanent Select Committee on Intelligence. It was an epochal period. The days of laissez faire oversight were over.[67]

Congressional investigations were not the only day-to-day challenge facing Colby and the agency's senior staff during the mid-1970s. The Vietnam War was ending—badly. In the wake of the American withdrawal, the South Vietnamese government fell to the communist forces—a blow for Colby, the architect of the Phoenix Program. Television cameras captured helicopters evacuating the last Americans as South Vietnamese supporters, including many CIA assets, thronged the U.S. embassy gates, hoping for their promised rescues.[68] As Nixon's power declined, the détente with the Soviet Union hardened. Helms was convicted of perjuring himself to Congress when testifying about the CIA role in the Chilean military coup.[69]

Beyond helping the agency weather the storms, Evans continued to tend the unending administrative minutiae of the seventh floor. For example, a March 1974 memo between Evans and Colby debated whether the DCI and his wife should attend the RAND Corporation annual dinner. Evans wrote the pros and cons: "It depends upon whether Bill has any great interest in the personalities there." If so, an "informal chat" could be helpful. On the other hand, the DCI was swamped with invitations, and if he attended the RAND dinner, the plethora of other organizations, "whom receive large government subsidies," would clamor to have him attend their dinners. After seeking Evans's concurrence, Colby sent his regrets.[70] Evans ran a tight ship. A 1976 memo scolded a large distribution list: "Far too often material is reaching the Director or his immediate office without going through the Executive Registry and over my desk."

As he had done earlier in his career, Evans continued to serve as a spokesman for the agency. In July 1976 he spoke to a group at Oatlands, a National Trust for Historic Properties in Leesburg, Virginia. "This is to thank you for the fantastically expert and interesting presentation that you gave the men at Oatlands last Friday evening on the subject of the current 'intelligence' situation in Washington," B. Powell Harrison wrote, mentioning an avid group clamoring to ask questions three and four at a time.[71]

Part of Evans's job was fending off demands for administrative time—especially if potentially troublesome. In one such exchange, Evans responded to the Army's Chief of Military History, who wanted CIA documents for a research project on Vietnam pacification operations from 1964 to 1973. The historian had expanded his initial information request to include the politically controversial "Enemy Order of Battle" topic. Given the Tet Offensive fiasco, that was a potential land mine. Evans politely demurred, estimating it would take a three-person task force several weeks off-site just to do an initial review, and then months to comply with all the clearance procedures. "The manpower for such an undertaking is currently unavailable," Evans wrote. He noted the army, which took part in most of the pacification operations, already had the material in their files.[72] Go away.

On January 30, 1976, Colby stepped down as director. Colby's successor, George H. W. Bush, was a contentious choice in the divisive post-Watergate era. As the head of the Republican National Committee, Bush had been a staunch defender of Nixon. A former congressman, Bush was the first politician to be tapped to be DCI. He was confirmed only after pledging to not run for president or vice president in 1976.

Evans helped orient Bush, preparing the briefing format for the director-designee. It listed the briefers and subjects and warned the distribution list to not overwhelm the new guy: "Experience shows that a new DCI is the victim of his own calendar growing out of external pressures to get up to speed on various topics for meetings he will be called on to attend."[73]

Bush inherited a bad situation. "It is perhaps the toughest job in government right now," he had written his siblings.[74] Relations between the CIA and

Congress were at a nadir following the Family Jewels investigations. Agency morale was at low ebb after all the public criticism. And the agency was headed for more major changes. On February 18, 1976, Ford issued Executive Order 11905, which established policy guidelines and restrictions on the intelligence agencies. The most extensive intelligence reform since 1947, the order called for a massive reorganization of the U.S. intelligence community to be completed in ninety days. It pretty much got done.

Scion of an East Coast dynastic family who had gone West to work the oil patch, the Ivy League-educated, consensus-building Bush had the right stuff for Evans. "Ben thought he was the best of the pack—the best of the CIA heads he served under," Jan said. "Bush fit in there; he wasn't above them."[75] And after years of organizational upheaval, Evans at last had some hope for order. In a memo titled, "An Eight-Year View of DCI Management," Evans depicted a seventh-floor culture that was personality-driven and not uncommonly dysfunctional. He aimed ire at Colby, whom Evans felt had consolidated power at the expense of good management. "DCI Colby's problem and perhaps his undoing was that there are 24 hours in a day rather than 34 hours in a day. The extreme centralism of his leadership caused him to give insufficient attention to our primary customer and his ultimate supervisor/ the president/ and this was, in my judgment, his undoing." Evans lauded Bush's reorganization of upper management. "With the advent of the new DCI and the shake/down cruise having been accomplished for Agency management, we now have a truly "first/time opportunity" to see if the Director and his Deputies can perform with the existing management plumbing."[76]

But Bush's term as DCI proved to be short—less than a year—serving from January 30, 1976 to January 20, 1977. The election of Jimmy Carter sealed Bush's fate. While he had briefed Carter both as a candidate and president-elect, there was too much momentum for change.[77] Carter named an Annapolis classmate, Admiral Stansfield Turner, to replace Bush. In his 355 days as DCI, Bush had calmed the CIA rank and file, developed a working relationship with the turf-jealous intelligence community, and established a tenuous trust with the wary White House and Congress.[78]

When Bush prepared to leave office, Evans sent him a farewell letter, writing, "As you step across the threshold to private life, I cannot resist the urge to say how much I'm going to miss you. Every day of service on your behalf has been a challenge <u>and</u> a joy."[79] Three days later, Bush sent a "Memorandum in lieu of fitness report" to the DDCI and personnel. Bush wrote, "Ben Evans has given me total support. He keeps the paperwork moving; I am always confident that his operation is being run in a thorough fashion." He praised Evans's follow-through and "sound advice." Bush stated, "He is dedicated to the CIA and this comes through in the warm and personal way in which he supports the DCI."[80] A month later, Bush wrote from Texas, asking Evans for some unclassified documents he could use in upcoming lectures at Rice University. Bush wrote, "I am getting back into the national political scene with an eye on '80," and signed off with "Best to all my friends, and they are my friends I feel so strongly."[81]

On the seventh floor, the executive secretariat's monumental workload continued to grow. Evans wrote in 1977, "During an average working day we assign actions on approximately fifty (50) pieces of actionable internal and external correspondence."[82] It took rock-solid composure, a keen work ethic and capacity to lead people to get the job done. Cormack talked about the executive secretariat during the Time of Troubles: "In our little domain, we just proceeded. There was some consternation about what was going on, but it really didn't affect our work at all. Ben was a great boss—smart, intelligent, completely above board. He was unflappable; really cool. I can't think of any missteps he made—which is remarkable."[83]

An abstentious Christian Scientist, Turner was the third admiral to serve as the director. Like his predecessors, he was grappling with complicated political conundrums. The intelligence community reorganization had given him broad responsibilities without commiserate authority. Despite his best efforts, centralized intelligence management under the DCI was an unrealized ambition. One CIA study concluded that centralized DCI management would take both White House leadership and "a heroic bureaucratic battle." Stymied by competing intelligence services and a waffling White House, Turner stated, "almost every President has walked up to the brink of giving the DCI control over the Intelligence Community. All have walked back from that brink."[84]

Turner emphasized technical intelligence (TECHINT) and signals intelligence (SIGINT) over human intelligence (HUMINT). Downgrading the covert services, Turner expended enormous resources to enhance U.S. reconnaissance satellites' global coverage. Yet, psychological warfare was still an important CIA tool. When Carter took office, he promulgated a U.S. foreign policy that was built on protecting human rights, particularly behind the Iron Curtain. At his directive, the CIA unleashed covert actions aimed at the Soviet Union, Poland, and Czechoslovakia. Once again the agency was in the publishing business, subsidizing dissident presses across the Eastern European communist bloc that were challenging the communist grip on information. Longtime CIA official Robert M. Gates, later to be director, stated, "Carter had, in fact, changed the long-standing rules of the Cold War."[85] The agency's psywar operation had an outsized impact on the now geriatric and teetering Soviet Union. It was the nudge that started the regime's long fall.

Carter also ordered the CIA to act against South Africa and Rhodesia, both controlled by white racists. He wanted the agency to change its previous course and apply political and economic pressure to end apartheid. The agency, historically engaged with fighting communists, was initially resistant. Carter's DDCI, Frank Carlucci, said, "nobody wanted to focus on Africa."[86] That is, until the South African issue was connected to the communists. The Soviets supported the anti-apartheid African National Congress, and its leader Nelson Mandela. The CIA worked closely with South Africa's repressive Bureau of State Security and had been instrumental in Mandala's 1962 arrest and imprisonment. That was then. Now the CIA was marshaling its energy to drive the Soviets out of southern Africa with the support of newly aligned black African governments.

Evans in Africa

Karla went to Africa in August 1978, when she was studying at Connecticut College. She was working in Tanzania with anthropologist Doctor Peter Schmidt, who specialized in African iron production.[87] She flew from East Berlin to the capital of Dar es Salaam on the Swahili coast of the Indian Ocean. Tanzania was a socialist country, so the air links were typically through Communist-bloc countries. Arriving in Dar es Salaam, she learned the hotel had lost her reservation, so a taxi driver took her to a brothel, where she spent the night with an open Swiss Army knife. The next day she relocated to a convent. Before heading into the field, she checked in at the U.S. embassy, where she visited with a CIA official her father had contacted. Her father had promised to send her a telegram if he heard of any trouble in Tanzania.

It was a two-and-a-half-day trip by train and bus up to the field site west of Lake Victoria, close to where Tanzania, Uganda, Rwanda, and Burundi meet. She was working a research project on ancient carbon steel, a product of sophisticated smelting done in the area two thousand years before. The anthropologists theorized the Iron Age metalworkers had accomplished the highly advanced smelting by utilizing the region's lush forests for charcoal to preheat their furnaces.[88] She and her colleagues had been working for a few months on the project, when "things started heating up," as Karla said. There were sanctions, then a petrol shortage, then MiG fighter jets were flying overhead.

Relations between Tanzania and Uganda had been strained since 1971, when Idi Amin had seized power in a coup. Tanzania gave sanctuary to the ousted Ugandan president and twenty thousand refugees fleeing Amin's bloodbath. In early October 1978 rebel Ugandan troops ambushed Amin in the presidential lodge in Kampala—though Amin escaped. Rallying his remaining loyal troops, he drove some of the mutineers into Tanzania, where anti-Amin exiles joined forces.

On October 30, 1978, Uganda declared war on Tanzania. Amin's troops invaded, intent on annexing the Kagera region, where Karla and her team were working. When the bombing started, Karla had to dive for a doorway as one exploded nearby.

Though caught unaware by the invasion, the Tanzanians quickly mobilized. Karla saw lorries on the road filled with young fighters, some as young as twelve and thirteen. "And then there were other troops in there—fifteen or so who were different." When the archeological team reached the nearby city of Bukoba, she saw three Cubans with the lorries transporting the child soldiers. She saw Russians and suddenly realized communist forces were aiding the Socialist Tanzanians. It was on-the-ground intelligence. The Americans needed to know; her father needed to know.

Karla and some of her teammates joined a United Nations Development Program convoy that was evacuating people from the front lines. "We drove through the night and got to the Serengeti," she said. "Found a ritzy game resort and checked in." At the resort, they encountered a mercenary. Karla said: "He was a guy in the business of getting people out of hot situations. He said, 'You can't tell anyone you've seen any fighting. You can't tell anyone you are American. No travelers checks. Don't show your passport.' And he said we needed to lay low."

When she got to Dar es Salaam, they were out of money. "I called the marines at the embassy and told them that we were in a pickle. How can you help us?" she remembered. The marines put them up in a garage. The next morning, she headed to the embassy to tell them about the fighting and the Cuban soldiers on the front lines. But the diplomats did not believe her—what war?[89]

It was a long journey through South Africa back to Washington. When she told her father she never got a telegram, he replied that one was never sent. The CIA did not know about the war. Karla was shopping with her mother at a DC sports store when they ran into Maryland congresswoman Beverly Byron, an old family friend. Byron said, "I understand you were in a tight situation." And Karla proceeded to tell the congresswoman about war and the Cuban troops in Tanzania. A few days later CIA director Turner was testifying at a national security hearing on the Hill. Byron pointedly asked him about the Cuban troops in Tanzania.[90] Turner returned to Langley, where he told Evans, "I just got a real grilling on the Hill about Cubans in Africa." Evans replied, "That must be my daughter."

When Evans got home, he told his daughter to expect a phone call from the CIA. "You are going to have answer their questions," he told her. She was a little nervous. She had only been to the CIA a few times. After she checked in, someone led her to the elevators where "four massive human beings—not in uniform" escorted her onto the elevator. The doors opened and there was her father and the director laughing. "We just thought we'd make it a little more fun for you," Evans said. "So daddy and I went to lunch," Karla recalled. "And then I was interrogated by the CIA." Turner later wrote Evans, "I would never contradict your daughter's word."[91]

By late 1978 Evans had served five DCIs, six DDCIs, and two Executive Directors. He wrote a memo in December to Turner: "An Opportunity to Remodel the Executive Secretariat." He recommended they have a "brief 'bull session'" to discuss "a more responsive Secretariat" that was adaptable to each DCI. By this time, Evans had been on the seventh floor for ten years, working through some of the CIA's most excruciating periods, yet he remained upbeat and positive. He wrote to Turner, "I've never had a dull day and perhaps due to some 'character flaw' enjoyed each one."[92]

18

DENOUEMENT

Since the early 1970s, the Central Intelligence Agency had been aggressively winnowed—a thousand officers cut under James Schlesinger's leadership alone—and the agency mood was grim. With Stansfield Turner's predilection for spy gadgetry, Covert Action was particularly hard hit. On October 7, 1977, the CIA memo DD077-8855 announced severe cuts in the clandestine service. More than eight hundred officers, most senior, were to be purged within fifteen months. The first to go received their pink slips on October 31. The demoralized officers called it the Halloween Massacre.[1]

There had been unease in the ranks for years. In early January 1977, CIA Deputy Director for Administration James F. Blake wrote a letter that noted the agency had lost 14 percent of the executive staff through resignations and voluntary retirements in the previous eighteen months. "It is our considered opinion that a great number of these individuals would not have departed if there had been a more equitable compensation arrangement." He stated, "The contribution which these officers might have made, and which now is lost, is impressive."[2]

Senior CIA officer David Martin lashed out during a classified internal interview a few months after the Halloween Massacre, saying that "Personnel policies are leading to institutional suicide. Can no longer count on the abundant supply of dedicated old hands." Martin continued, "Headquarters duty is stifling" and that the CIA personnel system built on "dedication and self-abnegation" was admirable, "but not up with times." He called for "incentives and recognition."[3]

The Management Advisory Group was a bellwether of rising discontent. The minutes of the October 4, 1977, MAG noted "general restiveness" about reductions in force, and "the need to feel appreciated." The minutes noted that Benjamin C. Evans Jr. recommended that MAG contact the inspector general about grievance procedures and ask the White House Fellow to address their group about "his perceptions of the Agency in about December."[4]

In late November 1978 Turner addressed the impact of the previous years' scandals in a speech at Harvard University: "It has been a traumatic experience for those of us in the intelligence community. It has damaged morale. The typical intelligence officer, for instance, feels like he is performing a difficult, patriotic task which requires great sacrifice on his part." Turner said that CIA officers "cannot help but feel that the country neither understands nor appreciates that sacrifice." Citing the agency's crucial intelligence work, Turner called for forbearance and understanding. He said, "In sum, it is not a perfect world. It is not an open world. It is a world in which we must balance idealism and realism in international affairs."[35]

Iran

As 1979 dawned Mohammad Reza Pahlavi, the Shah of Iran, continued to enjoy the enormous largess that the United States bestowed on one of its most important allies. Since 1953, when the CIA overthrew the democratically elected Prime Minister Mohammad Mosaddegh to place the shah on his Peacock Throne, Iran had received billions in U.S. military and development aid. Seeking intelligence on the Soviet Union, the CIA had deep ties with the shah's brutal secret police, SAVAK. The shah returned the favor, catering to the U.S. power elites. Iranian oil and Caspian caviar made a lot of friends in Washington.

The CIA had been filing thumbs-up reports on the shah for decades, but as an anti-Shah movement began to emerge in the mid-1970s, the agency finessed its position. A CIA classified memo that DCI George H. W. Bush hand carried to the White House in the summer of 1976 included two "Washington Merry-Go-Round" columns by influential journalists Jack Anderson and Les Whitten, which appeared to be the result of leaked CIA reports. One 1975 column cited a CIA psychological study of the shah that depicted an insecure leader emasculated by a cruel father, his Western puppet masters and his "feared impotence." According to the columnists, the CIA analysts predicted that the shah would overcompensate for his inferiority complex by pushing for higher global oil prices. The May 1976 column, entitled "Torture, Terror in Iran," depicted the weeklong American bicentennial extravaganza that the shah threw for 150 celebrities, including Elizabeth Taylor. The columnists contrasted the bash with "Iran's seamier side," an oppressive rule increasingly dominated by SAVAK, writing that "behind all the glitter, the Shah rules by torture and terror, which are the antithesis of the U.S. principles he pretends to honor." Anderson and Whitten wrote, "Intelligence reports claim that his authoritarian rule and imperial airs are alienating his people, that he is dangerously isolated and aloof."⁶

The shah's extravagant lifestyle, insensitive economic policies, and Western cant estranged the Iranian populace. The oil boom had ignited a shocking inflation, which worsened the lives of average people. There was widespread resentment against the tens of thousands of highly paid foreign technocrats who tended the wildly expensive American military equipment. A nascent religious movement began to coalesce in 1976, attracting a following among the conservative unskilled poor who had migrated to the cities.⁷

When President Jimmy Carter took office in 1977, the shah recognized the U.S. foreign policy focus on human rights could easily be coopted. The shah released a few hundred prisoners and let the Red Cross inspect the prisons. Carter fell for it. At a lavish state dinner on New Year's Eve 1977, the president toasted the shah, hailing his monarchy as "an island of stability in a sea of turmoil." If only.

An Islamic movement led by Ayatollah Ruhollah Musavi Khomeini had been rapidly growing. In the summer of 1978 there were riots in Iranian cities. In August CIA senior analysts sent a National Intelligence Estimate to Turner for his review. It predicted the shah would stay in power for another decade. Turner wrote, "Producing an intelligence estimate that the shah might not survive would have been seen as inviting that to happen." With street riots belying the analysts' soothing prediction, Turner wisely set the report aside. At a time when agency capacities were thin and covert officers were keeping their heads down, the CIA was ill prepared to assess the protest movement.⁸ "Almost all of us in the national security establishment had been to Iran under the shah," wrote Turner. "We had not noticed any instability, as we were treated royally, but limited where we could go and what we could see."⁹

The Iranian revolt accelerated with unprecedented speed. Black Friday, September 8, 1978, when the shah's security forces killed eighty-nine protestors in Tehran's Jaleh Square, proved to be pivotal. On January 16, 1979, the shah fled Tehran. Two weeks later Khomeini returned from exile to jubilant crowds of millions thronging the streets of Tehran. On February 11, 1979, the Iranian army, corrupt and coddled with U.S. military aid, collapsed. The same day, the Shah of Iran fell from power.¹⁰ Khomeini told his followers, "To achieve real independence, we have to remove all forms of American influence, whether economic, political, military or cultural."[11]

Thousands of Americans and other Western expats quickly fled the revolutionary Islamic theocracy. The U.S. embassy was reduced to a bare-bones operation. Four CIA officials manned the Tehran station. None of them had Iranian experience, or even a basic working knowledge of Farsi. But CIA operatives understood the import of the cable they received on October 21, 1979, notifying them that Carter had admitted the exiled Shah of Iran into the United States for medical treatment. Two weeks later, enraged Iranian students seized the U.S. embassy, grabbing fifty-three hostages. And with the hostages, the Iranians also captured the remainder of Carter's 444 days in office.[12] "We did not understand who Khomeini was, and the support his movement had," Turner later wrote. "As far as our failure to judge the shah's position more accurately, we were just plain asleep."[13]

Guidance and Counsel

Evans's work on the seventh floor continued unabated—roundelays of matters big and small. His minutes of an October 1979 staff meeting noted the "much-advertised coup in El Salvador" would "reportedly be consummated at 1100 this morning," and a reconnaissance flight over Cuba was cancelled due to weather.[14] A MAG meeting with Turner included the officers' briefing of their review of "Agency Policy and Practices Concerning Hiring or Retention of Persons Involved with Homosexuality or Cohabitation," as well as discussions of personnel policies, particularly relating to promotions and internal communications.[15] The redacted MAG homosexuality-cohabitation review concluded, "the Agency policy and practices are reasonable and are given to reasonable occasional review." The specific policies and practices were redacted.[16] Evans negotiated with his State Department counterpart about "the dissemination of sensitive political cables," and organizing a visit of eight university presidents, including the presidents of Tufts, Oregon State, Carnegie-Mellon, and Notre Dame, who were meeting with Turner at the CIA's Langley headquarters. The memo noted, "All have been cleared for and agreed to Secret briefings."[17] Evans did get occasional respites. At a lengthy (and tedious) March 1979 Executive Committee Meeting, Turner noted, "although Mr. Evans will not normally attend, he should be aware of the Committee activities," as well as suggest topics for the committee members to consider.[18] But most times, he was in the room. Evans received appreciation for his work. On January 19, 1977, as the inauguration of president-elect Carter neared, outgoing presidential adviser Douglas P. Bennett sent a letter from the White House, thanking Evans for his "guidance and counsel."[19]

Innumerable reports crossed Evans's desk. One report sent from the U.S. Missile Command in Redstone Arsenal, Alabama, documented "Remote Perturbation Techniques," under Project Grill Flame, which researched paranormal behavior using "an intellectual/mental process" to "perturb remote sensitive apparatus or equipment."[20] And then there were the internecine squabbles—especially about parking. There were long, testy memos debating the use of Denver boots on the cars of covert spooks who were scofflaw parking violators. How to enforce the agency's sacrosanct parking system without jeopardizing undercover officers?[21] Commuting was another subject of high-level attention. During one April 25, 1980, staff meeting, Evans recorded a lengthy discussion about the agency's response to the botched rescue attempt of the American hostages in Iran—then noted that carpools had increased 22 percent and the senior executives were considering a bike path along Route 123.

Dissident

Beyond her family and philanthropic activities, Jan King Evans continued her work in the Republican Party, which started in the northwest Washington precincts with Barry Goldwater's presidential campaign.[22] By 1972 she was serving on the Republican Party's national Rules Committee. Jan began efforts to elect Bush president in 1979, rallying her friends and organizing fundraisers. After cohosting a successful party with Woodland Drive neighbor, Pennsylvania Republican senator Hugh Scott, George and Barbara Bush wrote the Evanses thank-you notes for "all your hard work on making that reception such as success."[23] In a note to Jan's mother and stepfather, Karla and Eugene Harrison, George Bush thanked them for their support, and wrote, "I think the world of my great and admired friend Ben Evans."[24] On July 29, 1979, Barbara Bush sent her a note from the Bush compound in Kennebunkport, Maine, telling of their campaign travels: "George just returned from Alaska and I from Mass! Off to New Hampshire in the morning, but not together. It's a long hard fight, but I can see several giant steps forward to one backward."[25] By early 1980 Jan was one of the cochairmen of the District of Columbia Executive Committee for George Bush for President.[26] It was not Bush's year, as Ronald Reagan won forty-four primaries on his way to a nomination lock. Bush wrote Evans in late June, "It hurt to lose, but we did come a long way."[27]

In July 1980 Jan flew to the Republican National Convention in Detroit as a Bush delegate and member of the Platform Committee. She wanted to serve on the Human Resources Subcommittee to fight for the Equal Rights Amendment and abortion rights, but she was assigned to the Fiscal and Monetary Subcommittee. She thought the committee assignment was due to her service on numerous finance and development committees, as well as her personal dedication to thrift. She wrote, "My miserly reputation had extended further than I realized!"[28] The fifteen Fiscal and Monetary Subcommittee members were like-minded, unanimously concurring on a rock-solid Republican fiscal conservatism plank. Convention dealings were not always so copacetic. Jan's first skirmish came when she saw the platform stated the Republicans planned to "restaff" the intelligence branches, "particularly the C.I.A.," with "knowledgeable and dedicated" people. Lobbying her influential friends, she got the platform amended. "That's how you get things done," she said.[29]

When the ninety Platform Committee members met to review the Republican platform, Jan was one of only nine voting in support of the ERA. The platform also included a plank calling for a constitutional amendment to prohibit abortion. She argued the plank was not in the best interests of the party, as "we would alienate a large segment of potential Nov 4 Republican voters." Jan moved to delete the abortion section from the platform, "on grounds that it was a private matter and no place in the platform." Once again, she was in a distinct minority, as her idea was rejected by a voice vote.[30]

Recognizing that there was no environmental plank in the platform, Jan enlisted conservationist friends, including neighbor Russell Train, the administrator of the Environmental Protection Agency, to expeditiously draft an environmental plank. The draft included a poetic paragraph that recognized global interdependence and urged the United States to take the lead in international efforts to protect and conserve natural resources. With the document in hand, she deftly navigated the treacherous waters of Reagan-era Republicanism, and succeeded in getting the first environmental plank into the platform—albeit stripped of the poetic internationalist paragraph.

Because of her support of the ERA, Jan became a quiet member of the "Dissentient 9." The group had sent a letter asking Reagan, by then the Republican presidential nominee, to meet with them.[31] While Jan did not sign the letter, she was invited to a meeting with Reagan on the sixty-ninth floor of the Detroit Plaza, where sixteen dissident women gave him their perspectives about the ERA and abortion. "We were just the rebels," Jan said.[32] Sitting amongst the other disgruntled Republican women, Jan gave Reagan a piece of her mind. She said that the Republican Party had to accommodate differing viewpoints and had to "open and not close doors." She told Reagan that "if I were to get pregnant I didn't want anyone telling me I couldn't have an abortion—that I didn't believe in promiscuity or using abortion as a means of birth control, but said in our platform preamble that we believed in freedom of choice but then denied it in abortion." After their confrontation, the women were led down to a "lion's den" of journalists and photographers. Jan wrote about her convention experience, "I soon realized I was, as Sen. Bob Dole so aptly expressed it, for the first time in my life on the liberal fringe."[33]

Freelance Buccaneer

By the time Reagan was inaugurated, Carter's human rights initiatives had already been overcome by events. In 1979 U.S.-supported tyrants fell in Nicaragua, El Salvador, and Iran, triggering clandestine CIA counterinsurgency campaigns. The Soviet military support of the communist-leaning Afghanistan government prompted Carter to initiate a covert CIA assistance program to Islamic fundamentalist fighters—the mujahideen. A secret National Security Council memorandum sent to Evans in late 1979 "noted with concern" that elements in Pakistan were urging accommodation with the Soviets and their client communist government in Afghanistan. "Aside from the long-term problems this could cause us," the memo continued, "we are more immediately concerned that this could mean cutting off of even the limited support and safe-haven the Afghan rebels enjoy in Pakistan."[34] In 1979 the Carter administration authorized the CIA to support the Afghan fighters with a paltry $500,000 for psywar operations, cash, and some nonlethal equipment.[35] A year later, the CIA funneled more than $30 million to the jihadis.[36] When Reagan took office, the CIA's anti-Soviet mujahideen funding quickly jumped into the hundreds of millions annually. Over the next ten years, the agency's Operation Cyclone became the most expensive secret war in history.[37]

CIA covert action was back in vogue. The spooks were again unleashed, clandestine intervention was the order of the day, and the ghost of William J. Donovan stalked the corridors of Langley.[38] It was DCI William J. Casey's kind of action. Casey had served in the OSS before his fortune-making career on Wall Street. He segued to Washington posts, including chairman of the Securities and Exchange Commission, undersecretary of state for economic affairs, president of the U.S. Export-Import Bank, and a member of the president's Foreign Intelligence Advisory Board.[39] After serving as Reagan's campaign manager, Casey wanted to be the secretary of state, with director of central intelligence as the consolation prize. As rumpled as DCI Richard

Helms was polished, Casey was nonetheless equally brilliant. With his erudite gravitas and fierce iconoclasm, he had a distain for conventional wisdom, Congress, and the press. DDCI Admiral Bobby Ray Inman called Casey "a freelance buccaneer."[40]

When Casey arrived at the CIA in January 1981, he saw it as a hidebound organization. Casey quickly signed up John Bross, an Ivy League ex-OSS and CIA officer, as an "old-boy" consultant to help reorganize the agency. Evans agreed management needed reform and in July 1980 sent a memorandum to the DCI and DDCI, subject-lined "A Legacy." Evans wrote, "At the moment there is a real smorgasbord of diverse activity going on in the name of management," and called the internal management of covert actions programs "disorganized." He stated, "'Planning' is limping along in many sectors," and wrote, "discipline is lax because there is no senior official, other than yourselves, to anticipate problems or requirements and marshal the energies of various deputies and senior staffs." He urged the DCI and DDCI to reinstitute the position of Executive Director, who could "put some muscle into his job."[41]

Robert M. Gates, the CIA official who Evans had tapped for the Management Advisory Group many years before, had returned to the agency in late 1979. Gates described the CIA as "An Agency in middle age, bureaucratic, scarred by investigations and purges, having had six DCIs in eight years."[42] After serving briefly as director of the Office of Strategic Research's Strategic Evaluation Center, Gates was named as the Director of the DCI/DDCI Executive Staff in 1981, charged with sorting out "a front office in chaos," as he termed it.[43]

The CIA had recruited Gates out of Indiana University in 1966, when he was studying for his masters in Eastern European languages. First serving in the U.S. Air Force under CIA sponsorship, he rejoined the agency as an intelligence analyst. After earning a doctorate in Russian and Soviet history from Georgetown University in 1974, he left the agency to serve on the National Security Council staff.

As DCI/DDCI Executive Staff director, Gates was essentially serving as chief of staff for Casey and Inman. On September 23, 1981, Gates delivered a scathing assessment of the agency to his two bosses. He termed the CIA "very bureaucratic," which was "absolutely inimical to collecting information and producing the best possible analysis as well as the most effective covert operations." Gates blamed ineffective senior leadership for an agency "chock full of people simply awaiting retirement: some are only a year or two away and some are twenty-five years away, but there are far too many people playing it safe, proceeding cautiously, not antagonizing management, and certainly not broadcasting their horizons, especially as their own senior management makes it clear it is not career enhancing." Gates claimed the CIA had "advanced bureaucratic arteriosclerosis" and concluded, "CIA is slowly turning into the Department of Agriculture."[44]

However much buccaneer Casey agreed with Gates's fulminations, the call for institutional change was subsumed by the crises of the moment. Gates was soon gone from the Executive Secretary directorship, shifted to become the Director for Intelligence in January 1982. With Reagan and Casey both obsessed with the Soviet Union, the CIA's analysis and covert operations focused on the Eastern European Communist bloc. The Iron Curtain was beginning to corrode. In Poland the Solidarity trade union emerged in Gdansk in the summer of 1980. It was the Soviet bloc's first nongovernmental trade union, which morphed into a broad-based, nonviolent social movement opposed to communism. Solidarity eventually claimed a membership of 9.4 million Poles.

After more than a decade on the seventh floor, Evans remained in the thick of the action.[45] In February 1981 he sent a memo to DDCI Frank Carlucci about sensitive files assembled for Turner.[46] Given the chaos created by the Family Jewels, the CIA needed to gingerly handle their internal secrets. The "sensitive topic folders," which included documents relating to Iran, Afghanistan, congressional compliance, and whistleblowers, were placed in sealed envelopes, carrying a label that limited access to the DCI, DDCI, and Evans.[47] Another memo suggested Evans, who had good relations with senior staff and MAG officers, be assigned to organize topics and responses for the DCI to discuss with the CIA rank and file. Evans's senior staff meeting minutes continued to document the multitude of issues the CIA executives unceasingly managed.[48] After Casey became DCI, Evans had a new problem. Due to physical impediments and a constitutional guardedness, Casey was a notorious mumbler.[49] During meetings Evans had trouble understanding what his boss was saying. Tom Cormack, Evans's deputy, said about Casey, "He was the mumbler-in-chief. Bill Casey was not the most articulate of people."[50] Agency staffers joked that Casey was the only director of central intelligence who did not need a scrambler.[51]

The Highest Credit

By the time Casey became director in 1981, Evans had been serving as a CIA officer for more than twenty years. "Ben was anxious to retire," Jan said.[52] Ever the responsible officer, he wanted to wait until after the new DCI was confirmed and oriented. But in March 1979 Evans was already inquiring about his Civil Service annuity. The estimate calculated that based on his thirty-six years of military and agency service with his three highest years of salary averaging $47,500, Evans was going to receive a monthly pension of $2,858.[53] His projected date of retirement was May 1, 1981.[54]

A summary of Evans's CIA employment listed eleven areas of special competence, from policy and control management to strategic planning, public relations, and crisis management. He had served twelve consecutive years as Executive Secretary to seven successive DCIs and DDCIs under four different presidential administrations.[55] Evans had been carrying a heavy load for a long time.

His dedication did not go unrecognized. On April 30, 1981, Casey awarded Evans the CIA's Distinguished Intelligence Medal, a high honor given for outstanding service and performance. Prior recipients included Richard Helms, William Colby, James Jesus Angleton, and a host of other legendary spooks. The citation recognized Evans for his twenty-three years of CIA service that included "increasingly important operational and managerial positions, culminating in his assignment as Executive Secretary." The citation lauded his leadership skills and expansive expertise that were required to develop and maintain a "flawless system" of action management for the DCI and DDCI, as well as his diplomatic skills that facilitated effective liaison with the intelligence community, executive branch and the private sector. The citation concluded, "Mr. Evans' record of achievement upholds the finest traditions of the Federal service, reflecting the highest credit on himself and the Central Intelligence Agency."[56]

19

RETIREMENT

After decades of spy work, Benjamin C. Evans Jr. could at last live full time on his beloved farm. "When he retired, he was exhausted," Jan King Evans said.[1] Only fifty-seven years old, still slender with his West Point bearing, he was nonetheless careworn from his long service. He was looking forward to slowing down. "He really enjoyed retirement—it was bliss," Jan said. "He needed a place to just *breathe*."[2]

Evans reveled in his farm life. "Ben never liked the city; never liked where we lived," Jan said. "He thrived in nature and the out-of-doors." Mowing the fields on his John Deere tractor was his favorite pastime.[3] Self-contained after his professionally hermitic spook life, Evans was comfortable spending long, solitary hours working on the farm.

Once he retired, Evans kept remote from the Central Intelligence Agency, not even joining intelligence associations. "He thought he would like to teach," Jan said. He eventually taught an undergraduate course on the CIA and world politics at George Mason University. But after the sharp-edged work of Langley's seventh floor, he found academic life too tame. "He received the highest student evaluations," Jan said, "but he wasn't stimulated enough by the students. So he quit."

Wildest Dreams

Jan and Ben Evans were a handsome, accomplished couple, ready to enjoy the long autumn of their years. Their daughters were off on their own, after both graduating from college.[4] The Evanses were wealthy, courtesy of Jan's stewardship of her family's fortune, augmented by Evans's CIA compensation. In early 1983 the couple left on a two-month Pacific trip on the *Queen Elizabeth 2* luxury liner. Evans had become something of a homebody, so the trip was a departure in more than one way. "He had to travel when he was in the army—probably more than he wanted," Jan said.[5] The cruise appealed to Evans. Rather than moving from hotel to hotel, they had a home-base stateroom to travel internationally. Departing from Los Angeles in early February, the ship sailed to French Polynesia, the Cook Islands, New Zealand, Australia, New Guinea, Indonesia, Singapore, Thailand, China, Japan, and back through Hawaii to California. No longer a CIA officer who needed to be eternally watchful of security, Evans could travel with the abandon of a retiree.

The *Queen Elizabeth 2* docked in Singapore and Thailand, ports of call on Ben's covert round-the-world CIA trip in 1964. Then Japan, where they had chastely courted and spent their early years of marriage. On the ship they dined at a table for two, foregoing the social clatter of the captain's table for talk of their shared future. "Ben loved it. He had me all to himself," Jan said.[6]

Traveling for a week in the interior of communist China to see the major tourist sites was eye opening. The old cold warrior was bemused by his unexpected forays into the heart of what had been enemy territory only a few years before. "Ben said, 'I never thought in my wildest dreams that I'd be flying all over China in Russian-made planes,'" Jan remembered.[7]

Home Again

While introvert Evans was happy living on their Virginia farm, his wife found unrelenting country life to be socially stifling. "It was hard on me. I didn't want to be at the farm seven days a week," said Jan. "So after a while I would go into town and do all my ladies meetings, pick up the mail, meet friends. I couldn't be stuck out on the farm. All he wanted was me around."[8]

Jan continued her DC development work and invested in another Virginia hunt-country farm. After making a name for herself as a Republican feminist firebrand in 1980, she was asked to join the board of the Women's National Bank of Washington. Organized in 1977, the institution in 1986 changed its name to the Adams National Bank to honor of protofeminist Abigail Adams, wife of President John Adams.[9] The board position was the only paid job Jan held in her life—beside waiting tables for a few months at college, "to see what it was like," she said. The bank board was short-term employment, too. "I smelled the dead fish, so I got off," she said.[10] The Adams National Bank suffered a major default soon after.

Still active in the national Republican Party, Jan decided she wanted to be an ambassador. With their powerful Republican friends, who included Vice President George H. W. Bush, she figured she had the connections. New Zealand looked appealing. "It was a nice, small, friendly country. I spoke the language. I couldn't have made many mistakes," she laughed. But her husband nixed the idea. "Ben was supportive of everything I did, but he said, 'I cannot be the husband of the ambassador,'" Jan said, "He'd put up with me all those years, but he put his foot down."[11]

In August 1986 the family traveled to Oberusel, Germany, near Frankfurt.[12] They were there to visit Camp King, named after Jan's intelligence officer father, Colonel Charles B. King, who died in Normandy on June 1944. During World War II the camp was a notorious German interrogation center, whose officers the British later prosecuted in a war-crimes tribunal. After the war, the U.S. military repurposed the camp as an American field interrogation and intelligence center.[13] As part of the allied denazification effort, the camp housed important prisoners, including Reich Marshall Hermann Göring, commander of the German navy Grand Admiral Karl Doenitz, and the German-American propagandist Mildred Elizabeth Sisk, better known as Axis Sally.

The Latest Storm

That October Evans had a physical. His liver test was abnormal, but a change in diet seemed to clear up the problem. In December 1986 the couple went to a party. Later that evening Evans got sick. At first, they thought he had eaten some bad food, but his symptoms worsened. By January 1987 there was jaundice. And then he got weaker. In February Evans went to Johns Hopkins in an ambulance. Jan said, "They opened him up and everything was cancer and they closed him back up." It was malignant pancreatic cancer that had spread.

Evans was on morphine all that year, traveling to Georgetown University hospital for radiation treatment. Jan said, "He was in pain all the time." Louise Evans came home from New Zealand, where she had been visiting. Staying in a nearby cottage, she nursed her father, cleaning his incision and catheters, dispensing his medications, and driving him to treatments. "Loving each other unconditionally," she wrote, remembering him in his bed in the Groveton farmhouse with her orange cat lying beside him.[14] Karla Evans was living with her husband on a nearby farm. Wanting her father to have a grandchild, she got pregnant.[15] "I was glad he was able to be on the farm; to be with his two daughters," Jan said.[16]

Jan said about Ben's terminal illness: "This was the challenge of my life—especially since the relationship was always good. It was difficult to lose a husband. It was difficult being alive."[17] As her husband was dying, she determined he needed to be buried in Arlington National Cemetery. Given his military service, his ashes could be interred in Arlington's columbarium, but their daughter, Louise Evans Turner, was opposed to cremation. So once again Jan worked her contacts. Attending a party given by Barbara Bush, she asked her friend Meg Gregg for help getting her husband buried at Arlington. "I need to have him buried with my stepfather," Jan told Gregg. General Eugene Harrison, who died in June 1981, was buried in one of Arlington National Cemetery's best plots, on a hillside overlooking the Potomac River and Washington.[18] Gregg's husband, Donald Gregg, was serving as Vice President Bush's national security adviser. He called Jan that evening, explaining that only the president or secretary of the army could order the Arlington burial. He asked whether Bush should go up to President Ronald Reagan or down to Secretary of the Army John O. Marsh Jr. with the request. Reasoning that relations between Bush and Reagan were not the best, Jan told him, "Don't go up; go down."[19]

During Evans's final days, many friends visited him. They included his physician and close friend, Doctor Ed Richards, another temperamentally circumspect man. Richards would spend Wednesday afternoons visiting Evans, now confined to a hospital bed in the front parlor. Recognizing the doctor's footsteps on the porch, Evans would call, "Here comes my buddy; here comes my friend."[20] Corbin Davis had been his roommate at West Point. Davis said, "The last year when he was ill out on that farm, it was very difficult. He was suffering, both physically and emotionally."[21] Oscar Echevarria came often, sometimes bringing him Mapurite pills, an experimental antitumor herbal drug refined by Cuban exiles in Venezuela. One morning Evans told Echevarria the pills helped—he had eaten a good breakfast and "felt better."[22] Vice President Bush called.[23] Former DDCI Frank Carlucci sent a letter from the White House, where he was serving as Reagan's national security adviser. Carlucci wrote, "You always kept things running like a well oiled machine. You made us all look good. Always strong in the face of adversity, I have a feeling you're weathering this latest storm with your usual spirit."[24]

But Evans's decline continued. In the early stages, he could occasionally make short forays to Middleburg. Then a walk to the backyard pool was too far; then the bathroom. "He looked like death warmed over," Jan said. "I can't imagine a worse way to die." Eventually all Evans could eat was custard, wasting away as the disease took hold. He shrunk to under a hundred pounds. But the intelligence world could still occasionally stir him. Evans watched the Iran-Contra hearings wearing his West Point bathrobe with his now too-big class ring on his thumb. Karla was with him when Oliver North testified, giving Congress members a runaround that backfired on the administration. At one point during North's duplicitous testimony, Evans shouted at the television, "That's not true!"[25] He was stoic to the end. Jan recalled, "I said to him, 'Ben you never talk about your illness.' And he said, 'Jan, I keep thinking I'm going to get better.'"[26]

Evans died at his cherished farm on September 23, 1987. He was sixty-three years old.[27] When the hearse came to take him away, the funeral director had to ask a family member to retrieve their orange cat, which was outside sitting on the body bag. Louise wrote, "I thought that was a symbol of the loyalty my father inspired in those who were close to him." Evans's loved ones were left trying to make sense of his untimely passing. Jan said, "He was so sickly as a child, maybe he was just worn out." Louise thought the CIA was the cause. She said, "He got sucked up in to the CIA because he went to West Point and was in the Army and was smart. It probably killed him."[28] Karla reminisced, "Daddy had two qualities I really appreciated. He had a sense of humor that was really wonderful. And he knew how to be in the moment."[29]

Bells and Boots

On September 28, 1987, the Washington National Cathedral's Bourdon mourning bell began its somber tolling. On a warm early autumn day Ben Evans was being laid to rest. A huge crowd of friends and colleagues filed into the vast nave of Indiana limestone to honor his selfless service, courage, and visionary commitment to America's highest ideals. It was a unique gathering of the intelligence community, many of whom seldom congregated with one another.[30] Evans's West Point classmates walked down the center aisle as honorary pallbearers. The Boys Choir sang the old hymn, "Saint Anne," and the canon read Ecclesiastes 3:1–8:

> To everything there is a season, and a time to every purpose under the heaven:
> A time to be born, and a time to die; a time to plant, and a time to pluck up that which is planted;
> A time to kill, and a time to heal; a time to break down, and a time to build up;
> A time to weep, and a time to laugh; a time to mourn, and a time to dance;
> A time to cast away stones, and a time to gather stones together; a time to embrace, and a time to refrain from embracing;
> A time to get, and a time to lose; a time to keep, and a time to cast away;
> A time to rend, and a time to sew; a time to keep silence, and a time to

speak;
A time to love, and a time to hate; a time of war, and a time of peace.

There were more prayers and hymns and a homily by Reverend Canon Charles Martin. Friends and family spoke of Evans's many virtues. West Point classmate Major General Calvert Benedict read the Cadet Prayer that requested God's help to "keep ourselves physically strong, mentally awake and morally straight, that we may better maintain the honor of the Corps untarnished and unsullied."[31]

After the service, there was a ceremony at the Arlington National Cemetery, where Evans received full military honors. A soldier led a black, riderless horse with boots backward in the stirrups—the symbol of a fallen warrior. To the martial cadences of "Pershing's Own" United States Army Band, a platoon of tall, taut Old Guard soldiers escorted the funeral caisson to his Arlington gravesite. There on the hillside above the Potomac River, Evans was laid to rest. His grave marker read, "Duty, Honor, Family, Country."[32]

Image Gallery

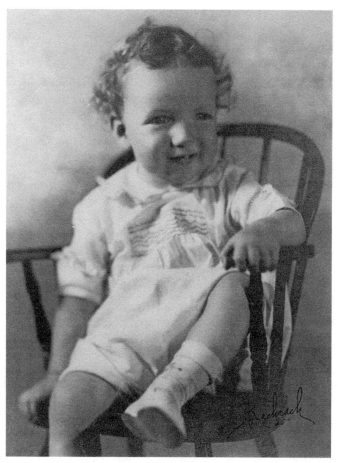

Benjamin C. Evans Jr. as a toddler.

Images courtesy Jan King Evans

Above and Opposite: Scenes from a Crawfordsville, Indiana, childhood, with brother Dan.

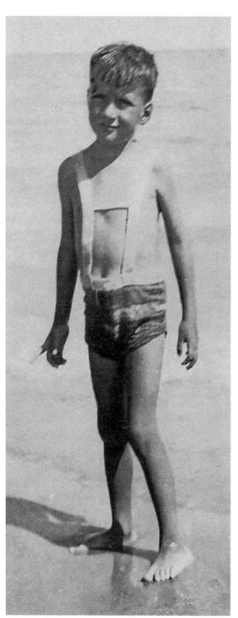

Opposite: *Ben at age five.* ***Above:*** *Ben and Dan at the beach in Florida.*

Ben and Dan Evans celebrate Christmas in Crawfordsville, 1935.

Ben Evans at Culver Military Academy.

Evans (at left in above photo) at the U.S. Military Academy.

Helping with earthquake relief in Fukui.

Evans, seen at the rear right, with General Douglas MacArthur at the Washington, DC, airport.

Flanked by their parents, Ben and Jan King Evans pose at their wedding reception at the Chevy Chase Club, Chevy Chase, Maryland.

Ben and Jan leaving their wedding reception.

Above: *Ben in Tampa, Florida with daughters Karla and Louise and in-laws Karla and Eugene Harrison.*
Left: *Skiing with Karla.*

Opposite, Above: (Left to right) Jan King Evans, Karla Harrison, Karla Evans, and Ben Evans greet Barbara Bush. **Opposite, Below:** Vice President George Bush talks with Ben Evans. Jan King Evans is behind the vice president. **Above:** Back home in Crawfordsville for fortieth high school reunion, class of 1942. Evans is fifth from left, third row.

Top: *At the farm with (from left to right) Karla, Ben, Louise, and Jan.* **Above:** *On vacation in Bermuda. (Left to right) Ben, Louise, Karla, Charles Griswold (son-in-law), and Jan.*

Ben and Jan.

Notes

Chapter 1

1. Jan King Evans U.S. diplomatic passport No. 18935, Jan King Evans archive.

Chapter 2

1. Benjamin Crabbs Evans Jr., "A Plain American," September 26, 1941, manuscript, Jan King Evans archive (hereafter cited as JKEA).

2. STATS Indiana, "Indiana City/Town Census Counts, 1900 to 2010," http://www.stats.indiana.edu/population/PopTotals/historic_counts_cities.asp.

3. James Insley Osborne and Theodore Gregory Gronert, *Wabash College: The First Hundred Years, 1832–1932* (Crawfordsville, IN: R. E. Banta, 1932), 22, 25. President George Stockton Burroughs wrote in his 1899 resignation letter, "The traditions of Wabash are, as you are aware, extremely conservative."

4. *Indianapolis Journal*, July 28, 1877. During the Bread or Blood labor unrest, Lew Wallace telegraphed his Montgomery Guards to hurry to Indianapolis: "the crisis has come here this afternoon. . . . Don't fail in this." The Montgomery Guard formed the core of the Wallace-led (and feared) Indiana Zouaves during the Civil War.

5. The Evans home was at 1405 East Main Street.

6. Daniel F. Evans, *It's All Relative, Part One* (Crawfordsville, IN: Indiana Printing Company, 1977), 4.

7. Richard Lyle Power, "The Hoosier as an American Folk-Type," *Indiana Magazine of History* 38 (June 1942): 107–22, and Phil Christman, "On Being Midwestern: The Burden of Normality," *The Hedgehog Review* 19 (Fall 2017).

8. Jan King Evans interview with the author, January 3, 2018.

9. Bina T. Sarver, diary manuscript, Daniel F. Evans Jr. archive (hereafter cited as Sarver diary). Bina T. Sarver and her husband Clifford began working as caretakers of Spring Ledge, the Evanses' estate in February 1919, and continued until 1937, when Clifford's health failed. Later to become a published poet and member of the Indianapolis Poet's Corner club, Sarver vividly chronicled the life of Spring Ledge and her times.

10. Sarver diary.

11. Crawfordsville Country Club, "Our History," https://crawfordsvilecountryclub.com/our-history/. Spring Ledge and the adjacent Crawford-

ville Country Club had been part of Lew Wallace's country home, "Water Babble," named after a winding spring-fed brook that hurried down to Sugar Creek. "The water fairly dances out of the earth, rushes over a bed of watercress . . . ripples down the hillside and creates music of its own, a laughing babble," Wallace wrote.

12. Letter from Daisy Stoddard to Benjamin Evans Jr., Christmas Time, 1947, Crawfordsville District Public Library, Genealogy Collection, Crawfordsville, IN.

13. Evans, *It's All Relative*, 60–62; "Crawfordsville: A Product Coming from Crawfordsville Has no Mean Birthplace," 1926 business directory, pp. 17, 31, Crawfordsville District Public Library, "Judge Howard Sommer Crawfordsville Recollections," oral history transcript, Crawfordsville District Public Library. Sommer, who began serving as an attorney for Evans, DeVore and Company in 1922, and was later chief counsel, remembered the firm in its heyday as having sixteen million dollars in five-year-termed mortgage loans on the books; "Soil Survey of Montgomery County, Indiana, Soil Conservation Service, August 1989, https://www.nrcs.usda.gov/Internet/FSE_MANUSCRIPTS/indiana/montgomeryIN1989/montgomeryIN1989.pdf.

14. *Crawfordsville Journal Review*, April 24, 1946.

15. Letter from Daisy Stoddard to Benjamin Evans Jr.

16. "A Planting Plan for the Estate of Frank C. Evans," Daniel F. Evans, Jr. archive; William H. Tishler, ed., *Midwestern Landscape Architecture* (Urbana: University of Illinois Press, 2000), 117–41; Robert Grese, *Jens Jensen: Maker of Natural Parks and Gardens* (Baltimore: John Hopkins Press, 1992), 199–212. Prior to his Spring Ledge design work, Jensen had made a name for himself in Indiana with his designs for auto industrialists James A. Allison (1911), Frank H. Wheeler (1912), and U.S. vice president Charles W. Fairbanks (1913). Jens Jensen Legacy Project, "Biography," http://www.jensjensen.org/drupal/?q=biography; The Cultural Landscape Foundation, "Jens Jensen," https://tclf.org/pioneer/jens-jensen; The Cultural Landscape Foundation, "Allison Mansion," https://tclf.org/allison-mansion. Soon after purchasing the land, Frank Evans contracted with Jensen to develop plans for Spring Ledge. Through his work as a Chicago park superintendent and landscape architect, Jensen was already a leader of the conservation-minded Prairie School, which endeavored to rigorously redesign and sculpt environments into romantic "natural" settings of indigenous plants and trees that sustained native fauna. Frank Evans was also buying social prestige: Jensen had prepared plans for

Allison, whose 64-acre Riverdale estate was situated on a bluff above Indianapolis's Crooked Creek. Clive Aslet, *The American Country House* (New Haven: Yale University Press, 1990). The early twentieth century was the Country Place Era, the period when industrialists and businessmen began to develop country estates to escape the crowded, commerce-blighted cities. Biltmore, the Vanderbilts' grand North Carolina estate built in the 1880s, is considered the first of its kind. Popularized in the early twentieth century by publications such as *Country Life in America*, lesser examples soon began popping up across the country. A notable early Indianapolis example was Oldfields (later known as the Lilly House and Gardens), which was built around 1910 near Crown Hill Cemetery. The estate included a naturalized garden designed by Percival Gallagher of the Olmstead Brothers Firm.

17. "Spring Ledge, A Bird Paradise Near Crawfordsville, Where Man's Kindness Has Been Fully Appreciated," *Indianapolis News*, March 6, 1920.

18. The winter of 1930 brought frigid weather as low as forty-five degrees below zero, then later freak rains that flooded parts of Indiana and Illinois, followed by a record blizzard. The spring was unseasonably hot and dry, the precursor to a disastrous drought and heat wave that wracked the prairie states.

19. John L. Stover, "The Farmers' Holiday Association Strike, August 1932," *Agricultural History* 39 (October 1965): 196–203; John L. Stover, *Cornbelt Rebellion: The Farmers' Holiday Association* (Urbana and London: University of Illinois Press, 1965). Stover indicated that 6 percent of farms in Iowa and the two Dakotas changed ownership in 1932 through bankruptcy or foreclosure, rising to 8 percent the following year. On 1920s agricultural commodity and land price declines, especially in Indiana, see Dean Albertson, *Roosevelt's Farmer: Claude R. Wickard in the New Deal* (New York: Columbia University Press, 1961), 32–33; Purdue University agricultural historian Fred Whitford interview with the author, November 9, 2017.

20. "How Crawfordsville and Nation May Join War Against Destitution," *Crawfordsville Journal Review*, September 12, 1932; Alissa C. Wetzel, "New Deal Photographs of the Hoosier State: Farm Tenancy, the Great Depression, and the Young Girl Who Lived through It All," *Indiana Magazine of History* 109 (September 1, 2013): 262, https://scholarworks.iu.edu/journals/index.php/imh/article/view/19950.

21. Evans, *It's All Relative*, 62; Sommer references the logistics of Evans, DeVore and Company foreclosures in his oral history transcript.

22. Stover, "The Farmers' Holiday Association Strike."

23. Stover, *Cornbelt Rebellion*, 90.

24. *Crawfordsville Journal Review*, September 19, 1932.

25. Ibid., August 6, 1932.

26. Ibid., August 15, 1932.

27. Ibid., August 13, 1932.

28. Evans, *It's All Relative*, 61.

29. Sarver diary. The early 1930s brought hard times, money was in short supply, agricultural commodity prices continued to drop, farmers left thousands of acres unplanted, and hog prices plummeted. In mid-February 1933, Sarver noted, "Mr. Evans came out Tues p.m. and told us he would have to cut our wages by 150 dollars on the year, beginning Mar. 1." For those who had money, there were bargains to be had. A few days later, she noted, "Mr. Evans bought the Dave Gardner place." Evans, *It's All Relative*, 76. Frank Evans bought the sixty-acre (probably foreclosed) farm for five dollars an acre from an insurance company.

30. Thomas L. Purvis, ed., "Frazier-Lemke Farm Bankruptcy Act," *A Dictionary of American History* (Malden and Oxford: Blackwell Publishers, 1997), http://www.blackwellreference.com/public/tocnode?id=g9781577180999_chunk_g97815771809998_ss1-175. The courts had a say. In May 1935 the U.S. Supreme Court decision on *Louisville Joint Stock Land Bank v. Radford* ruled the Frazier–Lemke act was unconstitutional because it deprived secured creditors of their property rights, violating the Fifth Amendment. Evans, DeVore had a short reprieve. Congress quickly passed a revised Frazier–Lemke act, naming it the Farm Mortgage Moratorium Act, which limited the moratorium to three years. The act also gave secured creditors the right to a forced public sale, though farmers could redeem their farms by matching the sale price. This time the Supreme Court upheld the bankruptcy law.

31. In August 1932 there were massive strikes protesting wage cuts in the southern Illinois coalfields. After sheriff deputies fired into a crowd of picketers, killing one and wounding seven, there was a march of 25,000 to 30,000 miners. By September the governor called up the Illinois National Guard and imposed martial law. *Crawfordsville Journal Review*, August 22, September 21, 1932.

32. Harvey Klehr, *The Heyday of American Communism: The Depression Decade* (New York: Basic Books, 1984), 3–5.

33. James H. Madison, *Hoosiers: A New History of Indiana* (Indianapolis and Bloomington: Indiana Historical Society and Indiana University Press, 2016), x.

34. Evans, *It's All Relative*, 61.

35. Wetzel, "New Deal Photographs of the Hoosier State," 263, cites a February 4, 1938 *Indianapolis Times* article, "Farm Prices in State Best in Eight Years." The New Deal provided some labor for Frank Evans's projects. In November 1935, Bina Sarver noted that WPA workers were helping with the Scout camp. The next summer she wrote that "CCC boys" were working on soil erosion projects at two of the Evanses' farms.

36. Evans, *It's All Relative*, 62.

37. Ibid., 157, 167; King Evans interview, January 3, 2018.

38. Julia S. Evans memoir, January 2003, manuscript, JKEA.

39. Evans, *It's All Relative*, 197–221; King Evans interview, January 3, 2018.

40. Troop 9 Boy Scouts of America, Indianapolis, Indiana, http://www.troop9bsa.org/. The Boy Scouts of America incorporated on the East Coast in 1910, the same year "Chief" Francis Oliver Belzer founded Troop 9 in Indianapolis as one of the nation's first troops, David L. Eby, "America's Oldest Boy Scout Camps," http://scoutcamp.org/oldestcamps.asp. Belzer organized the 130-acre Camp Chank-Tun-Un-Gi along Indianapolis's Fall Creek. Camp Chank-Tun-Un-Gi, meaning "loud, happy place," was one of America's earliest organized Boy Scout campgrounds, Evans, *It's All Relative*, 77. Frank Evans donated "the Gardner Place" to the Boy Scouts in 1934. It eventually became Camp Rotary.

41. Martin Dedman, "Baden-Powell, Militarism, and the 'Invisible Contributors' to the Boy Scout Scheme, 1904–1920," *Twentieth Century British History* 4, no. 3 (January 1, 1993): 201–23, https://doi.org/10.1093/tcbh/4.3.201.

42. Frederick Rohm, "Eagle Scouts and Servant Leadership," *Servant Leadership: Theory & Practice* 1, no. 1 (August 2014): 68–90, http://www.sltpjournal.org/uploads/2/6/3/9/26394582/7_rohm_-_print_v1_i1_2.pdf.

43. Benjamin C. Evans Jr. obituary, *Crawfordsville Journal Review*, September 23, 1987; Oratorical contest award: King Evans interview, September 21, 2017. Ben's older brother, Daniel F. Evans, also won the state award. Trophy in Daniel F. Evans Jr. archive.

Chapter 3

1. Robert B. D. Hartman, "CMA History," Culver Academies, https://alumni.culver.org/page.aspx?pid=436.

2. "Summer Cavalry Camp," booklet (Culver, IN: Culver Military Academy, 1941), 7.

3. The *Culver Vedette*, July 27, 1935, lists Benjamin C. Evans of Crawfordsville visiting on Woodcrafter Father's Day.

4. Robert B. D. Hartman, *Pass in Review: Culver, A Century in the Making* (Culver, IN: Culver Educational Foundation, 1993), 34.

5. Hartman, *Pass in Review*, 9, and Hartman, "CMA History."

6. Robert B. D. Hartman, *The Grand Parade, Volume One* (Culver, IN: The Culver Centennial Series, 1994), 43.

7. Hartman, *Grand Parade*, 37–43, and Paul Musgrave, "A Primitive Method of Enforcing the Law: Vigilantism as a Response to Bank Crimes in Indiana, 1925–1933," *Indiana Magazine of History* 102 (September 2006): 187.

8. Hartman, *Pass in Review*, 15.

9. "Summer Cavalry Camp," 53, and "Hours and Earnings in the United States, 1932-40" (Washington, DC: U.S. Government Printing Office, 1942), https://fraser.stlouisfed.org/files/docs/publications/bls/he_bls_1942.pdf.

10. "Summer Cavalry Camp," 13.

11. Gignilliat proved to be a promotional genius. In the spring of 1897 the recently organized Culver Black Horse Troop served as Indiana governor James Mount's honor guard at the massive Grand Army of the Republic Encampment in Richmond, Indiana. At Gignilliat's invitation, the governor and his staff were soon at the Culver graduation, reviewing the Corps of Cadets. Mount was the first of many powerful figures to enhance Culver's image.

12. L. R. Gignilliat, *Arms and the Boy: Military Training in Schools and Colleges; Its Value in Peace and Its Importance in War with Many Practical Suggestions for the Course of Training and with Brief Descriptions of the Most Successful Systems Now in Operation* (New York: Bobbs-Merrill, 1916), and John A. Coulter II, Cadets on Campus: History of Military Schools of the United States (Lubbock: Texas A&M University Press, 2017).

13. Hartman, *Pass in Review*, 26.

14. "Summer Cavalry Camp," 28–29.

15. Hartman, *Grand Parade*, 21–24.

16. Jeff Kenney, "Culver's Cuban Connection," Culver Academies History Facebook Page, April 5, 2016, https://www.facebook.com/groups/CulverAcademyAlumni78andThereabouts/permalink/10153772520608557/.

17. Jeff Kenney, "The Crown Prince of Siam at the Forefront of Culver's Asian History."

18. Benjamin Crabbs Evans Jr., "A Plain American," September 26, 1941, manuscript, Jan King Evans archive (hereafter cited as JKEA).

19. "Summer Cavalry Camp," 49. Evans's Troop B also included a young trooper from Dayton named Jonathan Winters, who later found fame as a madcap comedian.

20. *The Athenian* (Crawfordsville: Crawfordsville High School, 1942), 13, 54–55, 69.

22. Oratorical prize noted in "Ben Evans Will Enter Academy," *Crawfordsville Journal Review* [?], undated; "B.C. Evans, Jr. will go to West Point July 1," undated and unidentified clippings, JKEA.

23. Evans, "Plain American."

Chapter 4

1. Theodore J. Crackel, *West Point: A Bicentennial History* (Lawrence: University Press of Kansas, 2002), 208. President Franklin Roosevelt ordered the West Point course to be abbreviated to three years on October 1, 1942.

2. Clifford J. Rogers, Ty Seidule, and Steve R. Waddell, *The West Point History of World War II*, vol. 1 (New York: Simon and Schuster, 2015), 290.

3. Anne Kazzel-Wilcox and P. J. Wilcox, *West Point '41: The Class That Went to War and Shaped America* (Lebanon, NH: ForeEdge, 2014), ix–21; Crackel, *West Point*, 201–10; Stephen E. Ambrose, *Duty, Honor, Country: A History of West Point* (Baltimore: Johns Hopkins Press, 1966), 295–99; and Lance Betros, *Carved from Granite: West Point since 1902* (College Station: Texas A&M, 2012), 127–30, 223–24.

4. "Certificate for Accredited College, University, or Technological School" application, West Point archive, indicated Ben Evans graduated from high school eighth out of seventy-six boys. The male and female students were tabulated separately. For the mention of Evans's riding team, see "Benjamin Crabbs Evans, Jr.," https://www.westpointaog.org/memorialarticle?id=ec701e37-93a4-4d9f-a5e6-057072412deb.

5. "Dan Evans Went to Abbott Hall," *The Bachelor*, January 14, 1944. The Wabash College newspaper article stated, "As a speaker, Dan was rated one of the best college speakers in the nation," indicating he won numerous oratorical contests, and finished second in the National Oratorical Contest held at Northwestern University. The article stated Dan took navy courses while at Wabash, with the intent of entering Midshipman School.

6. "Certificate for Accredited College, University, or Technological School."

7. Candidate Russell Willis gave the opening address at the massive political gathering at the southern Indiana farm of Homer E. Capehart, who served as U.S Senator from 1945 to 1962. Historians consider the Cornfield Confer-

ence to be the momentous beginning of Indiana's obdurate support for Republican conservative policies. See, William B. Pickett, "The Capehart Cornfield Conference and the Election of 1938: Homer E. Capehart's Entry into Politics," *Indiana Magazine of History* 73 (December 1977): 251–75, https://scholar works.iu.edu/journals/index.php/imh/article/view/10041/13794.

8. James T. Patterson, *Mr. Republican: A Biography of Robert A. Taft* (Boston, Houghton Mifflin, 1972), 242–46; "Indiana Senator Raymond E. Willis Speaking against the Lend-Lease Bill," Sound Recording 200.36, National Archives at College Park, College Park, MD, February 24, 1941, https://www.docsteach.org/documents/document/senator-willis-speaking-against-lendlease-bill. In 1946 the Indiana Republican "palace guard" pulled the rug from under the incumbent Willis, giving the Senate nomination to William Jenner, former Republican state chairman, who went on to serve until 1959, "M. Clifford Townsend Is Demo Choice For Senator," *Post-Democrat* 27, no. 1 (June 28, 1946), https://newspapers.library.in.gov/cgi-bin/indiana?a=d&d=BALLM PD19460628-01.1.1. In the early 1950s Jenner was a staunch supporter of Senator Joseph McCarthy's anticommunist campaigns. Arthur Herman, *Joseph McCarthy: Reexamining the Life and Legacy* (New York: Free Press, 2000), 49, 55, 226, 290, 304–5, 311.

9. Tully C. Shaw to Jan King Evans, March 3, 2003, letter, in Jan King Evans archive (hereafter cited as JKEA). Shaw wrote: "I am pleased to say his Uncle Noble, my father, helped him get the appointment with the help of several Washington friends." Noble R. Shaw married into the Crabbs family (the "C" in Benjamin C. Evans's name) and joined the family's grain business, the Crabbs, Reynolds, Taylor Company, a successful seed distributor and grain elevator company. Both the Shaw and Evans families had a strong connection to Wabash College. Shaw graduated in 1919. Shaw was active in the Indiana Republican Party, holding several Indiana state and Republican positions, including being the Republican chairman of Montgomery County. Daniel F. Evans Jr., e-mail to author, January 18, 2018. Family lore also indicates Shaw was friends with Hoosier political heavyweight Will H. Hays, who also attended Wabash College. Jan King Evans interview with the author, January 17. 2018. Hays served as President Warren Harding's campaign manager, postmaster general, and as the chairman of the Republican National Committee. As the powerful head of the Motion Pictures Producers and Distributors of America from 1922 to 1945, Hays was the architect of the film-censuring standards, the Hays Code.

10. Family lore says Ben Evans first tried to get into Annapolis but was rejected because the physical revealed scoliosis had hitched one of his hips two inches higher than the other. Family members indicated that Evans then "learned how to stand" and passed the West Point physical. King Evans interviews, July 17–19, 2017 and Karla Evans interview with the author, July 18, 2017. A West Point photo of Evans showed that even when he stood with military bearing, his left shoulder was substantially higher than his right, indicating scoliosis. Ben's daughter, Louise, later wrote that when her father wore a swimsuit, she could see the substantial scoliosis, which she attributed to his childhood spinal meningitis. Louise Evans, "Remembrances of my father," in Oscar Echevarria, ed., *Benjamin C. Evans, Jr.: In Memory and Recognition* (Miami: Privately printed, 2014), 11. However, on his application to West Point, Benjamin Evans Jr. indicated that he had not previously applied to either Annapolis or West Point. "Certificate of Academic Work for Benjamin C. Evans, Jr.," United States Military Academy archive.

11. Betros, *Carved from Granite*, 224.

12. Corbin Davis interview with the author, September 28, 2017. The class of 1943 had only twenty-eight days away from West Point in the three years of its training.

13. John P. Lovell, *Neither Athens Nor Sparta? The American Service Academies in Transition* (Bloomington: Indiana University Press, 1979), 11, quoted in Crackel, *West Point*, 202.

14. "Certificate of Academic Work for Benjamin C. Evans Jr.," United States Military Academy archive; The mention of "goat" may be found in "Benjamin Crabbs Evans, Jr., 1946," West Point Association of Graduates, https://www.westpointaog.org/memorial-article?id=ec701e37-93a4-4d9f-a5e6-057072412deb.

15. Crackel, *West Point*, 215. West Point's football success continued through the 1940s. From 1944 through 1950, the army team won seventy games and only lost three. But in 1951 it was revealed that many of the football players had engaged in widespread cheating, a clear violation of the academy's honor code. After an inquiry, much of the team was dismissed from the service, and West Point's football fortunes plummeted.

16. "The Fields of Friendly Strife," The Vetruvian Man blog, July 20, 2011, https://www.thevitruvianman.org/the-fields-of-friendly-strife/. MacArthur's verse was also emblazoned above the entrance to the Cadet Gymnasium as far back as 1942. William H. Baumer, Jr., *West Point: Moulder of Men* (New York:

D. Appleton-Century Company, 1942), 196.

17. "Athletic and Activity Record for Benjamin C. Evans Jr.," United States Military Academy archive. For the mention of Evans's riding team, see "Benjamin Crabbs Evans, Jr."

18. Davis interview, September 28, 2017.

19. "Benjamin Crabbs Evans, Jr."

20. Bruce, Kauffmann, "The United States Military Academy at West Point," Bruce's History Lessons, March 14, 2012, https://historylessons.net/the-united-states-military-academy-at-west-point.

21. "Individual Delinquency Record, B. C. Evans," demerit notation May 21, 1944, U.S. Military Academy archive. Family archives includes a photo of a black cat sleeping on a steam grate in the West Point cadet barracks courtyard, photo, JKEA.

22. "Levy (DE-162)," Dictionary of American Naval Fighting Ships, Naval History Heritage Command, https://www.history.navy.mil/research/histories/ship-histories/danfs/l/levy.html; "USS *Levy* (DE-162), 1943-1974," Online Library of Selected Images, Naval Historical Center, https://www.ibiblio.org/hyperwar/OnlineLibrary/photos/sh-usn/usnsh-l/de162.htm; "USS Levy (DE 162)," Destroyer Escort Photo Archive, Navsource, http://www.navsource.org/archives/06/162.htm.

23. "United States Military Academy records for Benjamin C. Evans Jr.," U.S. Military Academy archive. Records indicate Evans was on sick leave from June 11, 1945 to July 13, 1945. King Evans interview, January 17, 2018; Betros, *Carved from Granite*, 225.

24. "Athletic and Activity Record for Benjamin C. Evans Jr., "United States Military Academy archive. For Ben Evans in choir, see Robert Channon, "Memories of Ben Evans and Roommates during Plebe Year." Manuscript in JKEA; "Benjamin Crabbs Evans, Jr.," https://www.westpointaog.org/memorial-article?id=ec701e37-93a4-4d9f-a5e6-057072412deb.

25. Davis interview, September 28, 2017.

26. Margaret Gresham Livingston interview with the author, January 22, 2018.

27. "A Glossary of West Point Slang," Combat, http://www.combat.ws/S4/MILTERMS/WP0SLANG.HTM.

28. Crackel, *West Point*, 105–6.

29. Alan Taylor, "Remembering Dresden: 70 Years After the Firebombing," *The Atlantic*, February 12, 2015, https://www.theatlantic.com/photo/2015/02/remembering-dresden-70-years-after-the-firebombing/385445/.

30. Kurt Vonnegut Jr., *Slaughterhouse-Five; or, The Children's Crusade* (New York: Delacorte Press, 1969).

31. Harry S. Truman, "The President's News Conference on V-E Day, May 8, 1945," Online by Gerhard Peters and John T. Woolley, *The American Presidency Project*, http://www.presidency.ucsb.edu/ws/?pid=12248.

32. "USS Levy (DE-162)."

33. Dan Evans witnessed history: The *Levy* was the site of the first surrender of an overseas Japanese post. Japanese Captain Masanori Shiga, commander of the forces on Mili Atoll in the Marshall Islands surrendered to U.S. Captain H. B. Grow on board the USS Levy, which later hosted similar surrender ceremonies at Jaluit Atoll and Wake Island. "*USS Levy (DE-162)*"; "First Japanese Surrender on Board USS Levy DE 162," Destroyer Escort Sailors Association, https://www.desausa.org/Stories/uss_levy_japanese_surrender.htm; Photo from the Destroyer Escort Sailors Association included Daniel F. Evans saluting Captain Shiga boarding the *Levy*, https://www.desausa.org/Stories/japanese_board_levy.htm.

34. Cadet Service Record for Benjamin C. Evans Jr., U.S. Military Academy archive. Only 875 cadets graduated out of the incoming plebe class of more than 1,200. While Evans's rank was not stellar, he graduated higher than the sons of the high-echelon officers, including General George Patton's son, who also attended West Point during the war years. Davis interview, September 28, 2017. Davis said, "The pressure there was exhausting. We were physically and mentally spent by graduation."

35. Benjamin Crabbs Evans Jr. Discharge Report, National Personnel Records Center, Saint Louis, MO.

36. "Charles B. King, 1928," West Point Association of Graduates, https://www.westpointaog.org/memorial-article?id=c02efebb-ed78-4754-b5db-ffbdd317f0c7; "The OCS Story," pamphlet (Headquarters, Department of the Army, October 1969), p. 3, http://www.benning.army.mil/Library/content/Virtual/OCS/OCSStory_DAPam601-1_October1969.pdf; "The Passing Parade," OCS Class No. 47-5 (Columbus, GA: Columbus Office Supply Co.), http://www.benning.army.mil/library/content/Virtual/OCS/Yearbooks/OCS_1940s/OCS_Class_47-5.pdf. The West Point officers who developed the training programs were colonels R. R. Coursey and F. A. Todd Jr. and Major Charles B. King. King was the father of Jan King, later to marry Ben Evans Jr.

37. Livingston interview, January 22, 2018.

38. According to Evans family lore, the racial climate in Alabama discom-

fited Ben, who felt the Gresham family had an expectation that he would settle in Birmingham with Margaret after his five-year military obligation was satisfied. Recognizing the disjuncture, he and Margaret mutually decided to go their own ways some months later, when he was shipping out to Japan. King Evans interview January 3, 2018, and Livingston interview January 22, 2018.

Chapter 5

1. Ben Evans Jr. to "Dearest Folks," July 1, 1948, letter in Jan King Evans archive (hereafter cited as JKEA).

2. Stephen Buono, "Commission and Omission of History in Occupied Japan (1945–1949)," *Binghamton Journal of History* (Fall 2011), https://www.binghamton.edu/history/resources/journal-of-history/stephen-buono.html.

3. "Significant Earthquake," National Oceanic and Atmospheric Administration's National Centers for Environmental Information, https://www.ngdc.noaa.gov/nndc/struts/results?eq_0=3884&t=101650&s=13&d=22,26,11,12&nd=display.

4. "Fukui, Surrounding Towns Destroyed," *Indianapolis Star*, June 29, 1948.

5. Telegram from Dad and Mother to Lieutenant Ben C. Evans, June 29, 1948, JKEA.

6. Ben Evans, Jr. to "Dearest Folks," July 5, 1948, ibid.

7. "Earthquake, fires take severe toll in western Japan," *New York Times*, June 29, 1948; "Significant Earthquake," National Oceanic and Atmospheric Administration's National Centers for Environmental Information, https://www.ngdc.noaa.gov/nndc/struts/results?eq_0=3884&t=101650&s=13&d=22,26,11,12&nd=display.

8. "Japan, Worse than B-29s," *Time,* July 12, 1948; Ben Evans Jr. to "Dearest Folks," July 1, 1948, JKEA.

9. John W. Dower, *Embracing Defeat: Japan in the Wake of World War II* (New York: W. W. Norton, 1999), 43–45; Kenneth B. Pyle, *The Making of Modern Japan*, (Lexington, MA: Heath, 1996), 207–26; Peter Frost, "The Allied Occupation of Japan," Japan Society, https://web.archive.org/web/20161004053655/http://aboutjapan.japansociety.org/the_allied_occupation_of_japan; "Political and Economic Changes during the American Occupation of Japan," Columbia University, http://afe.easia.columbia.edu/special/japan_1900_occupation.htm.

10. Dower, *Embracing Defeat*, 61–64; Theodore Cohen, *Remaking Japan: The American Occupation as New Deal* (New York: Free Press, 1987), 3–4.

11. Cohen, *Remaking Japan*, 7, 100.

12. Ibid., 8–13, 57. MacArthur reported to the Joint Chiefs of Staff. A September 1945 memo that was signed by President Harry Truman laid out MacArthur's supreme powers during the occupation: "Our relations with the Japanese do not rest on a contractual basis, but on unconditional surrender. Since your authority is supreme, you will not entertain any questions from the Japanese as to its scope."

13. Dower, *Embracing Defeat*, 23.

14. Cohen, *Remaking Japan*, 8; Dower, *Embracing Defeat*, 73, 573n. The culminating document that provided occupation agenda guidance to SCAP was the secret Joint Chiefs of Staff directive: "Basic Initial Post Surrender Directive to Supreme Commander for the Allied Powers for the Occupation and Control of Japan (JCS1380/15)," http://www.ndl.go.jp/constitution/e/shiryo/01/036/036tx.html.

15. Cohen, *Remaking Japan*, 14–48; Akito Okada, *Education Policy and Equal Opportunity in Japan* (New York: Berghahn Books, 2011), 33.

16. The New Education doctrines were promulgated through the *Report of the United States Education Mission to Japan,* published in March. 1946. Civil Information and Education team officers termed it "the bible." In March 1947 two pieces of Japanese legislation, *The School Education Law* and *The Fundamental Law of Education* codified the "democratizing" doctrine. William Nimmo, ed., *The Occupation of Japan: The Grass Roots* (Norfolk, VA: General MacArthur Foundation, 1991), 49, 50; Marcus B. Jansen, *The Making of Modern Japan* (Cambridge MA: Belknap Press, 2000), 222–23.

17. Lane Earns, "'Dancing People are Happy People:' Square Dancing and Democracy in Occupied Japan," Square Dance History Project, https://squaredancehistory.org/items/show/219.

18. *Education in the New Japan* (Tokyo: General Headquarters, Supreme Commander for the Allied Powers, Civil Information and Education Section, Education Division, 1948).

19. Dower, *Embracing Defeat*, 248. Nimmo, ed., *Occupation of Japan*, 45–92. These symposium proceedings included papers by members of the Civil Information and Education teams working on the prefecture level, as was Lieutenant Ben Evans.

20. Dower, *Embracing Defeat*, 247–48; Eiji Takemae, *Allied Occupation of Japan* (New York: Continuum, 2003), 362; Stephen Buono, "Commission and Omission of History in Occupied Japan (1945–1949)," https://www.binghamton.edu/history/resources/journal-of-history/stephen-buono.html.

21. Dower, *Embracing Defeat*, 269.
22. Ibid., 268–71; Nimmo, ed., *Occupation of Japan*, 47; Cohen, *Remaking Japan*, 54.
23. Cohen, *Remaking Japan*, 191.
24. Jansen, *Making of Modern Japan*, 223–26; Cohen, *Remaking Japan*, 449–53; Dower, *Embracing Defeat*, 271–73.
25. Ben Evans Jr. to "Dearest Folks," July 11, 1948, JKEA.
26. Ibid.
27. Jan King Evans, "Jan's story, beginning of Ben Evans romance," 2006, manuscript, JKEA; "Eugene L. Harrison, 1923," West Point Association of Graduates, https://www.westpointaog.org/memorial-article?id=11f621dc-c07f-4e93-8bc1-3db969a844f0.
28. King Evans, "Jan's story"; "Earthquake, fires take severe toll in western Japan," *New York Times*, June 29, 1948, confirmed the relief train.
29. Ben Evans Jr. to "Dearest Folks," July 1, 1948, JKEA.
30. King Evans interview, December 12, 2017.
31. "Earthquake, fires take severe toll in western Japan"; "Significant Earthquake," National Oceanic and Atmospheric Administration's National Centers for Environmental Information, https://www.ngdc.noaa.gov/nndc/struts/results?eq_0=3884&t=101650&s=13&d=22,26,13,12&nd=display.

Chapter 6

1. Jan King Evans, "Jan's story, beginning of Ben Evans romance," 2006, manuscript, Jan King Evans archive (hereafter cited as JKEA).
2. Vista K. McCroskey, "San Augustine, TX (San Augustine County)," *Handbook of Texas Online*, https://tshaonline.org/handbook/online/articles/hgs01; "Eugene L. Harrison, 1923," West Point Association of Graduates, https://www.westpointaog.org/memorial-article?id=11f621dc-c07f-4e93-8bc1-3db969a844f0.
3. Bob Seals, "U.S. Army Captures World Polo Title: Polo and the United States Army Officer Corps during the Interwar Period," Military History Online, December 29, 2013, http://www.militaryhistoryonline.com/20thcentury/articles/poloinusarmy.aspx; Horace A. Laffaye, *Polo in the United States: A History* (Jefferson, NC: McFarland and Company, 2011), 175–79.
4. Charles M. Province, ed., *Military Essays and Articles by George S. Patton, Jr.* (San Diego: George S. Patton, Jr. Historical Society), 296, http://www.pattonhq.com/pdffiles/vintagetext.pdf. Quoting from George S. Patton, Jr.,

"Report of Operations of the Army Polo Team of 1922," *Cavalry Journal* 32 (April 1923).

5. Secretary of War Henry Stimson commended Gene for his "ability," "great skill," "sound judgment," "tact," "perfect discretion," and "outstanding loyalty." "Eugene L. Harrison, 1923."

6. John A. Adams, *General Jacob Devers: World War II's Forgotten Four Star* (Bloomington: Indiana University Press, 2015), 353–54.

7. Stephen J. Zaloga, *Operation Nordwind, 1945: Hitler's Last Offensive in the West* (Oxford: Osprey Publishing, 2010), 29; Douglas Waller, *Disciples* (New York: Simon and Schuster, 2015), 294; "An SD Agent of Rare Importance (U)," CIA and Nazi Warcrim. and Col. Chap. 1–10, Draft Working Paper, Central Intelligence Agency, Special Collection, Nazi War Crimes Disclosure Act, https://www.cia.gov/library/readingroom/docs/CIA%20AND%20NAZI%20WARCRIM.%20AND%20COL.%20CHAP.%201-10,%20DRAFT%20WORKING%20PAPER_0003.pdf.

8. Boris T. Pash, *The Alsos Mission* (New York: Award House, 1969), 139–56. Pash wrote about Harrison, "His friendly aid was later to contribute materially to Alsos success." "Alsos Mission," Atomic Heritage Foundation, June 6, 2014, https://www.atomicheritage.org/history/alsos-mission.

9. "Report of the Lovett Committee," November 1945, Central Intelligence Agency, Special Collection, Creating Global Intelligence, https://www.cia.gov/library/readingroom/docs/1945-11-06a.pdf.

10. William Nimmo, ed., *The Occupation of Japan: The Grass Roots* (Norfolk, VA: General MacArthur Foundation, 1991), 5. "The jeep was not only a symbol of America's technology, speed and ingenuity, but also a symbol of the power of the Occupation."

11. "Officer/Enlisted Aide Handbook," General Officer Management Office, August 2009, U.S. Army, https://www.themilitaryleader.com/wp-content/uploads/2017/03/Senior-Leader-Aide-Handbook-2009.pdf; Andy Brokhoff, "11 Tips for Succeeding as Aide-de-Camp," The Military Leader, https://www.themilitaryleader.com/11-tips-aide-de-camp/.

12. "Letter of Thanks," January 7, 1949, from a dozen Fukui citizens thanking "our Dear Lt. Evans," praising him as a chief of the "progressive democratization the land," JKEA.

13. The functions of the CCD censorship division and CI&E often overlapped with G2 in the tumultuous economic period of 1947–48, when fears of

communism triggered the conservative American "reverse course" campaign, which accelerated with the Korean War. "Understanding the anthropology of the occupation and Japanese attitudes under MacArthur: An interview with Wilton S. Dillon," Wilton Dillon, David Wang and Daniel A. Métraux, *Virginia Review of Asian Studies* 18 (2016): 34, https://virginiareviewofasianstudies.com/archived-issues/2016-2/; "Occupation and Reconstruction of Japan, 1945–52," Office of the Historian, Bureau of Public Affairs, U.S. Department of State, https://history.state.gov/milestones/1945-1952/japan-reconstruction.

14. Evans, "Jan's story."
15. Jan King Evans interview with the author, December 12, 2017.
16. Evans, "Jan's story."
17. Barbara Gamarekian, "The Lives of the Cave Dwellers," *New York Times*, March 26, 1985, http://www.nytimes.com/1985/03/26/us/the-lives-of-the-cave-dwellers.html; Sarah Booth Conroy, "D.C.'s First Families," *Washington Post*, June 14, 1987, https://www.washingtonpost.com/archive/lifestyle/1987/06/14/dcs-first-families/81dec9e0-dc0a-4736-a95b-a20feb2de0c9/?utm_term=.14d5e4d43a10. The article indicated the term dates to at least 1904, when an article in the *Delineator* magazine stated Cave Dwellers "are the really truly delightful 'residenters' of Washington, made up mostly of well-born, well-bred families, long distinguished at the Capital for other qualities than riches or official position." The article also noted Cave Dweller Jan [King] Evans founded the Century Club, for Washingtonians whose family roots reach back at least a hundred years.
18. "Charles B. King, 1928," West Point Association of Graduates, https://www.westpointaog.org/memorial-article?id=c02efebb-ed78-4754-b5db-ff5dd317f0c7.
19. Lowell Limpus, "U.S. officers in 90 days with a West Point touch," *New York Daily News*, July 22, 1941.
20. King Evans interview, February 7, 2018.
21. "D.C. Socialite, 90, Widow of Times Correspondent," *Washington Post*, October 4, 1978, https://www.washingtonpost.com/archive/local/1978/10/04/dc-socialite-90-widow-of-times-correspondent/425b0d1e-79b3-4405-92f9-89468ca90e69/?utm_term=.02a6cd93bbb9.
22. King Evans interview, July 17, 2017. "Son Receives Legion of Merit for Late Col. Charles B. King," *Washington Times-Herald*, November 14, 1944; "Charles B. King, 1928."

23. King Evans interview, February 14, 2018.

24. Theodore Cohen, *Remaking Japan: The American Occupation as New Deal* (New York: Free Press, 1987), 465. Karla King Harrison's capacity to collect Japanese antiques was amplified by the extremely favorable dollar-yen exchange. The postwar yen plummeted against the dollar. From 3.4 yen to the dollar in 1934–36, the yen slid to 13.5 yen to the dollar in August 1945. By June 1947, it was 142 yen to the dollar. By the end of 1948, the exchange rate was 324 yen to the dollar.

25. "Frank C. Evans dies in Chicago; Funeral Friday," undated and unidentified clipping, JKEA. Frank Evans died April 23, 1946 at age seventy-one of a heart attack while attending a Boy Scout convention.

26. Ben Evans to "Dearest Family," July 5, 1948, JKEA.

27. King Evans interview, January 31, 2018.

28. Evans, "Jan's story."

Chapter 7

1. The Military District of Washington had its roots in the Civil War, when the Union army headquarters was charged with organizing the defense of the capital. During World War II, it was a joint command with responsibilities for the air, ground, and naval defense of Washington and the newly built Pentagon. MDW also was the home of the army's official ceremonial units, air support, military justice, and cemetery operations, including Arlington National Cemetery. "About MDW," U.S. Army Military District of Washington, http://mdwhome.mdw.army.mil/.

2. Jan King Evans interview with the author, March 2, 2018.

3. "Fort Myer History," Joint Base Myer-Henderson Hall, U.S. Army, http://www.jbmhh.army.mil/WEB/JBMHH/AboutJBMHH/FortMyerHistory.html.

4. King Evans interview, February 19, 2018. About leading the Arlington ceremonial company in the early days of the Korean War, Jan Evans said, "That really got to him."

5. William Wright, *Heiress, the Rich Life of Marjorie Merriweather Post* (Washington: New Republic Books, 1978), 198–202; Nancy Rubin Stewart, *American Empress: The Life and Times of Marjorie Merriweather Post* (New York: Villard, 1995), 273–74, 321–25. Born in Illinois, heiress Marjorie Merriweather Post relocated her primary residence to DC from her Long Island estate after her 1955 divorce from her third husband, Joseph E. Davies. However, Post had a long relationship with Washington from her school days at Mount

Vernon Seminary and College, when her father, C. W. Post, resided in DC to lobby the government on behalf of his cereal company. Perle Skirvin Mesta, *Perle: My Story* (New York: McGraw-Hill, 1960), 31. Perle Mesta, "the hostess with the mostest," was a Michigan native and Pittsburgh steel heiress who relocated to DC from Newport, Rhode Island, in 1940. She famously felt unaccepted by Pittsburgh society.

6. King Evans interview, March 22, 2018. Okemah, Oklahoma, sited where two railroads were supposed to intersect the highway, had been established only a few years before Norma Bowler left. Located in what was the Creek Nation of the Indian Territory, Okemah was a town of about a thousand in Bowler's day. Folksinger Woody Guthrie was born in Okemah in 1912, he too fled, joining the great Depression-era flight from the Dust Bowl. Carolyn S. Burnett Price, "Okemah," *The Encyclopedia of Oklahoma History and Culture*, http://www.okhistory.org/publications/enc/entry.php?entry=OK004.

7. "D. C. Socialite, 90, Widow of Times Correspondent," *Washington Post*, October 4, 1978, https://www.washingtonpost.com/archive/local/1978/10/04/dc-socialite-90-widow-of-times-correspondent/425b0d1e-79b3-4405-92f9-89468ca90e69/?utm_term=.40ea55abcede.

8. "Milestones," *Time*, June 26, 1939, http://content.time.com/time/magazine/article/0,9171,931337,00.html.

9. King Evans interview, March 22, 2018. Jan King Evans said about her grandmother, "She moved in the highest circles."

10. Ibid., February 14, 2018.

11. Ibid., March 22, 2018.

12. Mark Twain and Charles Dudley Warner, *The Gilded Age* (New York: Oxford University Press, 1996), 217.

13. Patricia O'Toole, *The Five of Hearts: An Intimate Portrait of Henry Adams and His Friends, 1880–1918* (New York: Simon and Schuster Paperbacks), 65.

14. Twain and Dudley, *Gilded Age*, 221.

15. Mark Elliot Benbow, *The Nation's Capital Brewmaster: Christian Heurich and His Brewery, 1842–1956* (Jefferson, NC: McFarland and Company, 2017), 36–37.

16. Ibid., 9–10.

17. Ibid., 38. The partner was Paul Hugo Ritter.

18. Christian Heurich, "From My Life, 1842–193" (Washington, 1934; translation 1985), 1, typescript, Heurich House Museum Archives, Washington, DC.

19. Douglas A. Wissing, *Indiana, One Pint at a Time* (Indianapolis: Indiana Historical Society, 2010), 13–29, 43–83.

20. Benbow, *Nation's Capital Brewmaster*, 52–53, 76.

21. Ibid., 50.

22. Ibid., 76, 96–100, 132–35.

23. King Evans interview, March 2, 2018.

24. The Heurich Mansion, known as the Brewmaster's Castle, is now an historical house museum. Heurich House Museum, http://www.heurichhouse.org/.

25. Benbow, *Nation's Capital Brewmaster*, 90–93. Christian Heurich remained extraordinarily vital through his long life. At the repeal of Prohibition, he relaunched his brewery, though he was ninety years old, becoming the nation's oldest brewer. In 1937 at ninety-four, he won the *Washington Herald's* Old Dad Race for being the oldest DC father. "Heurich Wins Old Dad Race in Camera Finish," *Washington Herald*, June 17, 1937. He died at the age of 102.

26. Kimberly Bender interview with the author, June 30, 2017.

27. Benbow, *Nation's Capital Brewmaster*, 89; Christian Heurich, "I Watched America Grow: By Christian Heurich as told to W.A.S. Douglas, Book One 1842–1872," pp. 103–104, manuscript, in Jan King Evans archive (hereafter cited as JKEA).

28. "Washington was smaller then, less partisan. The representatives stayed in town, broke bread together. The leadership was more homogenous, with shared norms," King Evans interview, March 22, 2018, December 13, 2017.

29. King Evans, "Jan's story, beginning of Ben Evans romance," 2006, manuscript, JKEA.

30. King Evans interview, June 17, 2017.

31. Ibid., November 24, 2017, February 19, 2018.

32. Ibid., November 29, 2017.

33. Ibid., February 19, 2018.

34. Ibid., March 2, 2018. Al Haig, later President Richard Nixon's Chief of Staff, was an aide-de-camp in occupied Japan who married his general's daughter. Elisabeth Bumiller, "Alexander Haig, Returning Fire," *Washington Post*, June 24, 1984, https://www.washingtonpost.com/archive/lifestyle/1984/06/24/alexander-haig-returning-fire/76a04e99-507d-4a13-ad7f-1e22981a3647/?utm_term=.bca44576439f; Major General David G. Barr's

daughter, Virginia, likewise married her father's occupied Japan aide-de-camp, Lieutenant James R. Cavanaugh.

35. Karla Evans interview with the author, July 18, 2017.

36. Benjamin Crabbs Evans Jr. Discharge Report, National Personnel Records Center, Saint Louis, MO.

37. King Evans interview, February 19, 2018.

38. Norma Richards interview with the author, March 1, 2018.

39. "Ben" to "Dearest Jan" letter, hand-dated "Spring '51?" JKEA.

40. Ben Evan's study of psychological warfare at Columbia was noted in "Miss Jan King, Capt. Evans Are Engaged," *Washington (DC) Sunday Star*, December 23, 1951.

41. King Evans interviews, October 12, 2017, March 22, 2018. Jan Evans indicated Ben Evans's address in Manhattan was 444 Central Park West, Apt. 15D.

42. King Evans interview, February 19, 2018.

43. "Jan Allison King Betrothed to Captain Benjamin Evans," *Washington Times-Herald*, December 23, 1951.

44. Ben Evans Jr. to Jan King letter, April 4, 1952, JKEA.

45. Amelia Heurich was Christian Heurich's third wife and the mother of his three children, Anita, Chris, and Karla. His first two wives died. Benbow, *Nation's Capital Brewmaster*, 187.

46. "Several Parties Planned Here for Jan King and Capt. Evans"; "Party Honors Engaged Pair"; "Hurleys Fete Engaged Pair"; Engaged Pairs Are Honored"; "Dinner Held for Couple," undated and unidentified clippings, JKEA.

47. "Jan King married in capital church," *New York Times*, September 13, 1952. Among the other articles was the wedding account in the *Washington Journal*, the German-language paper that published in ornate Fraktur type. Honeymoon newspaper coverage in "Smiles Across the Board," *Washington Times-Herald*, September 25, 1952.

Chapter 8

1. Jan King Evans interview with the author, March 7, 2018.

2. "Columbia University Bulletin of Information Commencement Number 1953," Columbia University Rare Book & Manuscript Library archive, New York, NY. The newlyweds lived at 5620 Netherlands Ave., a seven-story brick apartment building in the Riverdale section of the Bronx.

3. King Evans interview, April 19, 2018. Evans indicated Harrison episodically served as Fort Riley's acting commander, though had no direct connection to the psywar division.

4. William E. Daugherty and Morris Janowitz, *A Psychological Warfare Casebook* (Baltimore: Johns Hopkins Press, 1958), 29.

5. Paul A. Linebarger, *Psychological Warfare*, 2nd ed. (Washington: Combat Forces Press, 1954), 249; Daugherty and Janowitz, *Psychological Warfare Casebook*, 1–2, for "Organization and Personnel" chart of U.S. government PsyWar units, see 143.

6. A family photo shows Ben's father standing in front of his Cadillac parked in the Columbus carport, Jan King Evans (archive hereafter cited as JKEA).

7. "John F. Kennedy Special Warfare Center and School," Wikipedia, http://www.wikiwand.com/en/John_F._Kennedy_Special_Warfare_Center_and_School; Alfred H. Paddock, Jr., "Major General Robert Alexis McClure, Forgotten Father of US Army Special Warfare," "PsyWarrior.com, http://www.psywarrior.com/mcclure.html. McClure served with General Eugene Harrison in Europe on the Alsos mission that focused on German nuclear bomb development. For Cold War psychological warfare history, see Daugherty and Janowitz, *Psychological Warfare Casebook*, 135–43; Terance H. Qualter, *Propaganda and Psychological Warfare* (New York: Random House), 122, 125–32; Linebarger, *Psychological Warfare*, 246–55.

8. Norman Sklarewitz, "PsyWar—Beam of Hope to Captive Asia," *Stars and Stripes*, March 20, 1956; Norman Sklarewitz, "PsyWar Effective? The Reds'll Tell You," *Stars and Stripes*, March 21, 1956, has a photo of Capt. B. C. Evans reviewing "Communist books." During the war, U.S. bombers dropped more than four billion flyers over North Korea.

9. King Evans interviews, December 6, 2017, January 31, 2018.

10. Linebarger, *Psychological Warfare*, 1–24, 37.

11. Qualter, *Propaganda and Psychological Warfare*, 102.

12. Jo Fox, "The Legacy of World War One Propaganda," British Library, January 29, 2014, https://www.bl.uk/world-war-one/articles/the-legacy-of-world-war-one-propaganda.

13. Roger Hesketh, *Fortitude: The D-Day Deception Campaign* (Woodstock, NY: Overlook Press), 12–13, 34–39, 70, 80, 84–85, 90–91, 176–84.

14. "Psychological Operations Quotes," Psywarrior, http://www.psywarrior.com/quotes.html.

15. Ibid.

16. King Evans interview, March 7, 2018.

17. John W. Dower, *Embracing Defeat: Japan in the Wake of World War II* (New York: W. W. Norton, 1999), 525–64; Theodore Cohen, *Remaking Japan:*

The American Occupation as New Deal (New York: Free Press, 1987), 52–54. The American occupation of Japan officially ended on April 28, 1952, but SCAP had ceased to play a major role in Japan when the Korean War erupted and the "reverse course" American policy began.

18. King Evans interview, July 17, 2017.

19. Donald Gregg interview with the author, February 19, 2018; Donald P. Gregg, *Pot Shards: Fragments of a Life Lived in CIA, the White House, and the Two Koreas* (Washington, DC: New Academia Publishing, 2014), 36, 40.

20. King Evans interview, July 17, 2017.

21. Ibid., January 10, 2018. Jan Evans indicted that regardless of denomination, Ben found his ultimate religion in nature, stating that "Ben always felt that being in nature was like being in church. He felt closer to God in nature."

22. Ibid., January 26, 2018, March 29, 2018; Daniel F. Evans, *It's All Relative, Part One* (Crawfordsville, IN: Indiana Printing Company, 1977), 201. Ben Evans's mother, Ruth Fraley Evans, died on November 9, 1955.

23. King Evans interview, April 19, 2018.

24. Oscar A. Echevarria, ed., *Benjamin C. Evans, Jr.: In Memory and Recognition* (Miami, FL: Privately printed, 2014), 3. Ben received a citation for meritorious service from the Headquarters United States Army Far East and Eighth United States Army: Commendation Ribbon with Metal Pendant (First Bronze Oak-Leaf Cluster), which recognized his intelligence work, and highlighted his successful liaison work with various military and State Department entities. The citation noted his "diplomacy, tact and good judgment."

25. Daniel Evans Jr. interview with the author, September 20, 2017.

26. "Benjamin Crabbs Evans, Jr., 1946," West Point Association of Graduates, https://www.westpointaog.org/memorial-article?id=ec701e37-93a4-4d9f-a5e6-057072412deb; A twenty-one-year-old MiG-15 pilot, Kum-Sok No, did defect with his highly advanced Soviet jet on September 21, 1953, prior to Evans's offer. Kum-Sok No, J. Roger Osterholm, *A MiG-15 to Freedom: Memoir of the Wartime North Korean Defector Who First Delivered the Secret Fighter Jet to the Americans* (Jefferson, NC: McFarland Publishing, 1996).

27. King Evans interviews, January 26, March 7, April 19, 2018.

28. Jan King Evans, "Jan King Evans Houser," manuscript and Evans's passport, JKEA.

29. Ben Evans's inclusion on the early promotion "Outstanding List" is noted in "Benjamin Crabbs Evans, Jr., 1946," https://www.westpointaog.org/memorial-article?id=ec701e37-93a4-4d9f-a5e6-057072412deb.

30. "To ELH [Eugene L. Harrison] from BCE [Benjamin C. Evans]," hand-dated "Spring 1956 – Tokyo," letter, JKEA.

Chapter 9

1. President Roosevelt established the OSS with a presidential military order issued on June 13, 1942. "About the Records," World War II Records, U.S. National Archives and Records Administration, https://www.archives.gov/research/military/ww2/oss; Douglas Waller, *Wild Bill Donovan: The Spymaster Who Created the OSS and Modern American Espionage* (New York: Free Press, 2011), 69–74.

2. "A. B. Krongard Remarks at OSS Conference," Central Intelligence Agency, Speeches & Testimony Archive 2002, June 7, 2002, https://www.cia.gov/news-information/speeches-testimony/2002/ossconference_06022002.html; Waller, *Wild Bill Donovan*, 93–96. Tim Weiner, *Legacy of Ashes: The History of the CIA* (New York: Doubleday, 2007), 4, 7.

3. Weiner, *Legacy of Ashes*, 16; S. J. Hamrick, *Deceiving the Deceivers: Kim Philby, Donald Maclean and Guy Burgess* (New Haven: Yale University Press, 2004), 185.

4. National Park Service, "Postwar Period: End of the OSS and Return to the Park Service," 2. https://www.nps.gov/articles/postwar-period-end-of-the-oss-and-return-to-the-park-service.htm.

5. Weiner, *Legacy of Ashes*, 7.

6. "Postwar Period," 5.

7. Ibid., 10; Richard Dunlop, *Donovan: America's Master Spy* (Chicago: Rand McNally, 1982), 473–74. The OSS event was held in the Riverside Skating Rink.

8. "Postwar Period," 20, 22.

9. Ibid.

10. "Presidential Reflections on U.S. Intelligence: Harry S. Truman," Central Intelligence Agency, 2010 Featured Story Archive, https://www.cia.gov/news-information/featured-story-archive/2010-featured-story-archive/presidential-reflections-harry-truman.html.

11. "Donovan and the Interim—August 1945 to January 1946," Central Intelligence Agency, Special Collection, Intelligence, Policy, and Politics: The DCI, the White House, and Congress, https://www.cia.gov/library/readingroom/docs/Misc-006.pdf.

12. Weiner, *Legacy of Ashes*, 10.

13. "Report of the Lovett Committee," Central Intelligence Agency, Special Collection, Intelligence, Policy, and Politics: The DCI, the White House, and Congress, November 6, 1945, https://www.cia.gov/library/readingroom/docs/1945-11-06a.pdf.

14. Michael Warner, "Salvage and Liquidation, The Creation of the Central Intelligence Group," Central Intelligence Agency, CSI Publications, https://www.cia.gov/library/center-for-the-study-of-intelligence/csi-publications/csi-studies/studies/96unclass/salvage-and-liquidation.html.

15. Joseph J. Trento, *The History of the CIA* (New York: MJF, 2007), 45. FBI officials, including J. Edgar Hoover, and ex-OSS officers, such as Allen Dulles, contributed to the Red Scare leaks.

16. Weiner, *Legacy of Ashes*, 24.

17. L. Britt Snider, *The Agency and the Hill: CIA's Relationship with Congress, 1946–2004* (Washington: Center for the Study of Intelligence, 2008), 141, https://www.cia.gov/library/center-for-the-study-of-intelligence/csi-publications/books-and-monographs/agency-and-the-hill/08-The%20Agency%20and%20the%20Hill_Part2-Chapter5.pdf; Nicholas Dujmovic, "Review of 'Legacy of Ashes: The History of CIA,'" *Studies in Intelligence: Journal of the American Intelligence Professional* 51, no. 3, https://www.cia.gov/library/center-for-the-study-of-intelligence/csi-publications/csi-studies/studies/vol51no3/legacy-of-ashes-the-history-of-cia.html.

18. Weiner, *Legacy of Ashes*, 40.

19. Ibid., 28–29; Ben Steil, *The Marshall Plan: Dawn of the Cold War* (New York: Simon and Schuster, 2018), 315–16.

20. Weiner, *Legacy of Ashes*, 49–51.

21. Ibid., 24.

22. CIA historian Nicholas Dujmovic wrote in his critical *Legacy of Ashes* book review, "No objective observer of Agency history can fail to note that CIA in its history has failed—sometimes miserably—in what it set out to do or was ordered to do." Christopher Andrew, *For the President's Eyes Only: Secret Intelligence and the American Presidency from Washington to Bush* (New York: HarperCollins Publishers, 1995), 184–99.

23. Weiner, *Legacy of Ashes*, 57.

24. General James Doolittle's 1954 "Report on the Covert Activities of the Central Intelligence Agency" to President Eisenhower highlighted the problem of low-performing, incompetent CIA officers. The report stated the need to raise "the Agency personnel competence level." The report recommended,

"Elimination of personnel who can never achieve a sufficiently high degree of competence to meet the C.I.A. standard. This will entail a substantial reduction in present personnel. There is no place in C.I.A. for mediocrity." And the report urged review and improvement of recruitment policies to obtain "higher quality applicants for Agency jobs." James H. Doolittle, "Report on the Covert Activities of the Central Intelligence Agency (CIA)," Central Intelligence Agency, https://archive.org/stream/CIA-Covert-Activities-Doolittle-Report/doolittle_report_djvu.txt.

25. Weiner, *Legacy of Ashes*, 75.

26. Donald P. Gregg, *Pot Shards: Fragments of a Life Lived in CIA, The White House, and the Two Koreas* (Washington, DC: New Academia Publishing, 2014), 36, 40.

27. Weiner, *Legacy of Ashes*, 55.

28. "To ELH [Eugene L. Harrison] from BCE [Benjamin C. Evans]," hand-dated "Spring 1956 – Tokyo," letter, Jan King Evans archive.

29. Jan King Evans interview with the author, July 17, 2017. Jan told his Arlington National Cemetery memorialists: "He thought he could stop the next war." "Benjamin Crabbs Evans, Jr., 1946," West Point Association of Graduates, https://www.westpointaog.org/memorial-article?id=ec701e37-93a4-4d9f-a5e6-057072412deb.

30. There was a presidentially directed hiring freeze at the CIA in 1956. "CIA History—CIA Support Functions Organization and Accomplishments of the DDA-DDS Group, 1953-1956," Central Intelligence Agency, https://archive.org/details/CIAHistoryCIASupportFunctionsOrganizationAndAccomplishCIAHistoryCIA-DDSGroup1953-1956.

31. King Evans interviews, September 6, 2017, December 13, 20, 2018, January 26, May 10, 2018. According to Jan, Ben's West Point roommate, Corbin Davis, offered him an international executive position with the Blue Bird Bus Company, a large Georgia-based manufacturer. The State Department's Chief of Protocol Office, Wiley Thomas Buchanan, a family friend of Lady Lewis, offered Ben a protocol position, which he also declined. "Wiley Thomas Buchanan Jr. (1914-1986)," Office of the Historian, Bureau of Public Affairs, United States Department of State, https://history.state.gov/departmenthistory/people/buchanan-wiley-thomas.

32. King Evans interview, May 10, 2018.

33. Ibid., December 13, 2017. Walter Bedell Smith served as CIA director from 1950 to 1953, when he ordered the Guatemalan coup. He then moved to

the position of undersecretary of state. After the Guatemalan coup, the United Fruit Company named Smith to its board of directors. David Talbot, *The Devil's Chessboard: Allen Dulles, the CIA and the Rise of America's Secret Government* (New York: HarperCollins, 2015), 259.

34. King Evans interview, January 3, 2018.

35. Hoyt Vanderberg served from June 10, 1946 to May 1, 1947 as the second Director of Central Intelligence (DCI). "Hoyt Vanderberg, Lieutenant General, US Army (Army Air Force)," Central Intelligence Agency, https://www.cia.gov/library/center-for-the-study-of-intelligence/csi-publications/books-and-monographs/directors-and-deputy-directors-of-central-intelligence/vanden.html.

36. King Evans interviews, October 18, 2017, January 17, 2018.

38. Richard Helms, *A Look over My Shoulder: A Life in the Central Intelligence Agency* (New York: Random House, 2003), 83, 168–69; Hamrick, *Deceiving the Deceivers*, 189–90. Hamrick cites critical memos from special operations CIA officers who "resigned in disgust" due to negative views of "Wrong-Way" Galloway's performance as head of special operations, as well as a scathing assessment from Frank Wisner, who ran the CIA's first covert-action arm, the Office for Policy Coordination.

39. King Evans interview, May 10, 2018.

40. Ibid., November 14, 2017.

41. Hamrick, *Deceiving the Deceivers*, 193. When he returned from Italy in November 1947, James Angleton had served as special assistant to Galloway.

42. King Evans interview, November 29, 2017.

43. Ibid., December 13, 2017.

Chapter 10

1. The Farm, or its official name of Camp Peary, was established in 1942 as a training camp for Navy Seabees and later a German prisoner-of-war camp. It was closed to the public in 1951, and at some point it was transferred from the U.S. Navy to the Central Intelligence Agency, which made Camp Peary its field operations training site.

2. Jan King Evans interview with the author, September 9, 2017.

3. H. Keith Melton and Robert Wallace, *The Official C.I.A. Manual of Trickery and Deception* (New York: HarperCollins, 2010), 15. The CIA commissioned magician John Mulholland to write two books of deception techniques for covert officials, whom were termed "tricksters." The manuals were "Some Operational Applications of the Art of Deception" and "Recognition Signals." Allen

Dulles, *The Craft of Intelligence* (New York: Harper and Row, 1963), 145–53. In his definitive textbook on intelligence, Dulles devoted a chapter, entitled "Confusing the Adversary," to deception.

4. Oscar A. Echevarria, ed., *Benjamin C. Evans, Jr.: In Memory and Recognition* (Miami, FL: Privately printed, 2014), 3.

5. "Administrative Divisions in the Western Hemisphere Countries," Central Intelligence Agency, CREST, General CIA Records, https://www.cia.gov/library/readingroom/docs/CIA-RDP79T01018A000100030001-7.pdf.

6. John Ranelagh, *The Agency: The Rise and Decline of the CIA* (New York: Simon and Schuster, 1987), 424. The Western Hemisphere Division grew 40 percent from 1960 through 1965, accelerated by Fidel Castro's revolutionary efforts in Latin America.

7. "Summary of Agency Employment, Benjamin C. Evans," manuscript, Jan King Evans archive (hereafter cited as JKEA).

8. James A. Barry, "Managing Covert Political Action," *Studies in Intelligence*, 36, no. 5 (1992), Central Intelligence Agency, https://www.cia.gov/library/center-for-the-study-of-intelligence/kent-csi/vol36no3/html/v36i3a05p_0001.htm#top.

9. Peter Grose, *Gentleman Spy: The Life of Allen Dulles* (Boston: Houghton Mifflin Company, 1994), 446; Arthur Schlesinger Jr., *Robert Kennedy and His Times* (Boston: Houghton Mifflin Company, 1978), 454–56.

10. Schlesinger, *Robert Kennedy and His Times*, 456.

11. Ranelagh, *The Agency*, 424–25.

12. Mark E. Benbow, *The Nation's Capital Brewmaster: Christian Heurich and His Brewery* (Jefferson, NC: McFarland and Company, 2017), 215, 231. The CIA, after it was established in 1947, also had offices in the same complex the OSS used. National Park Service, U.S. Department of the Interior, "Postwar Period: End of the OSS and Return to the Park Service," p. 16, https://www.nps.gov/articles/postwar-period-end-of-the-oss-and-return-to-the-park-service.htm; Lawrence K. White, *Red White Memoirs* (Kearney, NE: Morris Publishing, 1999), 141. The Heurich Brewery site was considered for the new CIA headquarters that was eventually built in Langley, Virginia.

13. King Evans interview, May 17, 2018.

14. "The CIA Campus: The Story of Original Headquarters Building," Central Intelligence Agency, 2008 Featured Story Archive, https://www.cia.gov/news-information/featured-story-archive/2008-featured-story-archive/original-headquarters-building.html.

15. King Evans interviews, August 3, 2017, May 24, 2018.

16. Walter Bedell Smith served as director of Central Intelligence from 1950 to 1953.

17. King Evans interview, May 17, 2018.

18. Ibid.

19. Ibid. Jan indicated that her husband showed her a building near the Sixteenth Street hotels where he had an office at one point during his early days with the agency.

20. King Evans interview, January 10, 2018; Echevarria, ed., *Benjamin C. Evans, Jr.*, 19, indicated Ben's State Department title was Second Secretary of the Political Section. The State Department commonly used the Foreign Service Reserve designation as a cover for covert CIA officials, to the point that it almost was a marker for a spy on assignment. Robert G. Kaiser, "Diplomatic Titles Often Used to Protect Intelligence Aides," *Washington Post*, December 5, 1979, https://www.washingtonpost.com/archive/politics/1979/12/05/diplomatic-titles-often-used-to-protect-intelligence-aides/e57eec6c-e41e-4e6d-b193-1ebab1341dad/?utm_term=.afa2db397bad.

21. King Evans interview, May 17, 2018.

22. Ibid., May 3, 2018.

23. Thomas G. Patterson, *Contesting Castro: The United States and the Triumph of the Cuban Revolution* (New York: Oxford University Press, 1994), 217–25.

24. Jack B. Pfeiffer, "Official History of the Bay of Pigs Operation, Vol. III: Evolution of CIA's Anti-Castro Policies, 1959–January 1961," December 1979, p. 13, https://nsarchive2.gwu.edu/NSAEBB/NSAEBB355/bop-vol3.pdf.

Chapter 11

1. Oscar A. Echevarria interviews with the author, December 13, 2017, January 10, 2018; Oscar A. Echevarria, ed., *Benjamin C. Evans, Jr.* (Miami, FL: Privately printed, 2014), 19–25.

2. Echevarria interview, January 10, 2018.

3. Ibid., September 1, 2017. Echevarria said, "My father was a genius—he got professors to write books." While working for his father, Oscar Echevarria also ran a recycled-oil distributorship he'd started with a Villanova chemical professor.

4. Ibid., January 10, 2018. "My father owned businesses. He was anti-Batista," Echevarria said.

5. Ray Batavis, "Crosby's Luck," *FBI Studies*, November 2015, 44–48, http://fbistudies.com/2015/11/21/crosbys-luck/. The Evanses became longtime friends of Ken and Peggy Crosby, extending to Washington, where years later, the Evanses attended pool parties at the Crosbys' Spring Valley home. Photo of pool party, Jan King Evans archive (hereafter cited as JKEA).

6. Echevarra, ed., *Benjamin C. Evans, Jr.*, 19.

7. Echevarria interviews, September 1, December 13, 2017, January 10, 2018.

8. T. J. English, *Havana Nocturne: How the Mob Owned Cuba—And Then Lost It to the Revolution* (New York: William Morrow, 2007), xiv. Direct American investment in Cuba soared from $142 million in 1946 to $952 million by the end of the 1950s. Natasha Gelling, "Before the Revolution," *Smithsonian*, July 31, 2007, https://www.smithsonianmag.com/history/before-the-revolution-159682020/.

9. English, *Havana Nocturne*, 210–11.

10. Jesús Arboleya, *The Cuban Counterrevolution* (Athens: Ohio University Center for International Studies, 2000), 43–50.

11. Ibid., 43.

12. Jack B. Pfeiffer, "Official History of the Bay of Pigs Operation, Vol. III: Evolution of CIA's Anti-Castro Policies, 1959–January 1961," December 1979, p. 19, https://nsarchive2.gwu.edu/NSAEBB/NSAEBB355/bop-vol3.pdf.

13. "31 July 1959, Memorandum for the record, Subject: Debriefing of Jose Marcos Diaz, 28–29 July 1959, Tampa, Florida." Signed by Ben C. Evans, FIOA Crest archive. Author thanks investigative journalist Emma Best for providing the memo.

14. A November 6, 1959 CIA Related Mission Directive laid out the bifurcated policy. A December 11, 1959 CIA Western Hemisphere Division summarized the plans with the objective: "The overthrow of Castro within one year." Pfeiffer, "Official History of the Bay of Pigs Operation," 27–29.

15. Jeff Kenney, "Culver's Cuban Connection," Culver Academies History Facebook Page, April 5, 2016, https://www.facebook.com/groups/CulverAcademyAlumni78andThereabouts/permalink/10153772520608557/. In the 1950s then-Cuban President Fulgencio Batista's sons attended Culver. In 1955 eleven cadets from the Republic of Cuba attended Culver.

16. Jan Evans to Ann Heagney letter, hand-dated September 8, 1959, manuscript, JKEA. The letter referenced receiving a bouquet from the Heagney

family when the Evanses arrived "last Thursday," and described the Malacón apartment where they were residing. *Benjamin C. Evans, Jr.*, 15. Elena Falla de Echevarria indicated she met Ben Evans in the Havana embassy in May 1959.

17. King Evans interviews, August 3, 22, September 6, October 6, 2017.

18. A declassified 1960s CIA document that summarized a Cuban agent's information and contacts lists included "Ambassador Carrillo," who went into exile in 1958 and returned to Cuba after the revolution, serving as a protocol officer and as an ambassador. "Contact Report: Meetings of 22 June 1965 at Hotel Roosevelt and 23 June 1965 at the Tudor Room of the Hotel Commodore," June 28, 1965, National Archives, JFK Assassination Collection, https://www.archives.gov/files/research/jfk/releases/104-10183-10424.pdf.

19. King Evans interview, May 24, 2018.

20. "Bay of Pigs, 40 Years After: The Bay of Pigs Invasion/Playa Girón, A Chronology of Events," p. 8, National Security Archive, https://nsarchive2.gwu.edu//bayofpigs/chron.html. The report indicated that in late March 1960, David Phillips was assigned to be chief of political action for the counterinsurgency, with the responsibility of forming a government-in-exile to replace Castro's after the Bay of Pigs invasion.

21. King Evans interview, May 13, 2018; "Anglo-American Directory of Cuba 1960, Province of Havana," Cuban Information Archives, Document 0216, http://cuban-exile.com/doc_201-225/doc0216.html.

22. For the mention of the January 1960 Havana rally, see "238. Editorial Notes," *Foreign Relations of the United States, 1958–1960, Cuba, Volume VI*, Office of the Historian, Bureau of Public Affairs, United States Department of State, https://history.state.gov/historicaldocuments/frus1958-60v06/d238.

23. The number of political prisoners executed by the Castro government varies wildly. The Cuba Archive in Coral Gables, Florida, is considered to have a reliable database. See Cuba Archive, Free Society Project, Inc., http://cubaarchive.org/.

24. King Evans interviews, July 17–19, 2017; Karla Evans interview with the author, July 18, 2017.

25. Melvin Beck, *The Myth of Cold War Counterintelligence* (New York: Sheridan Square Books, 1984), 24–25. Beck depicted the organizational structure of the Havana Station.

26. Echevarria, ed., *Benjamin C. Evans, Jr.*, 15.

27. Elena Fala de Echevarria interview, October 5, 2017.

28. Ibid.

29. David A. Phillips, *The Night Watch* (New York: Atheneum, 1977), 78.

CIA officer Phillips wrote that in late 1959 operational security in Cuba had to become more "vigilant" and "complicated" after the Castro government executed an American businessman who was a CIA agent.

30. Pfeiffer, "Official History of the Bay of Pigs Operation" 29.

31. Ibid., 32–35.

32. Ibid., 4.

33. Ibid., 7.

34. Echevarria, ed., *Benjamin C. Evans, Jr.*; Arboleya, *Cuban Counterrevolution,* 77. Arboleya wrote the meeting took place in late February 1960 in Arlington, Virginia. Echevarria indicated the meeting was at Presidential Gardens in "northern Virginia," in late March 1960.

35. Echevarria, ed., *Benjamin C. Evans, Jr.*, 22–23.

36. "599. Memorandum From the Assistant Secretary of State for Inter-American Affairs (Mann) to the Secretary of State," October 28, 1960 *Foreign Relations of the United States, 1958–1960, Cuba, Volume VI*, Office of the Historian, Bureau of Public Affairs, United States Department of State, https://history.state.gov/historicaldocuments/frus1958-60v06/d599. The State Department memorandum summarized the FRD position and composition: "The constitutional manifesto of the FRD strongly condemns the dictatorial and communistic nature of the Castro regime. CIA states that the political orientation of FRD leaders can be described as varying from moderately conservative to moderately liberal; the group has been carefully constituted so as to attract the widest possible popular support in Cuba while avoiding extremes or the inclusion of persons who have become discredited on the basis of past political activities." The "discredited" persons reference related to those with strong Batista connections. The FRD eventually was comprised of five major anti-Castro groups, including the military wing, Brigade 2506.

37. In 1962 Soviet press attaché Alexander Fomin conveyed a back-channel message from Nikita Khrushchev to Kennedy administration liaison John Scali at the Occidental that helped defuse the Cuban missile crisis. "History," Occidental Grill & Seafood, http://www.occidentaldc.com/history/.

38. Echevarria, ed., *Benjamin C. Evans, Jr.*, 22.

39. "Bay of Pigs, 40 Years After," 6.

40. Pfeiffer, "Official History of the Bay of Pigs Operation," 29.

41. Ibid., 43. Footnote on 29–30 notated Dulles's handwritten revisions, which clarified the CIA counterrevolutionary plans in late 1959 and early 1960 did not yet include the intent to assassinate Castro.

42. Oscar Echevarria interview, September 1, 2017.

43. Arboleya, *Cuban Counterrevolution*, 78.

44. Daniel C. Walsh, *An Air War with Cuba: The United States Radio Campaign against Castro* (Jefferson, NC: McFarland and Company, 2012), 16–20; Lawrence C. Soley and John S. Nichols, *Clandestine Radio Broadcasting: A Study of Revolutionary and Counterrevolutionary Electronic Communication* (New York: Praeger, 1987), 163–84; Kenneth Van Belkum, "Radio Swan: Seabees Part of Cold War History," *SeaBee Magazine* (June 20, 2013), http://seabeemagazine.navylive.dodlive.mil/2013/06/20/swan-island-seabees-fifty-three-years-ago/. Greater Swan Island, where the transmitter was located, was about two-and-a-half miles long by a half-mile wide.

45. Nicholas, *Clandestine Radio Broadcasting*, 178.

46. "Worldwide Propaganda Network Built by the C.I.A.," *New York Times*, December 26, 1977, https://www.nytimes.com/1977/12/26/archives/worldwide-propaganda-network-built-by-the-cia-a-worldwide-network.html.

47. "Excerpts from History: Western Hemisphere Division," 282–283, Mary Ferrell Foundation, Miscellaneous CIA Series, https://www.maryferrell.org/showDoc.html?docId=48905#relPageId=1&tab=page; *Night Watch*, 90. Phillips wrote the CIA front company was the Gulf Steamship Company, though the longtime CIA spook may have been characteristically dissembling about the name when he wrote the book in the 1970s. Later renamed Radio Americas, the station was then titled to Vanguard Service Corporation, another CIA proprietary shell company.

48. Haynes Johnson, *The Bay of Pigs: The Leaders' Story of Brigade 2506* (New York: W. W. Norton, 1964), 18. U.S. officials claimed by July 1960 Cuba had nationalized United States-owned property worth $700,000,000.

49. Leland L. Johnson, "U.S. Business Interests in Cuba and the Rise of Castro," Rand Corporation, June 1964, 9, https://www.rand.org/content/dam/rand/pubs/papers/2008/P2923.pdf.

50. King Evans interview, May 17, 2018.

51. Oscar Echevarria e-mail to author, September 22, 2107. Echevarria provided the passage date and identified the ferry; 90 miles to Key West, Blogger, http://90milestokeywest.blogspot.com/.

52. Ginger Pederson, "How about a drive to Cuba—it was possible in the 1950s," *Palm Beach Past*, http://www.palmbeachpast.org/2011/06/how-about-a-drive-to-cuba-it-was-possible-in-the-1950s/.

53. Echevarria, ed., *Benjamin C. Evans, Jr.*, 22–23.

54. King Evans interview, May 3, 2018.

55. Falla de Echevarria interview, October 5, 2017. During the chaos following the failed Cuban counterrevolution, Elena Falla and Oscar Echevarria lost touch. Many decades later, the two married.

Chapter 12

1. "Flashback: Flying behind the Coconut Curtain," https://airwaysmag.com/traveler/flying-behind-the-coconut-curtain/. In 1960 Pam Am still had two daily Miami-Havana flights, down from eight daily flights. National Airlines continued service to Havana's Rancho-Boyero (Bull-Drover Ranch) Airport through much of 1961.

2. Eugenio Suárez Pérez, "Cuba nationalizes U.S. companies," *Granma*, August 10, 2015, en.granma.cu/cuba/2015-08-10/cuba-nationalizes-us-companies

3. David A. Phillips, *The Night Watch* (New York: Atheneum, 1977), 83. CIA officer Phillips provided an on-the-ground account of the last days of the CIA Havana Station.

4. Fabian Escalante, *The Secret War That the CIA Lost* (Melbourne: Ocean Press, 1995), 69, https://archive.org/stream/FabianEscalanteSecretWarCubaCIA/Fabian%20Escalante%20Secret%20War%20Cuba%20CIA_djvu.txt. Escalante, the former head of the Cuban State Security, detailed U.S.-Cuban relations in the years after the revolution.

5. Jesús Arboleya, *The Cuban Counterrevolution* (Athens: Ohio University Center for International Studies, 2000), 78.

6. Jack B. Pfeiffer, "Official History of the Bay of Pigs Operation, Vol. III: Evolution of CIA's Anti-Castro Policies, 1959–January 1961," December 1979, 136, https://nsarchive2.gwu.edu/NSAEBB/NSAEBB355/bop-vol3.pdf.

7. Ibid., 143.

8. Ibid., 137–40.

9. Ibid., 143. The CIA historian wrote about a botched Havana surveillance operation in September 1960 that involved the bugging of the New China News Agency office in the twenty-three-story Edificio Seguro Medico building in Vedado. CIA declassified documents detailed Cuban G2 officers arresting three CIA technicians, operating under the names of David L. Christ, Walter E. Szuminski, and Thornton J. Anderson, in the apartment, corroborating Pfeiffer's account. The bugging operation was codenamed Escalade. CIA documents concerning the incident: "Memorandum for: Director of Central Intelligence, Summary of Escalade," https://www.archives.gov/files/research

/jfk/releases/104-10066-10076.pdf; "Coup d'etat In America," https://archive.org/stream/CoupDetatInAmerica/NODULE%2012%20CIA%20TSD%20GENIUS%20DAVID%20CHRIST%20ROTTED%20IN%20CUBAN%20PRISON%20WHILE%20JFK%20SCREWED%20MARYLIN%20MONROE_djvu.txt.

10. Oscar A. Echevarria, ed., *Benjamin C. Evans, Jr.* (Miami, FL: Privately printed, 2014), 23. In Echevarria's uncorroborated account of the arrest, he wrote it related to the bugging of the Military Mission of Communist China, which had a FOSCA Building apartment, adjacent to Evans's agents' safe house, which was rented by a redheaded Vassar graduate who worked at the embassy. Echevarria indicated that after officers of the Defense Intelligence Agency bugged the military mission office, the Chinese detected the bugs, threatening exposure of the Cuban agents. "Memorandum for: Director of Central Intelligence, Summary of Escalade"; "Coup d'etat In America." CIA documents indicated that two women who worked in the embassy, Carolyn O. Stacey [Stacy] and Marjorie Lennox, assisted with the covert operation by renting the apartments in their names. G2 also arrested Marjorie Lennox, after bursting into her El Medico apartment about 1:00 a.m. She was soon released. The three CIA technicians were sent to Isle of Pines prison camp, until James Donovan negotiated their release in 1963. Prior to their release, the Cubans did not discover their true identities and importance.

11. Oscar Echevarria interview with the author, September 1, 2017.

12. Kathlyn Gay, *Leaving Cuba: From Operation Pedro Pan to Elian* (Brookfield, CT: Twenty-first Century Books, 2000), 18–19.

13. Robert A. Wright and Lana Wylie, eds., *Our Place in the Sun: Canada and Cuba in the Castro Era* (Toronto: University of Toronto Press, 2009), 12.

14. Yvonne M. Conde, *Operation Peter Pan: The Untold Exodus of 14,048 Cuban Children* (New York: Routledge, 1999), 16.

15. Daniel C. Walsh, *An Air War with Cuba: The United States Radio Campaign against Castro* (Jefferson, NC: McFarland and Company, 2012), 18.

16. Conde, *Operation Peter Pan*, 25. Citing a declassified 1960 State Department document, Conde wrote that FRD counterrevolutionaries on a multination Latin American publicity tour told the Costa Rican press about the nonexistent law.

17. Nelson P. Valdes and Saul Landau, "The CIA, Cuba and Operation Peter Pan," *Counterpunch* (December 16, 2011), https://www.counterpunch.org/2011/12/16/the-cia-cuba-and-operation-peter-pan/. According to the article, a Cuban counterrevolutionary, Antonio Veciana, said that David Atlee

Phillips, a CIA colleague of Ben Evans in Havana, instructed him to "wage psychological warfare" on the Castro regime by dissembling about the bogus CIA-forged law. Valdes and Landau also reported that Angel Fernandez Varela, who was one of Evans's agents, told his family "he had been one of those responsible for drafting the false law that gave rise to the hysteria." Maria de los Angeles Torres, *The Lost Apple: Operation Pedro Pan, Cuban Children in the U.S, and the Promise of a Better Future* (Boston: Beacon Press, 2004), 106–42. Torres, a Pedro Pan child who later became a DePaul University professor, contended the CIA used Operation Pedro Pan as a Cold War propaganda tool to frighten the Cuban middle-class parents into sending their children abroad. According to Torres, the CIA lost interest in Pedro Pan after the Bay of Pigs. Victor A. Triay, *Fleeing Castro: Operation Pedro Pan and the Cuban Children's Program* (Gainesville: University Press of Florida, 1999), 28–29. Triay asserted that the CIA wanted to separate the children from their counterrevolutionary parents, who would then be more committed anti-Castro fighters. Fabian Escalante, *The Secret War That the CIA Lost*, 172. Former Cuban G2 head Escalante indicated that the Cuban press began denouncing the CIA psychological warfare operation in early October 1960, when reports were published that CIA agents were circulating copies of a false law that purportedly transferred power over children from parents to the revolutionary government. He blamed "this contrived hysteria" for thousands of children being sent by their families to the United States as part of Operation Pedro Pan, see Antonio Veciana, *Trained to Kill: The Inside Story of CIA Plots against Castro, Kennedy, and Che* (New York: Skyhorse Publishing, 2017). Veciana was a longtime CIA anti-Castro conspirator. He wrote: "Parents grew nervous that their children were being brainwashed . . . they were primed to believe anything. I went to an accountant I knew, Andres Cayon. . . . Cayon got two people to draw up an official looking piece of legislation. We printed thousands of copies and let the underground network filter it onto the streets . . . it sparked 'Operation Pedro Pan,' the exodus of more than fourteen thousand unaccompanied children sent out of Cuba by their parents with the help of the Catholic Church. . . . The CIA's Radio Swan (JMHOPE), under David Atlee Phillips' direction, helped fan the flames."

18. Conde, *Operation Peter Pan*, 123–28. Conde wrote that the nuns at the Saint Vincent orphanage in Vincennes, Indiana, inflicted brutal corporal punishment on the Cuban children, as well as psychological punishment, such as making recalcitrant Cuban boys imbued with Latin machismo wear girls'

clothes. Guadalupe Heriberto Hernandez, "History of Hispanics/Latinos in the City of Fort Wayne and Allen County," *History of Fort Wayne and Allen County, Indiana* (Fort Wayne, IN: Allen County-Fort Wayne Historical Society, 2005), 711. Hernandez wrote about Pedro Pan refugees in Fort Wayne: "Twenty-three boys were sent to Saint Vincent Villa, Fort Wayne, Indiana, in July 1961. At that time Monsignor [John] Reed superintendent of Catholic Charities. Monsignor [J. Williams] Lester was superintendent of Catholic schools during this time and was living at St. Vincent Villa. The Cuban teenagers looked to him for comfort, counseling, and understanding. He became their mentor and father figure, and he took them to movies, school games and other outings. Eventually, the parents arrived, and Monsignor Lester helped them find housing, jobs and medical services."

19. Triay, *Fleeing Castro*, 10, 103.

20. Jan King Evans interview with the author, May 31, 2018.

21. Ibid. Jan indicated the family took shelter at Clearwater's Fort Harrison Hotel, a flagship resort where Keith Richards of the Rolling Stones later dreamed up "(I Can't Get No) Satisfaction."

22. Irene Albert, "Foreign Service Wives Out Cuban Trouble," *Clearwater Sun*, October 30, 1960. A photo in the article shows the wives with their children, including six-year-old Kathleen Turner, later famous for her movie roles.

23. J. C. King, "A Brief History of Radio Swan," 1961, http://cuban-exile.com/doc_226-250/doc0241.html. The CIA Western Hemisphere Division head J. C. King stated in the history that the station's effectiveness and credibility "began to diminish." King indicated that while the station still had a wide listening audience among Cubans, they increasingly distrusted the broadcast news. King blamed the "selfish interests" of the competing counterrevolutionary groups and the "individual political ambitions" of powerful Miami-based Cuban exiles for self-serving, implausible programming.

24. National Security Archive, "Bay of Pigs, 40 Years After," 18–19, https://nsarchive2.gwu.edu//bayofpigs/chron.html.

25. Ibid., 20.

26. George Gedda, "Diplomat Recalls Cuba Break in 1961," ProCon.org, https://cuba-embargo.procon.org/view.resource.php?resourceID=005153#83.

27. Escalante, *Secret War that the CIA Lost*, 67–68.

28. Ibid., 67–68. According to Escalante, those attending the meeting were Colonel Samuel Kail, Eulalia Wall, Major Robert Van Horn, David Morales, Captain Charles Clark, Hugh Kessler, and Ben Evans Jr.

29. "Working the Cuban Beat—Central Intelligence Agency," CIA, https://www.cia.gov/library/readingroom/docs/DOC_0001192279.pdf. Accounts of burying materials and transferring money in the last days of embassy operation.

30. Pfeifer, "Official History of the Bay of Pigs Operation," 191, 235. The history indicated the CIA officers evacuated on January 4, 1961, when the personnel gathered at the embassy to convoy to the ferry.

31. "U.S. Cuba Staff Home: Not Surprised at Break," *Stars and Stripes,* January 6, 1961. Embassy press secretary Paul Bethel told reporters in Florida, "We were prepared for about anything—the way it was going."

Chapter 13

1. Joseph J. Trento *The Secret History of the CIA* (New York: MJF Books, 2001), 204–6; James A. Barry, "Managing Covert Political Action: The Chile Case," Center for the Study of Intelligence, https://www.cia.gov/library/center-for-the-study-of-intelligence/kent-csi/vol36no3/html/v36i3a05p_0001.htm.

2. Jan King Evans interviews with the author, June 7, 2018, May 31, 2018. Oscar Echevarria e-mail to author, June 18, 2108, confirmed Ben Evans was removed from the Cuba desk after he returned to DC in January 1961.

3. Speech of Senator John F. Kennedy, Cincinnati, Ohio, Democratic Dinner October 6, 1960, http://www.presidency.ucsb.edu/ws/?pid=25660.

4. Daniel C. Walsh, *An Air War with Cuba: The United States Radio Campaign against Castro* (Jefferson, NC: McFarland and Company, 2012), 22.

5. Ibid., 26.

6. Jeff Kenney, "Culver's Cuban Connection," Culver Academies History Facebook Page, April 5, 2016, https://www.facebook.com/groups/CulverAcademyAlumni78andThereabouts/permalink/10153772520608557/.

7. Tim Elfrink, "He Buried Che," *Miami New Times,* August 6, 2009, http://www.miaminewtimes.com/news/ten-signs-youre-a-miami-marlins-lifer-10466350. Villoldo narrowly escaped self-immolation when his plane had to land with a napalm bomb stuck in the bomb bay. Villoldo, a longtime CIA operative, got his revenge against Che Guevara. Villoldo was with the U.S. Army Rangers-trained Bolivian special forces team that caught and assassinated Guevara in the Andes. Villoldo watched as a Bolivian country doctor sawed off Guevara's hands to send to Argentina for fingerprint verification; Peter Kornbluh, "The Death of Che Guevara: Declassified," https://nsarchive2.gwu.edu/NSAEBB/NSAEBB5/index.html.

8. Jesús Arboleya, *The Cuban Counterrevolution* (Athens: Ohio University Center for International Studies, 2000), 83.

9. Odd Arne Westad, *The Cold War: A World History* (New York: Basic Books, 2017), 300–305; Peter Wyden, *Bay of Pigs: The Untold Story* (New York Simon and Schuster, 1988), 210–88; Jack B. Pfeiffer, "Official History of the Bay of Pigs Operation, Vol. III: Evolution of CIA's Anti-Castro Policies, 1959–January 1961," December 1979, 182, https://nsarchive2.gwu.edu/NSAEBB NSAEBB355/bop-vol3.pdf.; National Security Archive, "Bay of Pigs, 40 Years After," pp. 58–96; https://nsarchive2.gwu.edu//bayofpigs/chron.html; Richard Goodwin, "A Conversation with Commandante Ernesto Guevara of Cuba, August 22, 1961, https://nsarchive.files.wordpress.com/2012/02/che.pdf.

10. Trento, *Secret History of the CIA*, 206–8.

11. Arthur Schlesinger Jr., *Robert Kennedy and His Times* (Boston: Houghton Mifflin Company, 1978), 457. The CIA was far from done with covert operations against Castro's Cuba. Operation Mongoose (1961–68) involved seven hundred CIA officers running thousands of Cuban agents, including soldiers, assassins, saboteurs, propagandists, and economic destabilizers. The operation included the ZR/RIFLE assassination program in the early 1960s, when Hoosier native William Harvey, a legendary CIA agent, ran the program.

12. King Evans interviews, October 6, 18, 2017, May 24, 2018, on Ben's post-Havana removal from Cuba responsibilities.

13. Burton Hersh, *The Old Boys: The American Elite and the Origins of the CIA* (New York: Charles Scribner's Sons, 1992), 36, 437. Hersh quoted Walter Pforzheimer, a top Allen Dulles-era CIA executive, who stated, "The social side was very important to Allen, and occasionally it warped his judgment." Gene Coyle interview with the author, September 12, 2017. Retired CIA officer and Indiana University professor Coyle discussed potential factors that might have insulated Evans from the flawed Bay of Pigs operation, including a "Dutch uncle," who might have protected a promising well-connected protégé.

14. Oscar Echevarria interview with the author, December 13, 2017; Echevarria e-mail to author, June 30, 2018.

15. Oscar A. Echevarria, ed., *Benjamin C. Evans, Jr.* (Miami, FL: Privately printed, 2014), 24.

16. Neil Carmichael, "A Brief History of the Berlin Crisis of 1961," National Declassification Center, https://www.archives.gov/files/research/foreign-policy/cold-war/1961-berlin-crisis/overview/berlin-wall-overview.pdf; Donald P. Steury, "Bitter Measures: Intelligence and Action in the Berlin Crisis,

1961," Central Intelligence Agency, https://www.archives.gov/files/research/foreign-policy/cold-war/1961-berlin-crisis/overview/bitter-measures.pdf.

17. Karla Evans interview with the author, July 18, 2017.

18. Sandra McElwaine interview with the author, December 2, 2017.

Chapter 14

1. Jan King Evans interviews with the author, July 17, September 6, October 6, 2017.

2. David Wise and Thomas B. Ross, *The Invisible Government* (New York: Vintage, 1974), 235, 235n. The Deputy Directors of Plans, who led the Clandestine Service, were in the pantheon of U.S. spies. Allen Dulles was the first DDP, followed by legendary (and unstable) spymaster Frank Wisner, Desmond FitzGerald, Thomas Karamessines, Richard Helms, and William Colby.

3. Victor Marchetti and John D. Marks, *The CIA and the Cult of Intelligence* (New York: Alfred K. Knopf, 1974), 60–61, 70–72, 80. Most of the Clandestine Services' personnel were assigned to area divisions, which mirrored the State Department's geographical bureaus, since most overseas CIA operators were covert under State Department cover. In 1974 Marchetti and Marks indicated there were 16,500 personnel in the CIA, which had an annual budget of $750,000,000. The reported total did not include the many thousands of personnel working for the CIA proprietaries, such as the Pacific Corporation that ran Air America and Air Asia, which had almost 20,000 employees. Jeffrey T. Richelson, *The U.S. Intelligence Community* (Cambridge, MA, Ballinger, 1985), 235. Richelson reported a partial-year 1975 Covert Action Staff budget that showed paramilitary expenses were about three-quarters of the expenditures, with most of the balance for "political action support" and "other propaganda."

4. Marchetti and Marks, *CIA and the Cult of Intelligence*, 134–72. Business proprietaries included the CIA's massive air arm, including Air America, Air Asia, Civil Air Transport, and other air charter companies that flew globally, as well as businesses such as Double-Chek Corporation, a Miami-based "brokerage" that covertly enabled Cuban counterrevolutionary operations, and Interarmco, which sold military equipment to CIA-vetted paramilitary groups.

5. Jeff Wheelwright, "A Writer's Controversial Past That Will Not Die," *New York Times*, February 2, 2018, https://www.nytimes.com/2018/02/02/books/review/peter-matthiessen-paris-review-cia.html.

6. Richelson, *U.S. Intelligence Community*, 235; John Crewdson, "Worldwide Propaganda Network built by the CIA," *New York Times*, December 26, 1977,

https://www.nytimes.com/1977/12/26/archives/worldwide-propaganda-network-built-by-the-cia-a-worldwide-network.html.

7. Marchetti and Marks, *CIA and the Cult of Intelligence*, 60–61.

8. Charles R. Beitz, "Covert Intervention as a Moral Problem," in Jan Goldman, ed., *Ethics of Spying: A Reader for the Intelligence Professional* (Lanham, MD: Scarecrow Press, 2006), 209.

9. "A Short Account of International Student Politics & the Cold War with Particular Reference to the NSA, CIA, Etc." *Ramparts* 5 (March 1967), http://www.namebase.net:82/campus/nsa.html; Angus MacKenzie, *Secrets: The CIA's Secret War at Home* (Berkeley: University of California Press, 1999), 19.

10. Jan King Evans to Senator Ernest F. Hollings, June 11, 1980, letter, Jan King Evans archive (hereafter cited as JKEA). The letter, cowritten with Ben Evans's input, referenced Evans starting to work with TAF president Haydn Williams "in 1963 when Ben was in that office of his organization responsible for liaison with the Foundation." Oscar A. Echevarria, ed., *Benjamin C. Evans, Jr.* (Miami, FL: Privately printed, 2014), 3. The "A Brief biographical note" in the Echevarria booklet indicated that after leaving Havana, Evans transferred to the Covert Action Staff, where he was "involved with management of the staff's second largest proprietary" from 1963 to 1967, becoming branch chief in 1968, when the CIA's relationship was terminated. The same biographical note indicated that Evans "spent six years as Deputy Director and Director of an annual multimillion dollar program with resident managers and programs in several foreign countries." Both references tracked to Evans's relationship with TAF.

11. Marchetti and Marks, *CIA and the Cult of Intelligence*, 172–7; Richelson, *U.S. Intelligence Community*, 235–36; Crewdson, "Worldwide Propaganda Network built by the CIA," https://www.nytimes.com/1977/12/26/archives/worldwide-propaganda-network-built-by-the-cia-a-worldwide-network.html. TAF outreach included such programs as one begun in 1955 that paid the expenses of selected Asian journalists to study at Harvard with prestigious Neiman Fellowships.

12. Emma Best, "The Stolen History of the CIA and the Asian [sic] Foundation," *Muckrock*, https://www.muckrock.com/news/archives/2017/nov/02/taf-1/.

13. "Salary Scale Adjustment for the President of The Asia Society (TAF)," April 8, 1966, CIA, FIOA CREST. The 1966 fact sheet reported that "After twelve years operation, TAF is now firmly established in Asia with an excellent

range of contacts in the 13 countries where its Representatives are working closely with Chiefs of Station and Ambassadors to catalyze, support and make more effective Asian initiatives which advance U.S. policy objectives."

14. "Our Founders," The Asia Foundation, https://asiafoundation.org/our-people/founders/. Other trustees included the presidents of Stanford and UCLA, the chairman of Standard Oil of California, prominent corporate attorneys, and Paul Hoffman, the administrator of the Marshall Plan (which provided skims to the CIA for black ops).

15. Best, "Stolen History of the CIA and the Asian [sic] Foundation." Mining declassified CIA documents on DTPILLAR, Best reported the first Committee for a Free Asia president, George H. Greene, was a CIA official, as was Alan Valentine, who replaced him.

16. Emma Best, "Robert Blum, the spy who shaped the world," parts 1 and 2, Muckrock, https://www.muckrock.com/news/archives/2017/aug/17/robert-blum-spy-who-shaped-world-part-1/; https://www.muckrock.com/news/archives/2017/aug/18/robert-blum-spy-who-shaped-world-part-2/; "Robert Blum—The Asia Foundation," https://asiafoundation.org/people/robert-blum/.

17. "F. Hayden Williams—The Asia Foundation," https://asiafoundation.org/people/f-haydn-williams/.

18. Hayden Williams letter to Karla Evans, May 16, 2013, working manuscript for "Benjamin C. Evans, Jr.," booklet, David Evans archive. Williams wrote that he first met Ben Evans "when I was in the Pentagon." Williams served in the Department of Defense during both the Eisenhower and Kennedy administrations.

19. King Evans interview, October 6, 2017.

20. "Nixon for Governor Finance Commiittee-1962 General Election Campaign Statement," box 64, folder 18, 1962, p. 23, Richard Nixon Presidential Library Special Files Archive, Yorba Linda, CA; King Evans interview, September 6, 2017. Evans's conservatism was consistent. Jan said, "He voted for Goldwater in 1964. It was the first year District of Columbia residents could vote in national elections."

21. "CA/PEG Project Renewal Sheet," September 30, 1964, CIA, FOIA CREST.

22. Ibid., November 12, 1965.

23. Thomas G. Coffey, "Intelligence in Popular Literature," Center for the Study of Intelligence, https://www.cia.gov/library/center-for-the-study-of

-intelligence/csi-publications/csi-studies/studies/vol-59-no-1/Kim-Philby-Books.html; Malcolm Gladwell, "Trust No One," *The New Yorker*, July 28, 2014.

24. Odd Arne Westad, *The Cold War: A World History* (New York: Basic Books, 2017), 308–10.

25. For all round-the-world quotes, Ben and Jan Evans letters, January 22, 1964 through February 27, 1964, JKEA.

26. Ihsan J. Hijazi, "Charles H. Malik, 81; Was President of U.N. Assembly," *New York Times,* December 29, 1987, https://www.nytimes.com/1987/12/29/obituaries/charles-h-malik-of-lebanon-81-was-president-of-un-assembly.html.

27. "The Asia Foundation Celebrates Sixty Years in Pakistan," Asia Foundation, https://asiafoundation.org/resources/pdfs/TheAsiaFoundation60Years.pdf.

28. Douglas A. Wissing, *Funding the Enemy: How US Taxpayers Bankroll the Taliban* (Amherst, NY: Prometheus Books, 2012), 29–39.

29. "Geographic Support Study, Afghanistan," CIA Reading Room, https://www.cia.gov/library/readingroom/docs/CIA-RDP79T01018A000600100001-4.pdf.

30. "2007 Distinguished Graduate Award, BG Amos A. (Joe) Jordan," West Point Association of Graduates, https://www.westpointaog.org/page.aspx?pid=2022.

31. When Ben Evans arrived in Vietnam, U.S. soldiers had just recently concluded Operation Cedar Falls, a massive search-and-destroy operation to eliminate a Viet Cong stronghold near Saigon called "The Iron Triangle." It was the largest U.S. ground operation in the war. Hailed by U.S. commanders as a grand success, the operation proved to be inconclusive, at best a temporary victory, as most Viet Cong had withdrawn to sanctuaries in Cambodia. The military tactic of removing the entire civilian population to "New Life Villages" drove many Vietnamese peasants into support of the Viet Cong. Deportation, exfoliation, and free-fire zones didn't win hearts and minds. On August 25, 1964, six months after Evans stayed at the hotel, a bomb exploded on the Caravelle's fifth floor, where the American journalists stayed when they weren't drinking together on the rooftop bar that overlooked Saigon. The reporters were luckily all out in the field when the bomb went off, so there were no casualties. As the Vietnam War troop levels escalated through the 1960s, many Americans were not so lucky. Over the next decade, three million U.S. military served in Vietnam, where over 58,000 Americans were

killed in the conflict. Millions of Vietnamese combatants and civilians died in the war.

32. Max Boot, *The Road Not Taken* (New York: Liveright Publishing Corporation, 2018), 409. The Saigon Station chief was John "Jocko" Richardson, who oversaw Montagnard paramilitary operations by CIA officers, including William Colby and Lucien Conein.

33. Boot, *Road Not Taken*, xxiii-L. During his early days in power, Diêm was advised by Edward Lansdale, the legendary former OSS officer and U.S. Army general. Often cited as the model for *The Quiet American,* Graham Greene's perceptive novel of the Indochina war, Lansdale was the architect for post-World War II counterinsurgency, including an emphasis on psywar operations. Frances FitzGerald, *Fire in the Lake: The Vietnamese and Americans in Vietnam* (New York: Vintage Books, 1989), 97–98. Vietnam War chronicler (and daughter of Desmond FitzGerald, the CIA deputy director of plans and the agency's deputy director), Frances FitzGerald wrote about OSS veteran and black propaganda master Colonel Edward Lansdale in her 1972 *Fire in the Lake*. After his counterinsurgency success in the Philippines, CIA Director Allen Dulles assigned Lansdale to Vietnam. Frances FitzGerald summarized Lansdale: "He had faith in his own good motives. No theorist, he was rather an enthusiast, a man who believed that Communism in Asia would crumble before men of goodwill with some concern for 'the little guy' and the proper counterinsurgency skills." FitzGerald was also describing the perspectives of many other like-minded Americans, including Ben Evans.

34. "Episode 2, 1963–1965: CIA Judgments on President Johnson's decision to 'Go Big' in Vietnam," Center for the Study of Intelligence, https://www.cia.gov/library/center-for-the-study-of-intelligence/csi-publications/books-and-monographs/cia-and-the-vietnam-policymakers-three-episodes-1962-1968/epis2.html; Thomas L. Ahern, Jr., *CIA and the Generals: Covert Support to Military Government in South Vietnam* (The National Security Archive, 1998), 1–11, https://nsarchive2.gwu.edu/NSAEBB/NSAEBB284/1-CIA_AND_THE_GENERALS.pdf; John Prados, *Vietnam: The History of the Unwinnable War, 1945–1975* (Lawrence: University Press of Kansas, 2009), 73–74.

35. CIA Saigon station chief Jocko Richardson also opposed the November 1963 coup. John Prados, "JFK and the Diem Coup," The National Security Archive, https://nsarchive2.gwu.edu/NSAEBB/NSAEBB101/index.htm. Conversely, CIA official Lucien Conein served as Ambassador Henry Cabot Lodge

Jr.'s liaison to the coup conspirators and delivered at least $42,000 in cash to them on the morning of the coup.

Chapter 15

1. "A Short Account of International Student Politics & the Cold War with Particular Reference to the NSA, CIA, Etc.," *Ramparts* 5 (March 1967), http://www.namebase.net:82/campus/nsa.html.

2. John Prados, *Vietnam: The History of the Unwinnable War, 1945–1975* (Lawrence: University Press of Kansas, 2009), 170–71. In 1965 the Selective Service called up 170,000 men for military service. With Johnson's massive escalation of the Vietnam War, that number soared in 1966 to 768,000 men; Tim Weiner, *Legacy of Ashes: The History of the CIA* (New York: Doubleday, 2007), 286. Weiner wrote that in 1967 there were 75 urban riots, with 88 deaths, 1,397 injuries, 16,389 arrests, and $664.5 million in damages.

3. Angus Mackenzie, *Secrets: The CIA's War at Home* (Berkeley: University of California Press, 1997), 30, https://archive.nytimes.com/www.nytimes.com/books/first/m/mackenzie-secrets.html?_r=1. Mackenzie credited counter intelligence official Richard Ober with the *Ramparts* attacks. Ober was a Harvard grad, who had a Columbia University graduate degree in international affairs. He joined the CIA after serving in the army; "The Article in the February 1967 Issue of 'Ramparts,'" CIA digest and analysis, March 29, 1967, FOIA CREST. A typical smear in a CIA press release termed the *Ramparts* journalists as "communists, socialists, and radicals." Prados, *Vietnam*, 197. Prados, longtime historian of the intelligence services, wrote about the CIA counterintelligence operation against *Ramparts*: "The agency crossed the Rubicon of legality, conducting domestic operations that were explicitly prohibited by law." The operations included illegally inspecting the magazine's IRS returns for information to use against the group.

4. Mackenzie, *Secrets*, 31.

5. "The Ramparts Affair: 1967," globalsecurity.org, https://www.globalsecurity.org/intell/ops/ramparts.htm.

6. David Wise and Thomas B. Ross, *The Espionage Establishment* (New York: Random House, 1967), 157.

7. Ibid., 155–56; Karen M. Paget, *Patriotic Betrayal: The Inside Story of the CIA's Secret Campaign to Enroll American Students in the Crusade against Communism* (New Haven, CT: Yale University Press, 2015), 351–87.

8. "Telegram, Department of State, 144245 Circular," February 25, 1967, FOIA CREST.

9. Jan King Evans interview with the author, August 3, 2017.

10. "Gift for the Kennedy Center, *Washington (DC) Evening Star*, June 23, 1965.

11. Karla Evans interview with the author, July 18, 2017.

12. King Evans interviews, July 18, September 6, October 6, 2017, December 20, 2018, July 17, 2018; Karla Evans interview, July 18, 2018.

13. King Evans interview, July 18, 2018. Jan Evans indicated she thought the intended victim of the planned CIA assassination was a Latin American leader who went to West Point. Nicaraguan strongman Anastasio Somoza DeBayle, also known as "Tacho" and "Tachito," was a West Point 1946 graduate, a classmate of Ben. During the CIA's Cuban counterrevolutionary operations, then-President Luis Somoza, Tacho Somoza's father, was deeply involved with the agency, providing bases for training and the Bay of Pigs invasion.

14. Jan Goldman, ed., *Ethics of Spying: A Reader for the Intelligence Professional* (Lanham, MD: Scarecrow Press, 2006), 193–247.

15. Ibid., 223. An impassioned report about covert anticommunist operations given to President Dwight Eisenhower in 1954 referenced the moral tension created by clandestine operations undertaken by a free democratic country that valued honesty and fair play. The report stated that the "ruthless" though "necessary" covert actions required "a fundamentally morally repugnant philosophy."

16. David Talbot, *The Devil's Chessboard: Allen Dulles, the CIA and the Rise of America's Secret Government* (New York: Harper, 2015), 203.

17. John P. Quirk, *The Central Intelligence Agency: A Photographic History* (Guilford, CT: Foreign Intelligence Press, 1986), 9. CIA Director Richard Helms stated: "This is neither a boy scout game nor a boxing bout fought with Marquis of Queensberry rules. It's a job to be done," unintentionally speaking to Eagle Scout Ben Evans's moral tension; Goldman, ed., *Ethics of Spying*, 220. The 1970s-era Church Commission that investigated illegal and extralegal CIA operations reported it was "struck by the basic tension—if not incompatibility—of covert actions and the demands of a constitutional system."

18. King Evans interviews, August 3, 2017, May 17, 2018. Years later when he was no longer a covert agent, Ben likewise turned down Wabash College's request to feature him in an alumni article, writing the magazine he would rather not discuss his CIA work.

19. Ibid., July 17, 2017.

20. Joseph J. Trento, *The Secret History of the CIA* (New York: MJF Books,

2001), 191–202. The CIA had a codified policy on assassinations, which were typically top-secret operations organized in tightly sequestered units, such as Hoosier native Bill Harvey's ZR/RIFLE operation that plotted Castro assassination operations and other "executive actions" under extremely tight need-to-know security.

21. Chip King, "Remembering My Brother-in-Law," working manuscript for "Benjamin C. Evans, Jr." booklet, David Evans archive.

22. Donald Gregg interview with the author, February 19, 2018. Gregg said about the implicit moral quandaries of covert intelligence operations: "It's an ongoing part of life if you stay in that work." Gregg said he thought that if superiors gave Ben an assignment to arrange an assassination, it would have hit him hard psychologically.

23. Dr. Barney Malloy interview with the author, October 6, 2017.

24. Gregg interview, February 19, 2018.

25. "Subject: The Asia Foundation Financial Cover," May 6, 1966, CIA, FOIA CREST. The name of the "Chief, CA Support Group" was redacted.

26. "CA/PEG Project Record Sheet," September 26, 1966, CIA, FOIA CREST; Emma Best, "The Asia Foundation's public distancing of its relation with the CIA didn't end Agency's ties," muckrock.com, https://www.muckrock.com/news/archives/2017/nov/03/taf-2/.

27. "CIA and Asia Foundation Are Linked," UPI, undated, FOIA CREST. The UPI article reported that TAF indicated it spent between $4 million to $5 million a year; "CA/PEG Project Record Sheet," September 26, 1966, CIA, FOIA CREST. The secret memorandum memorializes an internal debate about CIA funding of TAF, which is noted as $8,510,000 for July 1, 1966 to June 20, 1967; Victor Marchetti and John D. Marks, *The CIA and the Cult of Intelligence* (New York: Alfred K. Knopf, 1974), 172. Marchetti and Marks indicated the CIA subsidy to TAF reached $8 million a year.

28. "Secret, Priority to All Action Addresses, DTPILLAR," February 25, 1967, CIA, FIOA CREST. Williams informed the staffers that "Trustees are holding line, normal business proceeding in home office."

29. "Morning Meeting of 22 March 1967," CIA, FOIA CREST.

30. "TAF Liquidation Plan, Approved 20 June 1967 by the DCI," undated, CIA, FIOA CREST. The memorandum from the CIA executive director/comptroller to deputy director of plans included a Memorandum of Understanding signed on August 17, 1976 by Haydn Williams and members of the board acknowledging delivery of the terminal funds, after which "the Sponsor [CIA]

ceases financial support and relinquishes claim to all TAF assets, "thereby terminating its proprietary relationship."

31. King Evans interviews, July 17, 2017, July 18, 2018. Jan said Ben told her he flew to San Francisco with $5 million in a suitcase. She indicated that Haydn Williams told her decades later that Ben delivered $20 million to TAF.

Chapter 16

1. Tim Weiner, *Legacy of Ashes: The History of the CIA* (New York: Doubleday, 2007), 271. Just in the six-year period from John Kennedy's inauguration until the 1967 scandals, there were three hundred major covert action operations, many with little or no oversight by the White House, Pentagon, or State Department.

2. Ibid., 284.

3. Ibid., 277.

4. Donald Gregg interview with the author, February 19, 2018.

5. Douglas Waller, *Disciples* (New York: Simon and Schuster, 2015), 50–51.

6. David Wise and Thomas B. Ross, *The Espionage Establishment* (New York: Random House, 1967), 133–37.

7. Jan King Evans interview with the author, November 9, 2017. Raborn was another Evans family friend, connected through the Cathedral School, where his daughter attended. Jan said at one point Raborn asked her for gossip. She indicated that the West Point bond between White and Ben was an important element in their work relationship, which was a "trusted" one, in her words.

8. Waller, *Disciples*, 432.

9. Jefferson Morley, *The Ghost: The Secret Life of James Jesus Angleton* (New York: Saint Martin's Press, 2017), 186–89. Fueled by liquid lunches and paranoia, Angleton was obsessed with enemies, both American and Soviet. He saw suspects everywhere, and lashed out accordingly. "The mole hunt had become a witch hunt," Morley wrote.

10. James Hanrahan, "An interview with former CIA executive director Lawrence K. "Red" White," CIA Library, https://www.cia.gov/library/center-for-the-study-of-intelligence/csi-publications/csi-studies/studies/winter99-00/art3.html.

11. Lawrence K. White, *Red White Memoirs* (Kearney, NE: Morris Publishing, 1999), 140–41.

12. "The people of the CIA . . . Lawrence K. "Red" White," CIA News &

Information, https://www.cia.gov/news-information/featured-story-archive/2011-featured-story-archive/lawrence-k.-red-white.html.

13. "An interview with former CIA executive director Lawrence K. "Red" White," https://www.cia.gov/library/center-for-the-study-of-intelligence/csi-publications/csi-studies/studies/winter99-00/art3.html; White, *Red White Memoirs*, 152. White wrote that his job was to coordinate management and administration, "leaving the Director and other Deputy Directors to concentrate on intelligence business."

14. "The people of the CIA."

15. White, *Red White Memoirs*, 184.

16. Oscar A. Echevarria, ed., *Benjamin C. Evans, Jr.* (Miami, FL: Privately printed, 2014), 3, 29–31.

17. "The Management Advisory Group," March 15, 1971, CIA, FOIA CREST.

18. Shirley Cornett interview with the author, November 13, 2017.

19. Echevarria, ed., *Benjamin C. Evans, Jr.*, 4.

20. Jan King Evans interview with the author, November 9, 2017.

21. Karla Evans interview with the author, July 18, 2017.

22. King Evans interviews, August 3, November 3, 2017.

23. Ibid., July 20, 2018. Jan indicated the transaction noted in Loudoun County Book 513, page 618 recorded that the Evanses closed on the farm on April 30, 1970, paying $96,000 for the 500-acre property, three houses, and a stone barn.

24. Tom Cormack interview with the author, October 4, 2107.

25. Echevarria, ed., *Benjamin C. Evans, Jr.*, 11; Carol Joynt, "Another One Bites the Dust," *New York Social Diary*, January 5, 2010, http://www.newyorksocialdiary.com/across-the-nationacross-the-world/2010/washington-social-diary.

26. King Evans interviews, October 26, November 24, 2017.

27. Penny Denegre interview with the author, November 22, 2017. Denegre has been the Master of the Middleburg Hunt for twenty years. She explained fox hunting protocol and argot. "The hounds are the stars," she said. The riders, called "the field," are the spectators. Landowners who permit fox hunting, such as the Evans[es], are crucial to the sport. She noted, "One of the main reasons this area, so close to Washington, has stayed country, is because of fox hunting."

28. Melissa Cantacuzene interview with the author, November 17, 2017.

29. Sandra McElwaine interview with the author, December 2, 2017.

30. King Evans interview, July 18, 2018.

31. Tom Cormack letter to the author, October 5, 2017. Cormack served as Ben Evans's deputy from 1973 until 1981, when he became the CIA executive secretary.

32. Echevarria, ed., *Benjamin C. Evans, Jr.*, 29–31. Listed among the executive secretary responsibilities, there was the task notation: "Promptly reviews all questionable crank mail addressed to the DCI or DDCI, with particular attention to threats on their persons or other senior officials and directs the material to the Office of Security for further evaluation."

33. Shirley Cornett interview with the author, November 13, 2017. Cornett noted that the three secretaries also processed work for Colonel "Red" White, who had a separate office that adjoined the anteroom.

34. "Morning Meeting Action Item," June 5, 1970, CIA, FOIA CREST.

35. Karla Evans interview, July 18, 2017.

36. Cormack interview, October 4, 2017.

37. Gene Coyle interview with the author, September 12, 2017. However grave the responsibilities and lofty the position, headquarters executives were held in a lower regard by "the street guys" in field operations. Longtime CIA officer Gene Coyle said, "Being an operations officer is a peculiar occupation—part pimp, part Mother Teresa." He described the spook hierarchy: "Operations guys, they say, 'that headquarters weenie' or talk about 'the staffers' in a derisive way."

38. Andrew R. Finlayson, "A Retrospective on Counterinsurgency Operations," CIA, Center for the Study of Intelligence, https://www.cia.gov/library/center-for-the-study-of-intelligence/csi-publications/csi-studies/studies/vol51no2/a-retrospective-on-counterinsurgency-operations.html.

39. John Prados, *Vietnam: The History of the Unwinnable War, 1945–1975* (Lawrence: University Press of Kansas, 2009), 327–28; Weiner, *Legacy of Ashes*, 287–93, 340.

40. "MAG Memorandum, 'CIA's Domestic Activities,' March 1971," National Security Archive, https://nsarchive.gwu.edu/.

41. Thomas Powers, *The Man Who Kept the Secrets: Richard Helms & the CIA* (New York: Alfred P. Knopf, 1979), 285–89; Weiner, *Legacy of Ashes*, 285.

42. Powers, *Man Who Kept the Secrets*, 261.

43. Henry Kissinger, *The White House Years* (Boston: Little, Brown, 1979), 1180–81. Kissinger claimed that CIA analysts under Helms constituted, "the most liberal school of thought in the government."

44. Weiner, *Legacy of Ashes*, 315.

45. Powers, *Man Who Kept the Secrets*, 254–75; Weiner, *Legacy of Ashes*, 308–13.

46. Cornett interview, November 13, 2017. "Mr. Evans was very conservative," Shirley said.

Chapter 17

1. "The Pentagon Papers," UPI, https://www.upi.com/Archives/Audio/Events-of-1971/The-Pentagon-Papers. Senator Birch Bayh from Indiana was one of the senators who defended the publication of the Pentagon Papers. Bayh said, "The existence of these documents, and the fact that they said one thing and the people were led to believe something else, is a reason we have a credibility gap today, the reason people don't believe the government. This is the same thing that's been going on over the last two-and-a-half years of this administration. There is a difference between what the President says and what the government actually does, and I have confidence that they are going to make the right decision, if they have all the facts."

2. Owen Edwards, "The World's Most Famous Filing Cabinet," *Smithsonian Magazine* (October, 2012), https://www.smithsonianmag.com/history/the-worlds-most-famous-filing-cabinet-36568830/; David Wise and Thomas B. Ross, *The Invisible Government* (New York: Vintage Books, 1974), x, 349n; Thomas Powers, *The Man Who Kept the Secrets: Richard Helms & the CIA* (New York: Alfred P. Knopf, 1979), 295–307, 329–30.

3. "Memorandum, Subject: Allegations of Agency Involvement in the U.S.," W. E. Colby, March 1972. Responding to the MAG concerns about blowback from illegal agency domestic operations against U.S. citizens, Colby provided "Allegations and Answers" to provide rebuttal fodder to CIA command-line officers and senior staff. It was not the whole truth.

4. St. John Hunt, *Dorothy, An Immoral and Dangerous Woman: The Murder of E. Howard Hunt's Wife, Watergate's Darkest Secret* (Walterville, OR: Trine Day, LLC, 2015), 66–67. The author, E. Howard Hunt's son, stated that his father was still working for the CIA when he was active in the White House plumbers, citing a CIA memo that detailed the extension of Hunt's top secret clearance into his "retirement," and his father's revelation to him that he was covertly reporting plumbers' activities back to the agency during the Watergate period.

5. Stanley I. Kutler, *The Wars of Watergate* (New York: W. W. Norton and Company, 1992), 188–91.

6. Gerald S. and Deborah H. Strober, *Nixon: An Oral History of His Presidency* (New York: HarperCollins, 1994) 312.

7. "Copy given to Ben Evans 5/30/73," pp. 00282-00359, MORI Doc ID 1451843, Digital National Security, George Washington University.

8. Kutler, *Wars of Watergate,* 221.

9. Tim Weiner, *Legacy of Ashes: The History of the CIA* (New York: Doubleday, 2007), 319–21.

10. "Government and the Law," *Indianapolis Magazine* (April 1985); Julie Slaymaker, "Are Lawyers taking over Indiana?" *2004 Indiana Super Lawyers,* March 2004, https://www.superlawyers.com/indiana/article/are-lawyers-taking-over-indiana/11ca754a-281f-48aa-9e56-0ae1d8220c47.html. After leaving Washington in 1973, Daniel Evans Jr. returned to Indianapolis, where he attended Indiana University School of Law, and ran a drug diversion program called Treatment Alternatives to Street Crime. In 1976 Evans served as Indiana governor Otis Bowen's campaign manager, before embarking on what became an illustrious law and corporate career.

11. Dan Evans, Jr., "Ben Evans, Jr.," unpublished manuscript, David Evans archive.

12. Jan King Evans interview with the author, March 22, 2018.

13. Oscar A. Echevarria, ed., *Benjamin C. Evans, Jr.* (Miami, FL: Privately printed, 2014), 24–25.

14. Karla Evans interview with the author, July 18, 2017.

15. Echevarria, ed., *Benjamin C. Evans, Jr.*, 12; Louise Evans Turner interview with the author, August 24, 2017. Turner said, "Dad was so proud of being from Indiana." The Evans family indicated Ben Evans had an almost paradisal view of his boyhood in Indiana.

16. Echevarria, ed., *Benjamin C. Evans, Jr.*, 24.

17. Evans Turner interview, August 24, 2017.

18. King Evans interview, November 14, 2017.

19. Norma Richards interview with the author, March 1, 2018.

20. Karla Evans interview, July 18, 2017.

21. Benjamin C. Evans, Jr. letter to Gene Harrison, March 8, 197, Jan King Evans archive (hereafter cited as JKEA). The Evanses embellished Groveton Farm with thousands of trees and a swimming pool behind the main house.

22. "Medical Summary, Benjamin C. Evans, Jr." September 7, 1973, JKEA.

23. "Benjamin C. Evans," obituary, *Crawfordsville Journal Review,* September 24, 1973.

24. Powers, *Man Who Kept the Secrets,* 178–80.

25. Ibid., 313–14.

26. "Oral History: Reflections of DCI Colby and Helms on the CIA's 'Time of Troubles,'" https://www.cia.gov/library/center-for-the-study-of-intelligence/csi-publications/csi-studies/studies/vol51no3/reflections-of-dci-colby-and-helms-on-the-cia2019s-201ctime-of-troubles201d.html.

27. Stanley I. Kutler, ed., *Watergate: A Brief History with Documents* (Chichester, West Sussex, UK: Wiley-Blackwell, 2010), 41–44.

28. King Evans interviews, July 17, 2017, August 22, 2017.

29. Tom Cormack interview with the author, October 4, 2017.

30. David Talbot, *The Devil's Chessboard: Allen Dulles, the CIA and the Rise of America's Secret Government* (New York: HarperCollins, 2015), 125–26.

31. Louise Evans Turner interview, August 24, 2017.

32. Donald Gregg interview with the author, February 19, 2018.

33. Meg Gregg interview with the author, February 19, 2018.

34. Jack Devine, *Good Hunting: An American Spymaster's Story* (New York: Farrar, Straus and Giroux, 2014), 224.

35. Ibid., 223. "The CIA had been my family, and my family had been shaped by the CIA almost as much as I had," Devine wrote.

36. King Evans interview, September 6, 2017.

37. Karla Evans interview, July 18, 2017.

38. King Evans interview, August 18, 2017; Karla Evans interview July 18, 2017; Turner interview, August 24, 2017.

39. King Evans interview, November 14, 2017.

40. Ibid., October 26, 2017.

41. "Establishment of the Executive Secretariat," July 24, 1973, CIA, FIOA CREST.

42. U.S. Arms Control and Disarmament Agency letter to Mr. Ben Evans, Executive Secretary, Room 7D6015, Washington, D.C. 20505, August 13, 1974, CIA, FIOA CREST.

43. "Copy given to Ben Evans 5/30/73," pp. 00282-00359, MORI Doc ID 1451843, Digital National Security Archive, George Washington University, Washington, DC.

44. Ben Evans, "Superior Accomplishment Promotions," November 7, 1973; "The Entertainment Question," December 19, 1973, CIA, FOIA CREST.

45. B. C. Evans, "Stationery," April 24, 1974; June 24, 1974 memo regarding an applicant; "First Class Travel," October 29, 1974, CIA, FOIA CREST.

46. Benjamin C. Evans Jr. letter to Gene Harrison, March 8, 1974.

47. Weiner, *Legacy of Ashes*, 273–75.

48. "Memorandum, CIA Matters, James A. Wilderotter, Associate Deputy Attorney General," January 3, 1975, Digital National Security Archive, George Washington University, https://nsarchive2.gwu.edu/NSAEBB/NSAEBB222/index.htm. This memorandum summarized Colby's Family Jewels briefing to the Department of Justice, which passed it on to the White House.

49. "Included in this folder are miscellaneous items . . . ," p. 00337, MORI Doc ID 1451843, Digital National Security Archive.

50. Seymour M. Hersh, "Huge C.I.A. Operation in U.S. against Antiwar Forces, Other Dissidents in Nixon Years," *New York Times*, December 22, 1974.

51. "Oral History: Reflections of DCI Colby and Helms on the CIA's 'Time of Troubles.'"

52. Weiner, *Legacy of Ashes*, 338–39.

53. Richard Helms, *A Look over My Shoulder: A Life in the Central Intelligence Agency* (New York: Random House, 2003), 429; Brent Durbin, *The CIA and the Politics of US Intelligence Reform* (Cambridge: Cambridge University Press, 2017), 142.

54. David Wise, "Colby: The Man Who Told the Secrets," *Los Angeles Times*, May 5, 1996, http://articles.latimes.com/1996-05-05/opinion/op-704_1_elbridge-colby.

55. Maureen Orth, "Former CIA Director William Colby: The Man Nobody Knew, *Vanity Fair*, September 22, 2011, https://www.vanityfair.com/news/2011/09/former-cia-director-william-colby--the-man-nobody-knew.

56. Charles E. Lathrop, *The Literary Spy* (New Haven, CT: Yale University Press, 2004), 352.

57. "U.S. Intelligence Agencies Probed in 1975," *CQ Almanac*, https://library.cqpress.com/cqalmanac/document.php?id=cqal75-1214373.

58. "Oral History: Reflections of DCI Colby and Helms on the CIA's 'Time of Trouble.'"

59. Echevarria, ed., *Ben Evans, Jr.*

60. Powers, *Man Who Kept the Secrets*, 9. Under the National Security Act of 1947, the DCI was charged with the protection of the CIA's sources and methods, so Colby's revelations about "bad secrets" created consternation for many veteran CIA officers.

61. Loch K. Johnson, *A Season of Inquiry: The Senate Intelligence Investigation* (Lexington: University Press of Kentucky, 1985), 193.

62. Echevarria, ed., *Benjamin C. Evans, Jr.*, 12.

63. Evans Turner interview, August 24, 2017.
64. Robert Wallace and H. Keith Melton, *Spy Sites of Washington, D.C.* (Washington, DC: Georgetown University Press, 2017), 190. William E. Colby lived at 3028 Dent Place NW, less than two miles from the Evans home.
65. King Evans interview, September 6, 2017.
66. B. C. Evans, "Memorandum for Review Staff," November 11, 1975, CIA, FOIA CREST.
67. John Patrick Quirk, *The Central Intelligence Agency: A Photographic History* (Guilford, CT: Foreign Intelligence Press), 157, 195, 197–99.
68. Frank Snepp, *A Decent Interval: An Insider's Account of Saigon's Indecent End Told by the CIA's Chief Strategy Analyst in Vietnam* (New York: Random House, 1977), 471–580.
69. "CIA History of DCI William Colby," National Security Archive, George Washington University, https://nsarchive2.gwu.edu/NSAEBB/NSAEBB362/index.htm.
70. "The RAND Corporation Invitation," March 20, 1974, CIA, FOIA CREST.
71. B. Powell Harrison to Benjamin C. Evans Jr. letter, July 30, 1976, ibid.
72. B. C. Evans to Brig. Gen. James L. Collins, Jr." April 28, 1977, ibid
73. B. C. Evans, "Briefing Format for DCI-Designee," December 21, 1976, ibid.
74. Douglas Garthoff, *Directors of Central Intelligence as Leaders of the U.S. Intelligence Community* (Washington, DC: Potomac Books, Inc, 2007), 111.
75. King Evans interview, April 19, 2018.
76. Ben Evans, "An Eight-Year View of DCI Management," "Ben Evans, Jr.," unpublished manuscript, David Evans archive.
77. "President-Elect Carter Briefing," November 18, 1976, CIA, FOIA CREST. The briefing included sessions on international oil and Soviet strategic objectives.
78. Garthoff, *Directors of Central Intelligence as Leaders of the U.S. Intelligence Community*, 126.
79. Ben Evans letter to George Bush, January 15, 1977, JKEA.
80. George Bush, "Memorandum in lieu of fitness report," January 18, 1977, ibid.
81. George Bush letter to Ben Evans, December 18, 1977, ibid.
82. "Memorandum," B. C. Evans, August 16, 1977, Digital National Security Archive.

83. Cormack interview, October 4, 2017.

84. Garthoff, *Directors of Central Intelligence as Leaders of the U.S. Intelligence Community*, 131, 147.

85. Weiner, *Legacy of Ashes*, 361. A graduate of Indiana University, where the CIA recruited him, Robert Gates was a hand-picked member of Ben Evans's Management Advisory Group and went on to become the Director of Central Intelligence.

86. Ibid., 363.

87. "Peter Schmidt," University of Florida, https://africa.ufl.edu/first-last/schmidt/; Peter R. Schmidt, *Iron Technology in East Africa: Symbolism, Science, and Archaeology* (Bloomington: Indiana University Press, 1997).

88. Peter R. Schmidt, ed., *The Culture and Technology of African Iron Production* (Gainesville, FL: University Press of Florida, 1996), 172–85, 277–317.

89. The Uganda-Tanzania War began October 30, 1978, and lasted until April 1979, when the Tanzanian forces took Kampala and forced Idi Amin into exile. The Tanzanians mobilized over 100,000 soldiers. The war's momentum dramatically shifted early in the conflict, after the Soviets provided the Tanzanian forces with powerful Katyusha rocket launchers and other heavy weapons.

90. Piero Gleijeses, "Cuba's intervention in Africa during the Cold War," OUPblog, https://blog.oup.com/2016/12/cuba-intervention-africa-cold-war/. Tens of thousands of Cuban troops served in Africa during the Cold War. More than 36,000 Cuban soldiers were in Angola during the civil war, when the United States and the Soviet Union each backed Angolan proxy forces. In the proxy wars in Africa, the Soviet Union typically provided the armaments and the Cubans served as trainers.

91. Karla Evans interview, November 15, 2017.

92. B. C. Evans to Admiral Turner, "An Opportunity to Remodel the Executive Secretariat," December 4, 1978, CIA, FIOA CREST.

Chapter 18

1. Smith Hempstone, "Halloween Massacre," CIA, FOIA CREST; Stansfield Turner, *Secrecy and Democracy: The CIA in Transition* (Boston: Houghton Mifflin Company, 1985), 195–205; Stansfield Turner, *Burn before Reading: Presidents, CIA Directors and Secret Intelligence* (New York: Hyperion, 2005), 188. Turner wrote, "In retrospect, I probably should not have effected the reductions of 820 positions at all, and certainly not the last 17."

2. John F. Blake, "Memorandum for: Mr. Theodore Sorensen," January 13, 1977, CIA, FIOA CREST. Sorensen was Carter's first nominee for DCI. Sorensen withdrew after opposition.

3. "David Martin interview," January 11, 1978, CIA, FIOA CREST.

4. "Minutes of the DCI/MAG Meeting," October 4, 1977, ibid.

5. Stansfield Turner, "Is the CIA accountable?" JFK School of Government, November 30, 1978, ibid.

6. "Memo for: Mr. George Springsteen, Jr.," June 21, 1976, ibid. The heavily redacted memo included the columns by Jack Anderson and Les Whitten, "CIA Study Finds Shah Insecure," *Washington Post*, July 11, 1975; Jack Anderson and Les Whitten, "Torture, Terror in Iran," *Washington Post*, May 29, 1976. The memo also noted that DCI Bush was the courier: "Mr. Bush handcarried the memo to the White House for the Secretary and General Scowcraft."

7. Baqer Moin, *Khomeini: A Life of the Ayatollah* (New York: Thomas Dunne Books, 1999), 163–64.

8. Tim Weiner, *Legacy of Ashes: The History of the CIA* (New York: Doubleday, 2007), 363–64.

9. Turner, *Burn before Reading*, 180; Dustin Byrd, *Ayatollah Khomeini and the Anatomy of the Islamic Revolution in Iran* (Lanham, MD: University Press of America, 2011), 12–15; Vanessa Martin, *Creating an Islamic State: Khomeini and the Making of a New Iran* (New York: I. B. Tauris, 2000), 147–56.

10. Moin, *Khomeini*, 182–222.

11. Ibid., 213.

12. Weiner, *Legacy of Ashes*, 370–71.

13. Turner, *Burn before Reading*, 180.

14. "Staff Meeting Minutes of October 15, 1979," CIA, FIOA CREST.

15. "Minutes of the DCI/MAG Meeting with Admiral Stansfield Turner," May 16, 1977, ibid.

16. "Subject: Management Advisory Group (MAG) Review of Agency Policy and Practices Concerning Hiring or Retention of Persons Involved [redacted]" April 26, 1977, ibid.

17. "University Presidents Visit, 15 February 1979," ibid.

18. "Memorandum For: Executive Committee Members," March 28, 1979, ibid.

19. Douglas P. Bennett letter to Mr. Ben Evans, January 19, 1977, ibid.

20. "Remote Perturbation Techniques," November 7, 1979, ibid.

21. Ben Evans, "Parking Violations on Agency Compound," March 31, 1978; "Note for [redacted]," September 6, 1978, CIA, FIOA CREST. The memo

directed some heat: "Apparently Ben didn't read the regs or elected to ignore both Mr. Gambino's note and the reg." Hell hath no fury like an unheeded bureaucrat.

22. Jan King Evans interviews with the author, September 21, October 12, 2017.

23. George Bush letter to Jan Evans, July 13, 1979, and Barbara Bush letter to Jan Evans, July 13, 1979, Jan King Evans archive (hereafter cited as JKEA).

24. George Bush letter to General and Mrs. Harrison, May 20, 1979, ibid.

25. Barbara Bush letter to Jan Evans, July 29, 1979, ibid.

26. "George Bush for President," March 6, 1980, ibid.

27. George Bush letter to Ben Evans, June 25, 1980, ibid.

28. Jan Evans, "The Saga of my Detroit trip as a D.C. Delegate on the Platform Committee," manuscript, ibid.

29. King Evans interview, September 21, 2017.

30. Robert G. Kaiser, "Republican Right Crushes Backers of ERA, Abortion," *Washington Post*, July 10, 1980. GOP cochair Mary Crisp, a supporter of the ERA and abortion rights, shocked the convention by stating that the party was "suffering from serious internal sickness," by not supporting women's rights.

31. Former director George H. W. Bush was Reagan's running mate. When Bush was elected vice president, the Evanses' social calendar took on even more gloss in the 1980s with invitations to formal Christmas parties at the official northwest Washington residence near Woodland Drive. In December 1981, Barbara Bush inscribed the Christmas party photo to Jan Evans, "our neighborhood leader."

32. King Evans interview, October 12, 2017.

33. Evans, "The Saga of my Detroit trip as a D.C. Delegate on the Platform Committee."

34. Christine Dodson, "Subject: Pakistan and Afghanistan," December 21, 1979, Digital National Security Archive.

35. Steve Coll, *Ghost Wars: The Secret History of the CIA, Afghanistan and Bin Laden, from the Soviet Invasion to September 10, 2001* (New York: Penguin Books, 2005), 46.

36. "Instruments of Statecraft: U.S. Guerilla Warfare, Counterinsurgency, and counterterrorism, 1940–1990, Chapter 13: The Carter Years," 30, www.statecraft.org/chapter13.html; John Prados, *Presidents' Secret Wars: CIA and*

Pentagon Covert Operations since World War II (New York: William Morrow, 1986), 360.

37. "Instruments of Statecraft"; Prados, *Presidents' Secret Wars*, 360. Prados estimated that the CIA's Ghost War funding levels for the mujahideen reached $625 million by 1984, topping out at $630 million in 1987. The funding for the CIA's secret anti-Soviet war totaled $2.5 billion.

38. Turner, *Burn before Reading*, 189–204.

39. Ibid., 192–93.

40. Weiner, *Legacy of Ashes*, 377.

41. Ben Evans, "Subject: A Legacy," July 3, 1980, "Ben Evans, Jr.," unpublished manuscript, David Evans archive. In a postscript to his memo, Evans chronicled the demise of the Executive Director position under William Colby, who abolished his own position in the interest of gaining a more powerful one. Evans then depicted the subsequent inertia of sequential DCIs, none of whom could wrangle the cumbersome bureaucracy into enough order to reestablish the position. Evans quoted DCI-designate Theodore Sorenson, who asked him, "Who runs this place?"

42. Robert M. Gates, *From the Shadows: The Ultimate Insider's Story of Five Presidents and How They Won the Cold War* (New York: Simon and Schuster, 1996), 225.

43. Ibid., 222.

44. Ibid., 223–24.

45. Jan Evans letter to Senator Fritz Hollings, June 11, 1980, and Senator Fritz Hollings letter to Jan Evans, June 17, 1980, JKEA. Some of Ben Evans's work was extracurricular. Though The Asia Foundation had not been a CIA proprietary for more than a decade, the Evanses continued their close friendship with its president, Haydn Williams. In June 1980 Jan wrote to Hollings, the chair of the Budget Committee, lobbying on behalf of TAF, stating that Ben found the five years of liaising with the foundation "most rewarding because of the widely held conviction that the Foundation's program was a true national asset in Asia." She urged Hollings to fund the foundation's request for a $2 million appropriation. Four days later, Hollings responded, writing that he and Senator Daniel Inouye did a legislative end run, appropriating $4.1 million to TAF. "Subject: NIC Activity Report, 2–8 August 1985," CIA, FOIA CREST. While no longer a proprietary, TAF maintained a close relationship with the U.S. intelligence community. A secret 1985 memo to the DCI noted a National Intelligence Council officer met with Williams to discuss the foundation's projects in China and the Philippines.

46. Frank Carlucci served as DDCI from February 1978 to February 1981. Admiral Bobby Ray Inman replaced Carlucci and served until June 1982.

47. Ben Evans memo to "Frank," February 5, 1981, CIA, FOIA CREST.

48. "Staff Meeting Minutes of 2 January 1981"; Staff Meeting Minutes of 26 January 1981," CIA, FOIA CREST.

49. Joseph E. Persico, *Casey: From the OSS to the CIA* (New York: Viking, 1990), 15, 24–25. During a boyhood boxing match, Casey sustained a blow to the throat, and he also had a thick palate, which both contributed to his speech impediment.

50. Tom Cormack interview with the author, October 4, 2017.

51. James Conaway, "Spy Master, the File on Bill Casey," *Washington Post*, September 7, 1983, https://www.washingtonpost.com/archive/lifestyle/1983/09/07/spy-master-the-file-on-bill-casey/2287d601-df1f-45b4-b58b-53bb8d4c6e43/?utm_term=.815abc653f9d.

52. King Evans interview, October 18, 2017.

53. "Civil Service Annuity Estimates," March 8 and 9, 1979, JKE archive; "Dollar Times," https://www.dollartimes.com/inflation/inflation.php?amount=96&year=1980. Adjusted for inflation, $47,500 in 1980 had the buying power of $152,671.32 in 2018.

54. Oscar A. Echevarria, ed., *Benjamin C. Evans, Jr.* (Miami, FL: Privately printed, 2014), 6.

55. "Summary of Agency Employment," May 1981, JKEA.

56. "Distinguished Intelligence Medal to Benjamin C. Evans, Jr.," April 30, 1981, certificate, ibid.

Chapter 19

1. Jan King Evans interview with the author, November 3, 2017.

2. Ibid., October 6, 12, 2017.

3. Ibid., October 12, 2017, September 5, 2018. "Grandmother Lewis bought Ben his tractor, which was his best friend," Jan said, speaking of her elderly grandmother, Lady Norma Lewis, who often stayed with them at Groveton, where Ben cooked and attended to her needs.

4. Karla Evans graduated from Connecticut College in 1980, and Louise Evans Turner graduated from Saint Lawrence University in the class of 1982, after finishing her degree work in December 1981.

5. King Evans interview, October 12, 2017.

6. Ibid., September 5, 2018.

7. Ibid, October 6, 2, 2017; "QE II cruise, 1/31-4/2/83" itinerary and Jan

Evans passport, Jan King Evans archive (hereafter cited as JKEA).

8. King Evans interview, October 12, 2017.

9. Abigail Adams National Bancorp, Inc. History," http://www.fundinguniverse.com/company-histories/abigail-adams-national-bancorp-inc-history/. The bank opened in May 1978 under the name of the Women's National Bank of Washington. In 1986 it was changed to the Adams National Bank. The Adams National Bank suffered a major default in 1988, when Citibank assumed control.

10. King Evans interview, August 3, 2017.

11. Ibid., September 21, 2017.

12. Ibid., September 5, 2018; Jan Evans passport.

13. Jack C. Spratt, "The History of Camp King," manuscript, 1993 [?], US Army Heritage & Education Center archive.

14. Oscar A. Echevarria, ed., *Benjamin C. Evans, Jr.* (Miami, FL: Privately printed, 2014), 13.

15. "Karla Evans, C. A. Griswold Have Nuptials," *New York Times,* August 26, 1979, https://www.nytimes.com/1979/08/26/archives/karla-evans-ca-griswold-have-nuptials.html. The article noted, "Her father is executive secretary of the Central Intelligence Agency."

16. King Evans interview, September 5, 2018.

17. Ibid.

18. "Eugene L. Harrison, Retired Army General," *Washington Star,* June 16, 1981, CIA, FOIA CREST. In June 1981, Ben Evan's great mentor, friend, and father-in-law, General Eugene Harrison, died in Florida at the age of eighty-two. Referencing his importance to the intelligence community, Harrison's obituary found its way into the CIA's classified files. The *Washington Star* clipping listed his many awards, including the Distinguished Service Medal and Legion of Merit. The article noted that he was a member of the post-World War II board that created the CIA.

19. King Evans interviews, November 29, 2017, February 17, 2018. General Eugene Harrison's gravesite was next to his best friend and West Point classmate, Colonel Donald Galloway, who was commander of Fort Myers that had responsibility for the Arlington National Cemetery. (Galloway was also an important figure in Evans's CIA career.) When Galloway's wife died, he accordingly picked out the best gravesite for her. Harrison's connections led to him obtaining a prime location in the adjacent gravesite.

20. Norma Richards interview with the author, March 1, 2018.

21. Corbin Davis interview with the author, September 28, 2017. Davis indicated that in Evans's final months, he particularly sought the presence of his wife, who was sometimes in DC. Davis said, "He knew she was an independent cuss and there was no roping her in."

22. "Benjamin C. Evans, Jr.," 27; "Anamú or Mapurite," http://www.plantasmedicinales10.com/articulo/anamu-mapurite.html. A traditional herbal remedy of the Americas, anamú, also known in its purified state as mapurite, was used by folk healers for many ailments, including cancer. It was reputed to have antitumor properties.

23. Karla Evans interview with the author, July 18, 2017.

24. Frank C. Carlucci letter to Ben Evans, March 3, 1987, JKEA.

25. Karla Evans interview, July 18, 2017; "Oral History: Reflections of DCI Colby and Helms on the CIA's "Time of Troubles," p. 6, https://www.cia.gov/library/center-for-the-study-of-intelligence/csi-publications/csi-studies/studies/vol51no3/reflections-of-dci-colby-and-helms-on-the-cia2019s-201ctime-of-troubles201d.html. Evans was not the only CIA official who found Oliver North's testimony aberrant. Former director William Colby warned agency officers against trying to fool Congress members. Colby said, "Sure, deal with them straight and don't try to run them around like that jackass Ollie North did."

26. King Evans interviews, October 12, 18, 2017.

27. "Benjamin C. Evans, Jr.," *Washington Post,* September 24, 1987; "Benjamin C. Evans, Jr.," *Chicago Tribune,* September 27, 1987; "Obituaries State," *Indianapolis Star,* September 25, 1987; "Benjamin C. Evans, Jr.," *Crawfordsville Journal Review,* September 25, 1987. Evans's obituaries spanned his life. The *Washington Post* wrote of Ben Evans the day after his death, citing his Indiana birth, his education at West Point and Columbia, his military service in Japan and Korea, and his long career with the CIA that culminated in his Distinguished Service Medal. The *Chicago Tribune* and *Indianapolis Star* both recorded his death, as did his hometown paper, the *Crawfordsville Journal Review,* which ran a lengthy obituary describing his illustrious military and intelligence career, as well as his many boyhood achievements as a member of a pioneer Hoosier family.

28. Louise Evans Turner interview with the author, August 24, 2017.

29. Karla Evans interview, July 18, 2017.

30. Turner interview, August 24, 2017. Turner said, "There were people [at the funeral] who should not have been seen together; covert people who put

their lives at risk to be there. They should never have been in the same room with each other."

31. Funeral Program, Benjamin C. Evans, Jr., September 28, 1987, JKEA; Daniel Evans e-mail to author, December 25, 1987; King Evans interviews, November 29, 2017, February 17, March 29, 2018; Turner interview, August 24, 2017.

32. King Evans interview, September 17, 2018

Index

Adams, John, 160
Adams, Sam, 119
Afghanistan, 155
Agee, Phillip, 140
Agricultural Adjustment Act (1933), 9
Alexander the Great, 53
Allende, Salvador, 125, 126
Amin, Idi, 146
Anderson, Jack, 150
Angleton, James Jesus, 64, 100, 118–19, 140, 158
Arlington National Cemetery, 161–62
Arms and the Boy: Military Training in Schools and Colleges (book), 15
Asia Foundation, The (TAF), 98–101, 102, 103, 110, 113, 114–15

Bacon, Robert Ogden (Bunny), Jr., 42
Baden-Powell, Robert, 11
Baker, James, 86
Batista, Fulgencio, 68, 71, 72, 74, 92, 93–94, 99, 118
Bender, Frank, 80
Benedict, Calvert, 112, 164
Ben-Hur: A Tale of the Christ, 3, 13
Bennett, Douglas P., 152
Berlin, Germany, 95, 96
Bissell, Richard, 94
Black Horse Troop, 13, 14, 16, 72, 73, 74, 122
Blake, James F., 149
Blum, Robert, 99
Bonilla, Raul Cepero, 71, 77, 78
Bonsal, Philip W., 75, 78, 88
Bonus Army, 9
Bowles, Chester, 104
Bowler, Norma. *See* Lewis, Norma Hull Bowler
Boy Scouts, 5, 11
Bradley, Omar, 37, 49
Brigade 2506, pp. 93, 94
British-Dutch Shell, 81
Bruce, Davis K. E., 66
Bush, Barbara, 153, 162
Bush, George H. W., 142–44, 150, 153, 160
Byron, Beverly, 147

Cabell, Charles, 94
Carlucci, Frank, 145, 157, 162
Carter, Jimmy, 143, 144, 151, 152, 155
Casey, William J., 120, 155–57
Castro, Fidel, 1, 68–69, 71, 72, 73, 76, 78, 79, 83, 84, 88, 89, 92, 93, 125
Castro, Raul, 78, 83, 84
Central Intelligence Act (1949), 62
Central Intelligence Agency (CIA), 34, 52, 57, 59, 61, 62–64, 65–67, 68–69; Cuban policy, 68–69, 73, 77, 78–80 84–87, 88; plans to invade Cuba, 88, 89, 92–94; Chile, 90; propaganda and clandestine operations, 97–101, 109–10, 118, 125, 126; publisher, 97–98, 144; Vietnam, 106, 109, 119, 125, 141; investigations of, 109–10, 114, 115, 134–35, 138–41, 143; psychological warfare, 112; assistance programs, 113; domestic operations, 125, 129–30, 138, 139; Latin America, 125–27, 141, 155; Watergate, 130, 131, 133–35, 138; internal secrets of, 138–45, 157; communism, 144–45; Soviet Union, 144, 157; Eastern Europe, 144; Africa, 145; cuts in ranks and personnel policies, 149, 150; Iran, 150–52, 155; Afghanistan, 155; Pakistan, 155
Chile, 90, 126, 141
Chin Yi, 106
Church, Frank, 140
Church Committee, 139, 140
Clay, Lucius D., 95
Clearwater Beach (FL) 87, 91
Colby, William, 130, 134, 137, 138, 139, 140, 141, 142, 143, 158
Cold War, 24, 51, 52, 83, 94–95, 101, 103, 110, 145
Colson, Charles, 133
communism, 52–53, 61–62, 66, 77, 81, 92, 97, 98–99, 104, 106, 126, 127, 144–45, 157
Cormack, Tom, 123, 124, 135, 144, 157
Cornett, Shirley, 120, 124
Coughlin, Charles, 9
Cox, Archibald, 135
Crawfordsville (IN), 1, 4, 5, 8
Crosby, Ken, 71–72, 75

Cuba, 126; revolution in, 68–69, 71–82; economy of, 72, 78, 81, 83
Culver, Henry Harrison, 13
Culver Military Academy, 1, 13–17, 72; Black Horse Troop, 13, 16, 72, 73, 74, 122

Davis, Corbin, 20, 21, 23, 162
Dean, John, 130, 134, 135
Dean, Mary, 4
Debs, Eugene V., 16
Devers, Jacob, 34
Devine, Jack, 136
DeVore, Lawrence E., 5, 10
Diem, Ngo Dinh, 106
Dietrich, Marlene, 72
Dillinger, John, 9
Doenitz, Karl, 161
Donovan, William J. (Wild Bill), 59–61, 155
Doolittle, James H., 65–66
Dresden, Germany, 24
Dulles, Allen, 62–63, 65, 66, 79, 80, 88, 94, 120, 135
Duong Van Minh. *See* Minh Diong Van

Earhart, Amelia, 6
Eastern Europe, 144
Echevarria, Oscar: works with CIA, 71, 72–73, 76, 77–78, 79, 80, 84; relationship with Ben, 72, 73–74, 75, 80, 131–32, 162; incarcerated, 78; encouraged to leave Cuba, 82, 85; leaves Cuba, 85; warned not to join Cuban invasion force, 94
Ehrlichman, John, 129, 135
Eisenhower, Dwight D., 1, 63, 65, 66, 78–79, 80, 81, 84, 88, 89, 91, 92, 99
Ellsberg, Daniel, 129, 137
Esso, 83
Evans DeVore and Company, 5, 7, 8, 9, 10
Evans, Beatrice McMahan, 133
Evans, Benjamin C. Jr.: army intelligence, 1, 35, 47; in Cuba, 1, 2, 68, 69, 83–90, 94; Culver Military Academy, 1, 13, 14–17; youth, 1, 3–4, 11, 12, 17; in Japan, 1, 27–32, 52–53, 54, 55, 107; leader of Arlington ceremonial company, 1; psychological warfare, 1, 48, 49, 51–54, 55, 65, 112; West Point, 1, 19–24, 35; aide-de-camp, 2, 33, 35–36, 41, 48; courtship of Jan King, 2, 47–49; family life, 2, 67–68, 101, 103, 104, 105, 107, 110–12, 113, 131–33; health, 4, 22, 112–13, 133, 161–63; love of nature, 4, 6, 11, 121; physical description of, 4, 17, 23, 35, 133, 159; relationship with grandfather, 5, 38; sense of responsibility, 10, 11; Boy Scouts, 11–12; personality of, 11; wins oratorical contest, 12, 17; Black Horse Troop, 13, 16, 72, 73, 74, 122; attends Wabash College, 19; military postings, 25, 41, 51–52; visits Indiana family, 25, 55; earthquake and relief, 28, 31, 32, 35; writes letters, 28, 31, 48, 63, 101, 102, 103, 105, 107; part of team to Westernize Japanese educational and cultural institutions, 28–31; equestrian skills, 35; interacts with Harrison-King family, 35–36, 38; wedding, 49; converts, 55; establishes psywar radio stations in Korea, 55; ponders leaving military and career options, 56–57; considers CIA career, 57, 63–64; gives speeches, 51, 68, 142; resigns from army, 63; work in covert operations, 65, 66, 67, 68, 69, 71–82, 85, 91, 94, 97, 98, 117; relationship with Echeverria, 72, 73–74, 75, 131–32, 162; social life, 75–76, 132; propaganda attacks on Castro, 77, 80, 86; accompanies family from Cuba, 81–82, 83; advises assets to leave Cuba, 82, 85; takes family to Florida, 83, 87, 91; comes to Florida for birth of second daughter, 87; closes Havana embassy, 89–90, 91, 95; keeps secrets, 96; The Asia Foundation, 98–101, 110, 113, 114–15; Republican and conservative, 99, 127; travel, 101–7, 159–60, 161; cannot fly commercial, 111; delivers CIA funds, 115; CIA executive, 117–27, 130, 133, 137–38, 141, 142, 143, 144, 147, 149, 152–53, 155, 156, 157; conceives Management Advisory Group, 120; enjoys farm life, 121–23, 159, 160, 162; family's knowledge of his work, 135–27, 141; work and correspondence with George H. W. Bush, 142, 143–44; Karla's trip to Africa, 145–47; distress at CIA exposure from congressional investigations, 140, 141; works on CIA management reform, 156; awards, 158; teaches, 159; burial in Arlington National Cemetery, 161–62; death, 163; funeral, 163–64
Evans, Benjamin C., Sr. (father), 5, 10, 133
Evans, Dan Fraley (brother), 4, 8, 11, 19, 22, 24, 157–58, 159–63

Evans, Daniel, Jr., (nephew), 7, 140
Evans, Frank C. (grandfather), 4–5, 10, 11, 15, 38
Evans, Jan King: ties to intelligence community, 1, 2, 55; Washington aristocracy, 1–2, 46; courtship of, 2, 47–49; homelife, 2; Fukui earthquake relief, 31–32; Harrison becomes stepfather to, 33, 38; takes interest in Ben, 35, 38, 39; childhood, 36–37; social positions of paternal and maternal grandparents, 41–46; education, 47–48, 51, 54; wedding, 49; fear of communism, 52–53; comments on return to Japan, 54; manages household finances, 54, 133, 160; residences, 54, 64, 67, 94, 111; travel, 55–56, 159–60, 161; reasons that Ben wants in CIA, 63, 64; cover story, 67; organizes moves, 68; serves on boards and committees, 68, 133, 161; living quarters and social life in Cuba, 74–76; leaves Cuba, 81–82; gives newspaper interview, 87; stays with parents in Florida, 87–88, 91; prepares for nuclear war, 95–96; shares Ben's letters with family, 101, 102; philanthropic activities, 102, 111, 153; activism in Republican Party, 111, 133, 153–55, 160–61; social life, 132; unaware about details of Ben's work, 135; works to have Ben buried in Arlington national Cemetery, 161–62
Evans, Kara, 1, 67, 75, 76, 81, 87, 103, 105, 107, 111, 112, 121, 122, 132, 145–47, 162
Evans, Ruth Fraley (mother), 4, 10, 11, 55
Evans family, 3–4, 5–6, 25, 28, 31

Falla, Elena, 76–77, 82, 93, 132
Farmers' Holiday Association, 7, 8
Federal Bureau of Investigation, (FBI), 59, 60, 130
Foggy Bottom, 45, 59, 67
Foldberg, Frank, 21
Ford, Gerald, 139, 143
Fort Benning (Georgia), 51, 52
Fort Bragg (North Carolina), 52, 60
Fort Meyer (VA), 33, 41
Fort Riley (Kansas), 51, 52
Fraley, Arthur, 7
Fraley, Daisy, 7
Frazier-Lemke Farm Bankruptcy Act, 9
Frederick A. Praeger (publisher), 97
Frei, Eduardo, 125

Frente Revolucionario Democrático (FRD), 79, 80, 84
Friedman, William G., 83–84
Fukui, Japan, 54; earthquake, 27–28, 31–32, 35

Galloway, Donald H., 64, 111
Gardner, Ava, 72
Gardner, John W., 110
Gaston, Melchor, 77
Gates, Robert M., 145, 156, 157
Gignilliat, Leigh R., 15
Goebbels, Joseph, 53
Goldwater, Barry, 153
Goodwin, Richard, 63
Göring, Hermann, 161
Grant, Ulysses S., 21
Gray, L. Patrick, 130, 134
Gregg, Donald, 54, 63, 112, 113, 117, 136, 162
Gregg, Meg, 54, 136, 162
Gresham, Margaret. *See* Livingston, Margaret Gresham
Groveton Farm (Virginia), 121, 122
Guatemala, 63, 66, 75
Guevara, Che, 93
Guzman, Jacobo Arbenz, 66

Haig, Alexander, 126
Haldeman, H. R., 130, 135
Harrison, B. Powell, 142
Harrison, Eugene Lynch, 31, 153; army intelligence, 1, 34, 35, 52, 64; Ben aide-de-camp for, 2, 33, 35–36; stepfather to King children, 33, 37–38, 49; secures new aide-de-camp job for Ben, 41; psywar, 51; Ben discusses career options with, 56; residences, 67, 111; Ben writes to, 63; helps Ben to get in CIA, 64; Jan and children live with, 87; death, 162
Harrison, Karla King Heurich, 153; marriages, 33, 36, 37, 38; social position of, 33; residences, 67, 111; helps Jan, 68
Havana, Cuba, 1, 68; embassy closed, 89–90
Heagney, William T., 75. 82
Helms, Richard, 64, 92, 110, 112, 118, 119, 120, 125, 126, 129, 130, 133, 134, 135, 139, 141, 155, 158
Hemingway, Ernest, 72
Herren, Thomas, 41

Hersh, Seymour, 138, 139
Heurich, Amelia, 48
Heurich, Christian, 43–46, 67
Heurich Brewery, 59, 111
Hinkle, Warren, 109–10
Hiroshima, 24, 29
Hiss, Alger, 100
Hitler, Adolf, 24, 53, 118
Hoover, Herbert, 6
Hoover, J. Edgar, 59
House Un-American Activities Committee, 62
Hull, John A. T., 42
Hull, Norma Bowler. See Lewis, Norma Hull Bowler
Humphrey, Hubert, 115
Hunt, E. Howard, Jr., 129, 130, 133
Hurley, Wilson Patrick, 49
Hyland, James, 27

Inman, Bobby Ray, 156
Inside the Company (book), 140
Iran, 63, 66, 150–52, 155

Japan: post-WWII occupation of, 1, 27–32; Communist Party, 30–31; unions, 30, 31; U.S. psywar unit in, 52–53, 54, 55
Japanese Communist Party, 30–31
Jefferson, Thomas, 19
Jensen, Jens, 5
Johnson, Lyndon, 109, 110, 117, 125, 129
Jordan, Amos A. (Joe), 104

Kalamatiano, Xenophon, 16
Katzenbach, Nicholas, 110
Katzenbach Commission, 110, 114, 115
Keeler, Christine, 100
Kennedy, John F., 72, 88, 91, 92, 93, 94, 95, 96, 99, 106, 118
Kennedy, Robert, 96
Khomeini, Ruhollah Musavi, 151, 152
Khrushchev, Nikita, 80, 95
Kidd, William, 3
King, Charles, 42
King, Charles (Chippe), 33, 36, 37
King, Charles B., 1, 36–37, 67, 111, 161
King, Donald, 33, 36
King, J. C., 77, 79
King, Jan. See Evans, Jan King
King, Karla Heurich. See Harrison, Karla King Heurich
King, Ludlow, 42

King, Ludlow, Jr., 42
Kirk, Grayson, 99
Kissinger, Henry, 125, 126, 140
Korea,1, 51, 52, 54, 55, 63
Kyoto, Japan, 27, 28, 31, 32, 33, 54

Lady Norma Lewis. See Lewis, Norma Hull Bowler
Lady Willmott Lewis. See Lewis, Norma Hull Bowler
Lambert, Barbara, 56
Langley (VA), 67, 78, 117, 147, 155
Latin America, 155
Lee, Robert E., 21, 41
Lenin, Vladimir Ilych, 54
Lewis, Norma Hull Bowler, 37, 42–43, 47, 48, 64, 68, 91, 111
Lewis, Willmott, 42
Liddy, G. Gordon, 129
Little, Arthur D., 132
Livingston, Margaret Livingston, 23, 25
Long, Huey, 9
Lovett, Robert A., 61, 66, 94
Lovett Committee, 34, 61, 66
Lugar, Richard, 131

MacArthur, Douglas, 21, 27, 29, 30, 59
MacMillan, Harold, 100
Maestri, Raul, 71–72
Magruder, John, 61
Malik, Charles, 102
Malloy, Barney, 113
Management Advisory Group, 120, 125, 129, 149, 152, 157
Mandela, Nelson, 145
Mansfield, Mike, 134
Marsh, John O., Jr., 162
Marshall, George C., 37
Marshall, Thomas, 15
Marshall Plan, 62
Martin, Charles, 164
Martin, David, 149
Martinez, Eugenio, 1229
McCarthy, Joe, 100
McClure, Robert A., 52
McCone, John, 100, 106
McCord, James, 129, 130, 134
McElwaine, Sandra, 95–96
McGovern, George, 131
McMahan, Beatrice. See Evans, Beatrice McMahan

Mellon, Bunny, 12
Mellon, Paul, 122
Michener, James A., 99
Minh Diong Van, 106
Mosaddegh, Mohammad, 66, 150
Mutual Benefit Life Insurance Company, 5, 10

Nagasaki, 24, 29
National Recovery Act, 9
National Security Act (1947), 62
National Student Association, 109, 110, 114–15
Nationalization Law (Cuba), 83
Ngo Dinh Diem. *See* Diem, Ngo Dinh
Ngo Dinh Nhu. *See* Nhu, Ngo Dinh
Nhu, Ngo Dinh, 106
Nixon, Richard, 92, 99, 124, 125, 126, 129, 130, 131, 133, 134, 135, 137, 141, 142
Noel, Jim, 71, 72, 75, 89
North, Oliver, 162
Nosenko, Yuri, 118, 119

O'Malley, Jimmy, 76, 85
Offices of Strategic Services (OSS), 59–61, 62, 66
Onassis, Jackie, 122
Operation Pedro Pan, 85–87

Pahlavi, Mohammad Reza, 66, 150–51, 152
Pakistan, 155
Park, Richard, Jr., 60
Patterson, Robert, 61
Patton, George S., 33, 53
Paul, Alice, 48
Pentagon Papers, 129
Pershing, John, 21
Phillips, David, 75, 94, 126
Pike Committee, 139
Post, Marjorie Merriweather, 111
Profumo, John, 100
Psychological war (psywar), 51, 52–54, 55–56, 80, 85, 88, 97, 99, 112

Quality Hill (estate), 43, 47

Raborn, William, 118, 120
Radio Free Europe, 97
Radio Liberty, 97
Radio Swan, 80, 86, 88, 93, 97
Ramon, Pepe San, 93
Ramparts (magazine), 109, 110, 114

Rasco, Josè Ignacio, 79
Reagan, Ronald, 153, 154, 155, 157, 162
Red Scare, 61–62
Reno, Milo, 8
Report of the Office of the Secretary of Defense Vietnam Task Force. See Pentagon Papers
Reyes, Tito, 93
Reynolds, Ann Cannon, 52
Rhodesia, 145
Richards, Ed, 162
Richards, Norma, 12, 47
Riley, James Whitcomb, 13
Rockefeller, Nelson, 139
Rockefeller Commission, 139, 141
Romney, George, 110
Roosevelt, Eleanor, 33
Roosevelt, Franklin D., 9, 33, 59–60
Rosenberg, Ethel, 100
Rosenberg, Julius, 100
Rossow, Robert, 14

Saint Vincent Orphanage (Vincennes, IN), 86–87
Sarver, Bina T., 4, 6, 7, 8, 10, 11
Schlesinger, James, 133, 134, 149
Schmidt, Peter, 145
Schneider, Rene, 126
Schorr, Daniel, 139
Scott, Hugh, 152
Shah of Iran. *See* Pahlavi, Mohammad Reza
Shaw, Noble R., 20
Silvas, Felipe, 93
Silvas, Mario, 93
Sinatra, Frank, 72
Sinclair, 83
Sisk, Mildred Elizabeth, 161
Slaughterhouse-Five, or, The Children's Crusade, 24
Smathers, George, 72
Smith, Mary, 67
Smith, Walter Bedell, 62, 65, 67, 112, 119
Souers, Sidney, 61
South Africa, 145
Soviet Union, 63, 66, 80–81, 103, 144, 157
Spring Ledge (Evans family estate), 4, 5–6, 9, 10
Sputnik, 66
Standard Oil, 81
Steeves, John M., 103
Stimson, Henry, 34, 41
Sun Tzu, 53

Sweet, Edwin S., 83–84
Swing, Joseph M., 31, 32, 35, 87
Sycamore Landing (estate), 42, 43

Taft, Robert, 20
Talbot, David, 135
Taylor, Elizabeth, 122, 150
Taylor, Rufus, 118–19
Taylor Committee, 93
Texaco, 81, 83
Thompson, Jim, 105
Tokyo, Japan, 52, 54
Tracy, Spencer, 72
Train, Russell, 154
Truman, Harry, 24, 51, 60, 61, 62
Tsurga, Japan, 28, 32
Turner, Louise Evans, 87, 103, 105, 107, 111, 112, 121, 122, 132, 136, 141, 162, 163
Turner, Mrs. Allen, 87
Turner, Stansfield, 143, 144, 147, 149, 150, 151, 152, 157
Twain, Mark, 43

U.S. Communist Party, 98
United Fruit Company, 66

Valdes, Ramiro, 77
Vanderberg, Hoyt, 64
Varela, Angel Fernandez, 74, 75, 78, 79, 84, 94
Vietnam, 109, 118
Villoldo, Gustavo, 93
Vonnegut, Kurt, Jr., 24

Wabash College, 3, 19
Wallace, Lew, 3, 13
Walsh, Bryan O., 86
Walters, Vernon, 130
Watergate, 130, 133; CIA, 130, 131, 133–35, 138
Watergate Committee, 135, 138
Webster, Jim, 105
West India Fruit and Steamship Company, 82
West Point, 1, 19–24
White, Lawrence K. (Red), 119, 120, 130
Whitten, Les, 150–51
Williams, Hayden, 10–11, 99, 100, 114, 115
Willis, Raymond, 19–20
Wilson, Woodrow, 15
Woodward, Bob, 133

World War II, 19, 22, 24, 34, 37, 53, 59, 60, 61, 105

Young, Eleanor (Cooky), 42

Zellerbach, James D., 99